Beyond the Systemic Crisis and Capital-Led Chaos

Theoretical and Applied Studies

P.I.E. Peter Lang

Bruxelles • Bern • Berlin • Frankfurt am Main • New York • Oxford • Wien

Rémy Herrera, Wim Dierckxsens & Paulo Nakatani (eds.)

Beyond the Systemic Crisis and Capital-Led Chaos

Theoretical and Applied Studies

Business & Innovation
No.9

This publication has been peer-reviewed.

Éditions scientifiques internationales
Brussels, 2014
1 avenue Maurice, B-1050 Brussels, Belgium
info@peterlang.com; www.peterlang.com

ISSN 2034-5402
ISBN 978-2-87574-183-7 (paperback)
ISBN 978-3-0352-6443-2 (eBook)
D/2014/5678/57

Printed in Germany

CIP available from the British Library and from the Library of Congress, USA.

Bibliographic information published by "Die Deutsche Nationalbibliothek".
"Die Deutsche Nationalbibliothek" lists this publication in the "Deutsche National-bibliografie"; detailed bibliographic data is available on the Internet at http://dnb.de.

En memoria a Reinaldo Carcanholo
Compañero, amigo y cofundador del Observatorio
Con todo nuestro afecto

Foreword

The world today is living in a capital-led systemic crisis. The mass media are fully committed to the great economic interests that control the planet and have no interest in informing the people objectively. This is not just a systemic crisis, but also a crisis of the Western civilization, which can jeopardize the entire future of humankind. This crisis comes along with high levels of hazards ever seen in history. The Soviet Union lost the Cold War, which resulted in its dismemberment. The United States and the Western world finally seem to be losing this war too, which is manifested in the present systemic crisis of capitalism. Hence, there have been no winners; all human beings lost. The present crisis of capitalism is thus a very critical period, but it is also an opportunity to move towards a civilized future. In this context, we all have the moral responsibility to participate in the struggle to overcome the crisis, and is the main reason behind organizing the international observatory of the crisis.

Since the 1980s, with neoliberal globalization, the productive sector tended to grow increasingly smaller; the speculative financial sector became dominant and fictitious capital turned into the core of the present crisis, which is at the same time financial, economic, political, social, military, ecologic, climatologic and cultural. We are reaching, and even surpassing, the possible global limits of the production of oil and other non-renewable resources of energy. There is competition between biofuel and food for the use of the land, which makes food increasingly more expensive, causing famines, especially in Africa. Water, the most vital source of life for human and natural species is becoming scarce. Mineral resources are becoming ever-scarcer and the extraction of strategic resources concentrated in the South has led to neo-colonial wars. Those resources are necessary for sustainable capital accumulation, which, in the long run, is impossible without growth. It becomes clear that this is a civilizational crisis, demanding a redrawing of the economic rationality as the logic of capital reaches its limits.

We work to show that the 21st century is not the end of the history but the beginning of a new civilization. This crisis of the Western civilization will be analysed in its different dimensions. We will look for opportunities to build a post-capitalism in practice and theory. We will analyse how the current crisis offers new opportunities to the social movements in their resistances against the current system. We will examine how the crisis offers opportunities for the establishment of new institutions or for the improvement of integration processes that have already started, as it is the case today in Latin America. We hope that this observatory will transcend the academic role and will be an instrument of information and documented alerts for the people in their struggles and for the creation of alternative proposals in the different spaces and regions of the world.

Wim Dierckxsens (sociologist and economist, The Netherlands), coordinator
Paulo Nakatani (economist, Brazil)
Rémy Herrera (economist, France)
Reinaldo A. Carcanholo (economist, Brazil)
Antonio Jarquín (physician and sociologist, Nicaragua)
Paulo Campanario (sociologist and demographer, Brazil)

Contents

Introduction

Wim DIERCKXSENS, Rémy HERRERA &
Paulo NAKATANI

International Observatory of the Crisis (IOC) and Ecumenical Research Centre (DEI), The Netherlands and Costa Rica

National Centre of Scientific Research (CNRS), France

and

Federal University of Espírito Santo (UFES), Brazil

In this book, our common statement is that we are entering 'the Great Depression of the 21st Century'. The current crisis is not merely an economic chaos or panic that is overwhelming us. One frequent error made in interpreting this crisis is that it is financial in nature and is contaminating the sphere of the 'real economy'. On the contrary, it is a crisis of capital, whose one of the most visible and publicized aspects has emerged within the financial sphere because of the extreme degree of financialization of contemporary capitalism. We are dealing with a systemic crisis that affects the very heart of the capitalist system, that is, the power centre of finance that has been controlling accumulation over the past three decades.

The crisis has worsened recently, mainly since 2006-2007, starting with the hegemonic centre of the world system and becoming more widespread. It is developing into a crisis that not only has socio-economic, political and humanitarian dimensions, but it also concerns food, energy and climate – and again, it is always financial, particularly affecting European countries, such as Iceland, Ireland, Greece, Portugal and Italy. Consequently, it is not 'the beginning of the end of the crisis', as perceived by some advisers to President Barack H. Obama. It is not a usual and conjunctural credit crisis, nor yet a temporary liquidity crisis, through which the system reorganizes and reinforces itself and begins to function 'normally', with a new growth of productive forces in a framework of modernized social relations. It is much more serious.

To analyse this particular capitalist crisis, or capitalist crises in general, it seems to us fundamental to refer to Marx because, in spite of numerous difficulties and uncertainties, Marxism – or Marxisms – provide(s) us with powerful tools, concepts, methods and theories for conducting such an analysis, even of political outcomes. It is the strongest and most useful theoretical framework for understanding and analysing the crisis and, above all, for comprehending the current transformations of capitalism and clarifying the post-capitalist transitions that are opening up and getting underway, for reasons and in conditions that we shall be developing here.

For some years now, there have been a number of Marxist thinkers who maintain that the devalorization of capital was inescapable and that it would be brutal and on a large scale. Basically, this crisis could be interpreted in Marxist terms as a crisis of over-accumulation of capital that ensues from the very anarchy of production, leading to a pressure on the tendency of the rate of profit to fall when countering tendencies – including new ones, linked to financial instruments, as we shall see – have dried up. This over-accumulation manifests itself through an excess of sellable production, not because there are not enough people who need or desire to consume, but because the concentration of wealth tends to prevent an increasingly large proportion of the population from being able to buy the merchandises.

Nevertheless, instead of it being a question of a standard over-production of goods, the expansion of the credit system makes it possible for capital to accumulate in money-capital, which can take forms that are increasingly abstract. By its nature, fictitious capital is complex, dialectic and both imaginary and real at the same time. Its nature is partly parasitical, but this kind of capital benefits from a distribution of surplus value – its liquidity gives its owner the power to convert it without loss of capital into money, 'liquidity par excellence'. Therefore, this capital nourishes an accumulation of additional fictitious capital, as a way of remunerating itself.

The current crisis is also the stage where different interests fight to manage the economic and political processes at a global scale. Fundamentally, it would seem that the conditions are combining so that a major consequence of this crisis could be the deepening of the North-South confrontation – in spite of co-optation within the G20. The North-South confrontation is taking place in a world where the levels of contradictions are becoming increasingly complex: between the ruling classes and the classes they dominate; between the different ruling classes that control the states; and between the countries of the South themselves. All this, however, is with the predominance, at the moment, of the contradictions between ruling classes, together with the rise of the 'emerging' countries – among them, China.

The crisis is the expression of the struggle to redistribute the global mass of real wealth. This redistribution no longer pits countries of the metropolis against each other, like in the past world wars. This time, financial capital engages in a warlike strategy to enlarge its areas of influence and to establish a global order under its hegemony through the creation of a global state without borders and citizens. By referring neoliberalism, defined as the doctrinal system on which the global strategy of domination of high finance is developed, to the functioning of the capitalist world system and class content, we entered into a casino-type economy, which is increasingly global in scope.

In the last decades, financial capital resorted to a significant expansion of credit to finance its commitments to the future. This translated into an increased expansion of assets in financial markets that was sustained by an inverted pyramid of credit without being backed by a major growth of the real economy. As long as the objective of appropriation and concentration of real wealth is maintained, credit will serve only to finance this speculative movement. This upward spiralling does not only generate (fictitious) profit, it is also a mechanism of appropriating the mass of real wealth produced in the world by a minuscule club of the super rich that have control over this process. Nevertheless, we believe that sooner or later, fictitious capital will disappear in an unprecedented financial collapse.

In Part I of this book, we propose a general framework to analyse the implications of this capital crisis. In Chapter 1, 'The Struggle for a New Civilization: Challenges and Threats', Wim Dierckxsens studies the strategy of those who possess this gigantic pyramid of portfolio investments to incorporate as many mechanisms as possible that allow them to hoard the lion's share of the productive or real wealth before or when the collapse takes place. According to him, the greatest fear of the Anglo-American financial capital is that the Eurozone will not only transform itself into Great Germany, but, worse, they will do so in alliance with China and Russia as part of the Euro-Asian Continental Bloc. The constitution of this mentioned Bloc would imply the definitive defeat of global Anglo-American capital. This idea clashes with unilateral and imperialist conservative forces in the United States and means a possible direct confrontation with China and Russia. We can hear the drums of war again of a direct confrontation among superpowers. The strategic objective of the Anglo-American project is not only to destabilize the euro, but also the dollar. Global bankers want to take advantage of the panic to replace the dollar and the Federal Reserve Bank with a global monetary authority controlled by the global bankers themselves, free of any state control, even of the US government. There is a faction inside the US power bloc that opposes this political project, and there are conservative forces that are trying at all costs to preserve the hegemonic power of the United States. Thus, it is important to them to keep the dollar as the leading global currency in order to fund their military might, but this current project looks more and more difficult to sustain.

In Chapter 2, 'A Critique of the Hegemonic Ideology and its Root', Paulo Campanario states that there is a Eurocentric dominant worldview that is held by most members of society, not just the West. A global power commands humankind today, without threats, but is unable to solve basic problems: unemployment, hunger, environmental destruction and others. Increase opposition movements, economic crises and geopolitical problems (Iraq and Afghanistan, China and India ascension). Despite its weaknesses and oppositions, this power still survives thanks to a strong ideology that justifies it, which is based on principles formalized in ancient Greece and accepted worldwide today. This thought is still alive, at the root of the hegemonic ideology. In the past, it sustained the ideologies of violent and unjust systems such as slavery, monarchy or feudalism. Consequently, it will probably continue to sustain and give life blows to the ideology of the global system until an alternative appears, which will replace the simplistic and Manichaean principles by others that are more appropriate to the complex challenges ahead and serve the interests of the greater part of the population.

After this general framework, we examine some global problems in Part II. Chapter 3, 'The Great Depression of the 21st Century and the Military-Industrial Complex', by Antonio Jarquín and Wim Dierckxsens, examines the war economy in order to explain current geopolitics. This leads us to understand the role of the war economy in times of a new Great Depression. The United States, or at least a conservative faction of its leaders, seems to be prepared to unleash a greater war, in view of maintaining its hegemonic place in the world. Today, US military spending looks really out of control, as it is the most important factor of indebtedness. By the 1950s, total indebtedness of the United States was already 150 per cent of its national income; today, it surpasses 350 per cent. We remember that heavy military burden had been one of the main causes of the breakdown and disintegration of the Soviet Union. This might be applicable today to the United States. Indeed, the latter increased its military expenditure by 83 per cent between 2000 and 2010. With negative GDP growth rates recently registered in real terms, the United States will see how this unproductive spending will impact heavily on its civilian economy. By focusing its economy on productive sectors and sustained growth, China can now afford to go deeper into this arms race. However, a sustained race could mean an ever-deeper crisis for the US economy, as happened in the case of the former USSR. In other words, the United States is digging its own grave, just as the Soviet Union did a few decades ago. Thus, we may today be close to the collapse of the US' hegemony, which is already in full crisis. In this context, a 'great war', that is, a war between core countries, may become a possibility. It will especially involve those powers that could represent a potential threat to the present established order. In our opinion, this definitely means a military conflict of the United States with China and perhaps also Russia.

In Chapter 4, 'Is a "New Green Deal" an Alternative?' Paulo Campanario, Antonio Jarquín and Wim Dierckxsens wonder whether there is a possibility of another 'New Deal' to rescue the capitalist economy. All conventional ways out of the crisis point towards a tacit and sine qua non condition: the necessity of sustained economic growth. Capitalist society clings to the myth of economic growth. Without it, sustainable accumulation is impossible. The myth holds that economic growth would be a necessary condition for people's welfare. Although, throughout history, growth may be (and has been) a major vehicle to create greater welfare, it is not a necessary condition for it. At certain degrees of capitalistic development, it is more likely to obstruct welfare. Without economic growth, it is only possible to accumulate capital temporarily, in which case it is based on a more unequal distribution of income and existing wealth, which will result in mortgaging the future. Another way to do so is by means of fictitious capital accumulation. This way of accumulation, however, reaches its limit sooner or later and henceforward produces a deep economic crisis. This evidences the impossibility of generating new profits without creating real wealth based on real value. The authors suggest that if we do not stop global economic growth, nature will destroy us due to our destruction of the natural resources necessary for our survival as human beings. Consequently, it is absurd to maintain the myth of sustainable growth. We are facing a deep crisis, mostly derived from the Western lifestyle. Its logic of practical, ideological and political performance rules the world today. Thus, the current crisis is not only one of this mode of production, but also of the Western 'civilization' itself.

In Part III, we concentrate on analytical approaches to these difficult problems related to the current capital crisis in order to contribute to the rebuilding of theory from a Marxist point of view. Chapter 5, by Reinaldo A. Carcanholo and Mauricio de Souza Sabadini, deals with 'Fictitious Capital and Fictitious Profit'. Here, the central issue is to try to identify the characteristics of the new stage of world capitalism that started in the late 1970s and early 1980s. Which are the perspectives of this system to go on and develop? Nowadays, these are extremely important questions, and the appropriate answers, as the authors point out, are related to the Marxist concept of 'fictitious capital'. This concept, described by Marx in *Capital*, Volume III, is not accepted well by those who owe something to positivist and metaphysical conceptions, whether they are Keynesians or not. The fact that fictitious capital is, at the same time, unreal and real, could seem a contradiction in terms. It is in this real-imaginary dialectic that this rarely assimilated concept acquires its complete relevancy. Similarly, the concept of 'fictitious profit' is hardly considered from a theoretical point of view, even by some that call themselves Marxists. First of all, it is not a concept that has been elaborated on by Marx and that can be definitive for many economists. At that time, the idea of a dominant 'fictitious capital' over substantive or real capital was far from being possible. To think that a part of the profit was derived from the surplus value or even from the surplus value of non-salary production forms was still contradictory. The authors precisely define the concepts of 'fictitious capital', parasitic speculative capital and explain what fictitious profit is.

In Chapter 6, 'The Great Depression of the 21st Century and Fictitious Wealth: On the Theoretical Categories of Fictitious Capital and Fictitious Profit', Reinaldo A. Carcanholo delves into this interpretation in depth. Starting from the Marxist theory of value and the nature of capitalistic wealth, he defines some forms of fictitious and parasitic capital with geopolitical relevance. He analyses the issue of bonds and public debt growth, which appears to be fundamental to understanding the present speculative behaviours against public debt in the core countries of the capitalist world system. In fact, the conversion of fictitious capital into real capital is another important geopolitical item to understand massive acquisitions of land in Africa to produce biofuels, for example. Such a conversion from fictitious to real capital also happens, the other way round, when the increase in military expenditures is financed by the expansion of public debt, which is obviously a central subject for the US economy today.

In Part IV, we move our investigations towards analytical approaches to rebellions and struggles. In Chapter 7, 'The Dialectical Unity of Capital and Non-Capital: The Role of Overpopulation in Popular Rebellion Today', Wim Dierckxsens and Andrés Piqueras state that throughout its history, capital has established a decisive form of discrimination, which has effectively strengthened its power against labour. Discrimination exists between an endogenous labour force (that is, integrated into the capitalist nexus, with some guarantees and rights) and an exogenous labour force (yet to be incorporated or integrated as 'heterochthonous', that is, without such guarantees and rights). The authors refer to the historical incorporation of the exogenous population from the non-capitalist to the capitalist nexus (with the consequent replaceability of the endogenous labour force) as absolute mobility. The more possibilities capital has of accessing a population in the non-capitalist nexus and of being able to incorporate it through absolute mobility into the capitalist nexus, the greater its unilaterality or class domination. In contrast, when these possibilities run dry, capital is more inclined towards reformism or negotiation. However, this absolute mobility has historically been combined with relative mobility of the labour force, which includes various processes, of which labour force migration is a key component. Both types of mobility are at the core of class struggles.

Following this reasoning, in Chapter 8, 'Notes on the *Class Struggle* in Late Capitalism', Andrés Piqueras focuses on the analysis of the subject of class struggle during neoliberalism. One of his main conclusions is that, these days, the connection between capitalism and employment is becoming increasingly harder. He explains that stable employment and social and economic security, which are the bases of middle-class and political stability, are becoming even scarcer. As a consequence, the attempts to solve the valorization crisis by means of a further impoverishment of the already disadvantaged populations or by cutting public debt affect the possibilities of profit realization even more. In the sphere of capital accumulation, democratic options are becoming more and more difficult to implement, and the logical effect is a growing de-legitimacy of the capitalist mode of production. This is the reason we are entering a new era of class struggle, which has deep implications.

In Part V, we examine China as a case study, which was mentioned earlier and seems crucial to be more systematically considered within the framework of our analyses. In Chapter 9, 'Financial System and "Chinese-Style Market Socialism"', Tony Andreani and Rémy Herrera suggest elements of answers to a series of questions related to the current Chinese financial system. It is important to wonder whether the present Chinese financial system, which is playing a key role in the overall economy, exhibits specific features. These issues, which are taking the form of deep and complex problems to be solved by China today, are: Which are the characteristics of China's market socialism? What is the place of market finance in a system that still remains based on credit? Are financial markets more efficient in allocating resources than banking credit? Do the Chinese state-owned enterprises have to function as private companies? Should the semi-administrated interest rates be completely liberalized? Should the Chinese banks be 'universal'? These are, according to the authors, some of the major challenges to be resolved by China to succeed in its 'emergence'.

Finally, in Chapter 10, 'Some Problems (and Paradoxes) Related to the Internationalization of China's Economy', Rémy Herrera examines and explains some of the most serious difficulties, and deep contradictions, encountered by the Chinese economy since its opening up in 1978. As a matter of fact, it appears that China's internationalization remains strongly articulated as a development strategy that is mainly orientated towards the inner economy, but that has not been implemeted without internal problems. Furthermore, this internationalization has produced, especially through exports of merchandises and capital, numerous contradictory effects, both on the Northern and Southern countries. In addition, these issues directly concern the internationalization of the national currency. Should the Chinese monetary authorities agree to 'internationalize' the renminbi? Such a decision would require conditions that, if they are achieved, would have huge implications, to be discussed, for the existing international monetary and financial order, the future trajectory of the Chinese economic system and the consolidation and improvement of its 'socialist transition'.

Part I

General Framework

Chapter 1

The Struggle for a New Civilization

Challenges and Threats

Wim Dierckxsens

International Observatory of the Crisis (IOC), The Netherlands and Costa Rica

Introduction

Towards the end of June 2011, the world faced, for the first time in recent history, the possibility of a financial collapse that not only threatened the periphery countries or one or two European countries, but also the US. Since then, panic has spread, the price of gold has skyrocketed and we increasingly hear about an imminent Great Depression. We are actually not confronting a new recession or a 'double dip', like the mainstream media wants us to believe, but are standing before the Great Depression of the 21st Century. Even the data of the US Bureau of Economic Analysis (BEA), readjusted for 2011, shows that the GDP of the US declined in the last quarter of 2008 by 8.9 per cent. According to other data reported by the BEA, which usually shows lower numbers after readjustments, 2009 registered a negative growth of 3.5 per cent. Per capita GDP at current prices demonstrates that the US had already entered a recession in 2005.[1] This is why we have to go further back in time to search for the causes of the depression.

By the end of the 1970s, the rate of profit had declined in the productive sphere. In other words, it had declined in those sectors where real wealth is produced: value and surplus value. This was because, since World War II, the average life of fixed capital had gradually dropped to the extent that the cost of technological innovation could not be compensated by a larger reduction in the cost of labour once the technology had been introduced. Driven by the need to be ahead of the competition in the development of

1 *The Economist*, 6 August 2011, p. 28.

cutting-edge technology, fixed capital's average lifespan was reduced at the expense of its rate of return. Since then, Keynesian economics had been in crisis and neoliberalism had come to take its place. The time was ripe to look for cheaper labour force outside the metropolis and/or to import cheaper labour force from the periphery. As labour became flexible globally, the reserve army of labour was to be found worldwide and the degree of exploitation in the real economy was intensified.

In the metropolis, we do not observe a new move of capital towards the productive sphere, instead we see how capital tries to abandon the productive sphere at all cost. Capital increasingly takes refuge in the fantastic world of the self-expansion of money. In other words, capital tries to realize profits and accumulate in the speculative and unproductive spheres of the economy. Profits here tend to be higher, but they do not contribute to increase in real wealth. They act as a form of entitlements that demand participation in real wealth, without having taken part in its creation. Thus, there is fictional capital and fictional profit, which develop as forms of dispossession and concentration of real wealth that has been produced at the global level. Such profits intensify the competition for the distribution of the mass of surplus value produced globally without affecting a real increase of it at the global level. In order to guarantee proper functioning of this economic logic, the deregulation of the financial system became necessary in the 1980s. The measures that were adopted promoted the exponential growth of investment banking and new financial instruments known as hedge funds and derivatives. Huge financial networks were created that functioned without any type of fiscal or legal control or constraint. In the last few decades, financial capital resorted to a significant expansion of credit to finance its commitments to the future. This translated into an increased expansion of titles in financial markets that was sustained by an inverted pyramid of credit, which was not backed by major growth of the real economy. In short, with neoliberalism we enter into a casino-type economy that is increasingly global in scope. As long as the objective of appropriation and concentration of real wealth is maintained, credit will serve only to finance this speculative movement. This upward spiralling does not only generate (fictitious) profit, but it is also a mechanism of appropriating the mass of real wealth produced in the world by a minuscule club of the super rich who have control over this process.

The actual size of the inverted pyramid of titles that is built on the ever-shrinking base of real wealth makes palpable the magnitude of fictional capital and its fictitious profits. The Bank for International Settlements (BIS), in its June 2011 issue of the *BIS Quarterly Review*, reported that it had received information that by December 2010, a total of 601 trillion dollars of derivatives had been issued. This sum is 10 times more than the net world GDP; however, the real number of derivatives issued is probably an underestimation as there is no obligation to report it. Trace Mayer (2009) estimates that the number of derivatives issued is 30 times the world GDP. In reality it is very hard to measure its real dimension. Sooner or later, fictional capital will disappear in an unprecedented financial collapse. The strategy of those who possess this gigantic inverted pyramid of investments is to incorporate as many mechanisms as possible that allow them to hoard the lion's share of the productive or real wealth before or when the collapse takes place. This is a politics of subordination to the global financial networks of not only countries of the periphery, like Latin America in the past, but also, in the final analysis, of even superpowers like the European Union and the US.

The creation of a Eurozone and the European Union was a political attempt by this continent to avoid being consumed by the tentacles of the two financial octopuses, the City of London and Wall Street. Today, we face the threat of bankruptcy of the European Union states and even the US. This demonstrates that not even the metropolis can stay safe from the encroachment of the global financial networks. We can see unified efforts of the financial octopuses through the Financial Funds of Global Investment (FFIG) and in the way big banking and corporations are strategically managed. It is a diversified network that operates with maximum anonymity and secrecy; it is where the struggle for the control of transnational capital takes place and where the financial octopuses are able to transform themselves into global financial networks. These networks function like 'private states without borders and citizens' that are accountable to no one. It is a form of capitalism without citizenship.[2]

How is a global financial network structured? The findings of a study conducted by Swiss researchers Stefania Vitali, James B. Glattfelder and Stefano Battison (2011) show that 737 companies control 80 per cent of the transnational network of corporations and that only 147 – what the researchers call the 'super entity' – control more than 40 per cent of this global network. Half of the 50 largest corporations are American. UK occupies the second place with eight corporations, followed by Japan and France at four each. Switzerland, Holland and Germany have two each, and China, Canada and Italy have one each. Here we can draw a comparison with the secret Bilderberg Group. We can also add that 12 of the 25 companies with the greatest nodes or connections are well-known financial institutions. They are, in order of importance: Barclays PLC, J.P. Morgan Chase, UBS AG, Merrill Lynch & Co., Deutsche Bank AG, Credit Suisse Group, Bank of New York Mellon, Goldman Sachs Group Inc., Morgan Stanley, Mitsubishi Financial Group Inc., Société Générale

2 See Dierckxsens (2000: 73-76 and 107-111).

and Bank of America Corp. The 'super entity' is no longer composed of mainly big corporations of the real economy; instead, it has increasingly been taken over by financial institutions, with Wall Street and the City of London at the forefront (See Figure 1.1).

These financial institutions have the capacity to speculate in the market and have privileged access to enormous quantities of information. Thanks to these researchers, we are able to understand how the great bubbles and financial crises that we have witnessed in the last few years have originated, and how these great corporations, in contrast to the majority of the population, can report great earnings in the context of the global economic meltdown. We can understand the phrase: they are too big to fail and, in reality, they are too powerful to fail. The major stockholders can exert massive influence through their connections with other transnational corporations, concentrating so much power in their hands that they are able to destabilize entire countries and even the US. It is clear that fictitious capital is concentrated in Wall Street and the City of London. The forces that subordinate productive capital at a large scale operate from these places and are in a position to control the metropolis.

Figure 1.1: The Super Entity of the World Economy

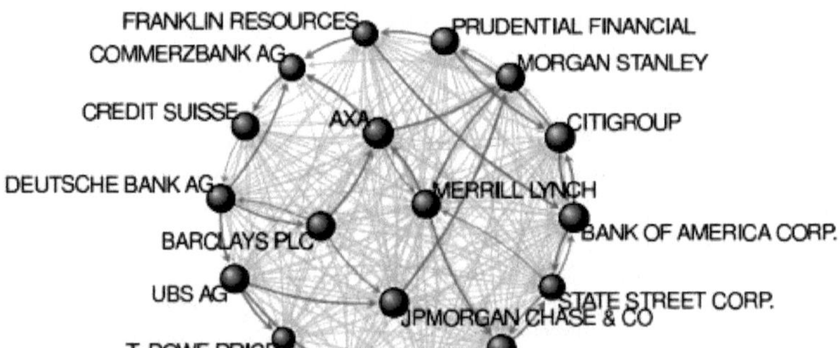

Source: New Scientist.

The Struggle to Restructure the World Order in the Current Crisis

The current crisis is not only a period of economic chaos or panic that overwhelms us, but it is also a stage where different interests struggle to manage the economic and political processes at a global scale. This crisis is the expression of the struggle to redistribute the global mass of real wealth. This redistribution no longer pits countries of the metropolis against each other, like in the past world wars. This time, financial capital engages in a warlike strategy to enlarge its areas of influence and establish a global order under its hegemony through the creation of a global state without borders and citizens. This newly created 'social territoriality' requires a new type of state: a state that, by means of a global financial network, has sovereignty over a social territory. This war will have winners and losers inside and among the great economic powers themselves that are based on territoriality. Two Argentinean authors, Formento and Merino (2011) emphasize that the imposition of global financial power responds to a logic that transcends the subordination of some countries to other countries or an imperial country. In the new world order, they say, 'the global networks need to supersede the US as the only world superpower and advance to a new form of imperialism that has no central country as hegemonic and exclusionary power.'

In the US, we observe how the conflict of economic interests uses the global financial crisis as a strategic political struggle that resembles a financial-political media war. The conflict of interests inside the divided Anglo-American financial power bloc is deepening and globalizing. Formento and Merino (2011: 9) talk about a conservative US American financial section led by J.P. Morgan and the Bank of America now steeped in crisis, and the globalist financial power section led by Barclays, Citi Group and Lloyd's Bank. Clearly, the global financial network is not monolithic. The latter group wants to create a type of state that is global, without geographical borders and citizens and is not anchored in any territory, not even the US territory. Its territory is social. Formento and Merino tell us that according to the global networks, 'there should be only colonies, no colonizing countries; colonizing countries themselves must be colonized territories'. Global financial networks have already been successful in incorporating many Latin American countries and are now targeting the European Union and the US. It is through the pyramidal multiplication of fictitious capital as entitlements or rights over the ever-expanding portion of the world's real wealth produced each year that they are able to effectively control the productive assets in the world and, thus, its process of reproduction. This internationalized power in the form of a global state seeks to impose its own global currency, and to accomplish this it is ready to destroy the area of influence of the euro and even the hegemony of the dollar (Formento and Merino, 2011: 21).

How can we envision the new imperial modality? It is a form of imperialism that is deployed as a hierarchical network of global financial cities, with New York and the City of London as its centre and other local nodes in Paris, Tokyo, Shanghai, Frankfurt, Moscow, Singapore, Hong

Kong, Dubai, Abu Dhabi, Mumbai, Sydney, Johannesburg, Sao Paolo, Buenos Aires, Mexico City and others. The principal nodes would give the global state its shape and there would be a global division of labour that assigns each region a specific role. In this context, the hegemonic power of the US as a unipolar, unilateral, or even trilateral, force in the world now becomes an obstacle to the realization of the Anglo-American globalist economic interests. The Anglo-American power bloc controls the largest portions of transnational financial capital and the largest financial network in the world under the leadership of Citigroup, Lloyd's Bank, HSBC, Rothschild, Shell, Barclays and others. The Democratic Party best represents the political interests of this group from the time of the Clinton administration, and now, with the Obama-Hillary Clinton administration.

The main characteristics of the global-state network can be summarized as follows: Constitution of a global government articulated within the G-20 as a unipolar, multilateral sphere. Opposing this trend is the multi-polar multilateralism of other power segments like the European Union that struggle not to be absorbed in this sphere. We can also mention the BRICS and China that present a degree of autonomy, and even UNASUR. It is not surprising then to watch how these groups support the euro to prevent the European Union from coming under the charge of dominant global financial capital. The development of an imperialist global network consists, first of all, of a network of financial cities as a mode of social territoriality. The state modalities are constituted by the structures of strategic management of the cities. The central command is constituted by the global financial networks that make up the FFIG. The aforementioned regional power segments oppose this trend. The emission of global electronic money through the granting of Special Drawing Rights (SDRs) will take place by the IMF or other ways of keeping the global financial networks always at the centre. This form of politics implies the elimination of the dollar as the leading currency and the dismantling of the Federal Reserve Bank as a global bank. This is opposed by the US financial bloc that seeks to maintain the hegemony of its country. The global state further goes for an optimum liberalization of global commerce through the WTO; the development of Global Armed Forces through NATO and the UN Peacekeeping forces; a fictional, virtual democracy composed of demobilized and disorganized majorities, in other words, a global citizenship under the sovereignty of financial media power.[3]

The global state further goes for an optimum liberalization of global commerce through the WTO; the development of Global Armed Forces through NATO and the UN Peacekeeping forces; a fictional, virtual

[3] See Formento and Merino (2011: 57-58).

democracy composed of demobilized and disorganized majorities, in other words, a global citizenship under the sovereignty of financial media power.

There is a section inside the US power bloc that opposes this political project. These are conservative forces that try at all cost to preserve the hegemonic power of the US. Thus, it is important to them to keep the dollar as the leading global currency in order to fund their military might. They also need to strengthen their position vis-à-vis other groups. Their politics still rests on the control of geographical areas. According to their logic, Latin America must be annexed through free-trade agreements and the consolidation of a continental defence strategy. Latin American projects, like the ALBA (the Bolivarian Alliance for the Peoples of Our America), Union of South American Nations (UNASUR), the Community of Latin American and Caribbean States (CELAC) and the South American Defence Council (SADC), go against these political projects of the North. The deployment of the US Fourth Fleet ran parallel to the installation of the SADC. At the very moment that the coup in Honduras was taking place to prevent the consolidation of an autonomous South American power bloc, the Pentagon was allowed to install seven military bases in Colombia.

This US American power bloc appears as a unipolar, unilateral strategy of the Pentagon and prefers building regional blocs that are kept under the leadership of the US, but this project is becoming increasingly difficult to sustain. The Pentagon and the financial segment of J.P. Morgan, Bank of America, Goldman Sachs, Big Pharma, Exxon Mobil of Rockefeller and others support this political strategy. The Republican Party under the George W. Bush administration best represented this group politically. The economic weakness and backwardness of this US American power bloc was compensated by its military strategy. After losing the midterm elections in 2010, the globalist Anglo-American section had serious difficulty in imposing its programme (Formento and Merino, 2011: 63-79). The re-election of Obama, however, may be interpreted as a victory of the globalists. As the globalist and nationalist forces appear to struggle with each other, a third force arises with the mass movement 'Occupy Wall Street' that may advance an alternative project. The more the two former parties struggle, the more the alternative forces will rise.

The current wave of speculative attacks targets the public debt that has been accumulated by the governments of the metropolis. In the context of a debt crisis, the creditor banks seek to exchange the most difficult debt titles to collect against productive assets, that is, in the real economy of the debtor countries. This type of regime was applied to Latin American towards the end of the 20th century, and it's the turn now of the countries of the metropolis. The importance of the ratings agencies in this speculative wave is significant. Many entities, like the pension funds that carry trillions in investments, are tied to these rating agencies of credit and are forced to submit themselves to their ratings. When the credit rating of a country is lowered (intentionally), the sale of bonds is massive and consequently they lose value, which simultaneously raises the interest rates for new credit. The new credit can only be obtained under severe conditions of structural adjustment policies that were very well known in Latin America during the 1980s. To ensure the installation of the global state without borders, it is necessary to subordinate the European Union and its Eurozone as well as the US and its dollar. The threat of bankruptcy is a weapon par excellence.

Through the Credit Default Swaps (CDS) one can engineer a financial coup against a particular country or several countries at once, like the so-called PIIGS countries (Portugal, Ireland, Italy, Greece and Spain). The CDS are derivatives of credits that act like insurance policies to protect themselves from debts (public debt in this case) that have become UN-payable due to the lowering of their ranking by rating agencies or by the increase of interest rates provoked by lower credit ratings. The CDS and the interest rate swaps are the market products of Wall Street and the City of London. The real objective of the Anglo-American globalists is not necessarily to bankrupt the countries on the periphery of Europe or to make them abandon the Eurozone, but to appropriate (steal) their assets that were produced in the real economy. Bankruptcies are a means to do so, but they are not the main objective.

The Globalist Anglo-American Forces and the Euro

There are several credit rating agencies in the world, but among the most important are Standard & Poor's Rating Services, Moody's and Fitch Ratings. During the international economic crisis, rating agencies play an important role in the daily fluctuation of financial markets. Any raising or lowering of the credit score (or any other similar indicator) of a particular nation has an immediate impact on the markets and the economy. Just as banks rank their clients using credit scores before granting a loan, international financial organizations have their own methods and objectives to rank countries in order to grant or deny them financial support.

Fitch Ratings is associated with the Bank of France and Renault and responds to the politics in Brussels. The purpose of cutting Greece's credit rating to junk status was a step towards a greater centralization of the European government in Brussels, and it appears to be working as it survived the speculative attacks at the end of the summer and the fall of 2011. Standard & Poor's has its headquarters at the City of London and is part of the most global financial network that works with Barclay and others. It was the first one to lower the credit rating of Spain causing a contagion effect over the whole European periphery, reaching even Italy. This gave way to the speculative attacks centred on insurance contracts (securities) or CDS, fearing the eventual bankruptcy of these countries.

French-German financial capital was able to put the European economy back on track after the experience with the Greek crisis. Through the rescue plan of the PIIGS, it was possible to transfer the risk of the peripheral countries to the central countries of the Eurozone. The Germans, Finnish, Dutch, Austrians and French must now pay tax to stabilize the peripheral countries of Europe. In actuality, it was all about rescuing German and French banks. It is in this context that a German-French project emerged to create the fiscal integration of Europe. This implied the transfer of taxes from the North to the South. This transference, which began taking place in the current crisis period, provoked an ultraconservative backlash in the North. Popular sectors demanded to leave the Eurozone. Global rating agencies were of the opinion that if the crisis did not break out in the South, it would break out in the North. The risk of having northern European countries leave the Eurozone was not great. Were they to abandon the Eurozone, their exports to the South of Europe would be in serious danger.

The ultimate goal of the German-French project was to avoid falling under the charge of Anglo-American financial capital. The German-France axis continued to consolidate as a power bloc with a hard currency and a fiscal integration to prevent its subordination to Anglo-American global financial forces. The politics is: (*i*) to deepen the gap between countries with trade and fiscal surplus, like Germany and China, and those with a trade and fiscal deficit, like the US and the UK; and (*ii*) to increase protectionist measures and economic warfare among blocs. To preserve its domain over the real economy, the German-French project will confront Anglo-American global capital with a politics of adjustment-savings-investment-production-export-commercial-surplus.[4]

To prevent subordination to Anglo-American global financial forces, European financial capital found tactical allies with other big banks in the US, like Goldman Sachs, which is one of the bigger banks in New York, not allied with the said Anglo-American forces. Since the euro crisis, Goldman Sachs became a central economic and political player in Europe. Mario Draghi, the current president of Europe's Central Bank, Mario Monti, who succeeded Silvio Berlusconi in Italy, and Lucas Papademos, the new prime minister of Greece, either are or were part of Goldman Sachs. In this context, it is clear that the real battle in the euro

4 See Formento and Merino (2011: 120-27).

crisis is between big bankers at a global scale. Will this alliance survive or will the Anglo-American global financial forces triumph, or will a more radical social movement emerge at a global scale against the bankers in general?[5]

Europeans found in the BRICS (Brazil, Russia, India, China and South Africa) tactical allies for their project. In the meeting of the G-20 in October 2011, it became clear that Russia and China would support the euro. Anglo-American forces meanwhile tried to snatch the real assets of Europe through the business of speculating with public debt and looking for bankruptcy of ever-larger countries. If they did not win this bet, the burden of the collapse of fictitious capital would fall on Wall Street and the City of London. Towards the end of November 2011, it looked like the global Anglo-American financial capital had lost an important battle: The creation of the European Fund for Financial Stability with external support represented a great loss for them. They lost another battle with Obama's re-election in the US, but the war continues. Amidst this confrontation of the forces of capital, a space has opened up for radicalized progressive forces that fight for de-globalization and a decoupling from neoliberal globalization. As the Great Depression of the 21st Century appears to turn into reality, these forces may become more radical and internationalized. If 2011 represented springtime, 2012 might be referred to as nearing harvest time.

The greatest fear of the Anglo-American forces is that the Eurozone is not only transforming itself into Great Germany but, even worse, it may do so in alliance with China and Russia as part of the Euro-Asian Continental Bloc. The constitution of this Bloc would imply the definitive defeat of global Anglo-American capital. The Euro-Asian Continental Bloc clashes not only with global Anglo-American capital, but also with unilateral and imperialist conservative forces of the US. In this context, we observe that actually the geopolitics of Anglo-American global capital promotes the transfer of the scenarios of war in oil-producing countries in Iraq and the Middle East (a major interest of US conservatives) towards countries that can break the integration of China and Russia. In the context of this encirclement of the Euro-Asian Continental Bloc we can expect an all-out war against Iran. This means a possible direct confrontation of the US with China and Russia. We can hear the drums of war beating among superpowers again.

The Anglo-American Forces and the Dollar

The strategic objective of the Anglo-American project is not only to destabilize the euro, but also the dollar. At the end of June 2011, Standard

---

5 See Marín (2011).

& Poor's lowered the credit rating of the US for the first time in history. This was a warning that the sole superpower of the world ran the risk of not being able to pay its debt. This caused immediate panic around the world. Global bankers seem to deliberately want to destroy the dollar and the current financial system. The purpose is to produce a shock effect in order to establish a new system. Global bankers want to take advantage of the panic to replace the dollar and the Federal Reserve Bank with a global monetary authority controlled by the global bankers themselves free of any state control, even of the US government.[6]

Moody's, the third credit rating agency, is associated with Goldman Sachs and the US conservative power bloc. It has recently threatened to lower the credit ratings of both the US and the UK and even find a way to integrate both countries into the formula of PIIGS.[7] In a scenario where the Anglo-American forces advance, the opposing poles that feel threatened must find a way to protect their interests as a bloc. Conservative US anti-globalist forces need to maintain the dollar as the leading international reserve currency, guarantee their domination through the military-industrial complex and the Pentagon, control the Middle East to tap into its oil reserves, and deepen their intervention in Latin America. This backward section of the Anglo-American financial power bloc is anchored in neo-conservatism and is the section that mostly takes the conflict to the terrain of politics and military intervention. It needs to perpetuate traditional US power and deploy a neo-conservative strategy that is both fundamentalist and militarist, and even neo-fascist.

As the conflict deepens, the division of the power blocs becomes more visible making possible the development of nationalistic social movements like the Tea Party. The internal struggles in the US reached new heights in November 2010. The midterm elections were won by the Tea Party. Bush's nationalistic and neo-fascist tendencies were strengthened in the process. In the event of a tie of hegemonic forces, the Tea Party began to mobilize against those they considered the enemy of the country: Obama and the global financial oligarchy embedded in Wall Street, New York, and the City of London. According to conservative groups, these centres of power want to destroy the 'American Dream'. The neo-conservative faction imposed its agenda of reducing public investment (except military expenditures), putting a stop to raising taxes, defending unilateralism and militarism in foreign policy and putting forward its cultural and ideological obscurantism. It looks now that this conservative bloc is losing the battle. The current tie between the two conflicting hegemonic forces has left the field open to new and alternative forces,

6 See Wolfe (2011).

7 See Formento and Merino (2011: 106-11).

such as Occupy Wall Street. As the Great Depression of the 21st Century becomes a fact, social and political movements may grow to new heights.

How to Save the People or the Struggle for a New Civilization

As we observed in 2011, the globalization project, which has been split by class warfare from above and shows no limits, has reached a climax. It has generated space for class warfare from below and made possible the emergence of a popular project beyond its borders. The popular sectors that have been historically subordinated in the US and Europe are taking advantage of the conflict of interests inside the global financial bloc. Occupy Wall Street and the 'outraged' (los 'indignados') in Spain best symbolize this new space. The Great Depression of the 21st Century involves the collapse of neoliberal globalization and opens new avenues for alternatives. The Great Depression is not only a threat, but it also constitutes a message of hope. A global rebellion is making its way in the world, creating a new collective actor that has the potential of achieving a change in civilization. The rejection of the bankers is becoming international with the movement of the 'indignados'. On 17 October, there were demonstrations against the bankers in a thousand cities in over a hundred countries. In Spain, there were a million demonstrators. Hungary has formally accused bankers of being responsible for the financial crisis in the country. Other countries will follow.[8]

The Great Depression of the 21st Century has provoked a crisis of legitimation of global proportions. It appears as if we have entered a new era of rebellions and revolutions that reminds us of those that took place in Europe in 1848. We can speak of a global political awakening and awareness. Although this new awakening manifests itself differently in every country and region, it is global in nature. It is no longer an isolated rebellion in one country or region like North Africa or Southern Europe; it could erupt in every corner of the world, even at the heart of the financial centres of New York and the City of London, as we saw with the events of 2011. Western civilization itself could be put to question.

Over the last decade, we have observed a deep questioning and decoupling from neoliberalism in Latin America. Since 2008, we have been witnessing popular uprisings in Sub-Saharan Africa due to famines. The year 2011 has seen famines in Somalia, Ethiopia, Eritrea and Kenya, and now the FAO warns us of a new generalized famine in Africa and other continents. This is due mainly to the increase in prices of staple grains and speculation. For decades now, we have been observing rebellions in North

---

8 See *Geab*, No. 58, 17 October 2011.

Africa, perhaps with the exception of Algeria, against labour instability and social insecurity. For several years, political stability was only achieved by installing dictatorships. As the opportunities for international migration diminished, the possibilities of realizing individual or familial projects outside of the home country were shattered. The 'American Dream' or the 'European Dream' wouldn't lead to a greater politicization in the country of origin. The crisis and unemployment in the metropolis posed serious obstacles to migration. The solution to the problems of millions and millions of migrants of the periphery since then could only be found in their own countries. This demanded collective action that had the effect of politicizing the population, in particular the young, who migrated in droves. Rebellions surged in Northern Africa; especially those in Egypt and Tunisia became more widespread. The uprisings in Libya and Syria, however, were provoked by external forces with imperialist objectives.

Economic depression and massive unemployment in Europe and the US have also provoked their own popular uprisings that one had not seen for ages. We can no longer say that it cannot happen in core countries. Today, rebellions can surge anywhere and at any moment. We are living in an era of rebellion as well as in an era of hope and opportunities to change the world. The economic rationality of today tends to deny life to an increasing portion of the world's population, both at the centre and the periphery; it tends to shorten the economically active life of workers causing great economic and social insecurity. The same logic destroys the shelf life of products, as they become disposable, and even the lifespan of machinery and business equipment are reduced in the race to have cutting-edge technology competing in the markets. It destroys the natural world to the extent that it destroys non-renewable resources. Capital negates life in all realms with its own logic of reproduction. It promotes the death of all that is incorporated in its logic. It, therefore, runs the risk of succumbing to its own rationality. It is our contention that as capital negates life and sows death in so many fields, it ends up, in the ultimate analysis, negating life in the reproduction of itself. In other words, it is a system that is programmed to self-destruct.

We believe that human beings are the product of history as well as the producers of history, and not least through labour. The possibility of building a political project that can change the economic rationality does not depend exclusively on the will of the people, nor is it predetermined by so-called objective conditions. Liberal democracy is not nearly the exclusive historical project of a social class. The same can be said of alternative projects, be it socialism, civilizatory change or simply another phase of global capitalism under the hegemony of a global state. The key is provided in the intersection between political will and historical moments that allow a change in the economic rationality. We think that the Great Depression of the 21st Century is characterized by a crisis of civilization of a specific historical moment that offers the opportunity to transcend borders based on a political project destined to change the current economic rationality.

The global crisis will promote and amplify the decoupling from neoliberalism. In the last decade, Latin America has tended to free itself from the politics of annexation of the most conservative wing of US politics. The non-approval of the ALCA as a politics of annexation was a deep disappointment for US politics. The politics of decoupling continued in Latin America with ALBA, Petrocaribe, UNASUR and CELAC. Ecuador and Bolivia joined Venezuela's politics of decoupling, and other countries followed suit. UNASUR, which was constituted in 2008, signified the emergence of a new regional power bloc and a new beacon of liberty. CELAC went even further. Today we are witnessing decoupling attempts from neoliberalism even in Europe and the US.

How to Confront Bankers

Global bankers were able to subdue entire countries by using the burden of debt, something that could only be achieved in the past through war. The imposition of a debt can be understood as a financial war and, therefore, as odious debt. National economies have the right to defend themselves before such aggressions the way Iceland did through two referendums. Iceland did not rescue the bank (Icesave); it rescued its people. Mainstream media tries, through all possible means, to hide from public view the historical lesson that Iceland has taught us. Greece was forced to save foreign banks rather than its people. The people of Greece had to rescue the banks by enduring a severe austerity programme and a deep recession. The usual credit rating agencies committed fraud by classifying the Greek debt to junk status. Debts that have been acquired through fraudulent acts or corruption are illegitimate, and even illegal. This odious debt can and must be wiped off. The odious character of the debt can be demonstrated through an audit of the people, an audit that we support.[9]

The more countries and regional blocs get involved in the fight against global corporate greed and the banks, the more possible it is to build an international mass movement that can rescue the people, and not the bankers. The Great Depression of the 21st Century creates the climate for the nationalization of banks to make them work for the common good of

---

9 See Eric Toussaint, 'Es necesario anular las deudas ilegitimas', interviewed by Sebastian Bruklez (2011).

the people. The nationalization of the Dexia Bank is a case in point. It is necessary to regulate banks, just as they were after the Great Depression of the 20th Century. It is imperative to impose on banks, where people deposit their money and savings, a financial discipline that does not merge investment with commercial banking. It is important to exclude securities from banking. It is also necessary to control and put limits on the flows and outflows of capital to a country, as it is now timidly being done in Europe with the CDS. Obviously, to accomplish this it will be necessary that governments are forced to change their economic politics radically by decoupling from neoliberalism.[10]

How to Engineer the Change in History

The project of globalist bankers is to subordinate the countries of the metropolis, including the US and the European Union by stealing their productive assets. The Multilateral Agreement on Investment (MAI) was the first attempt to destroy the self-determination of the world's nation-states in economic strategic matters. The attempt failed in 1998/1999 within the OECD. The present battle against the dollar and the euro has the same objective. Unlike Formento and Merino, we do not believe that the project of the globalist bankers will succeed. The autarchy of these so-called private states without borders and citizens is very dependent on the unsustainable investments in the unproductive sphere of the economy. The lack of commitment of these private states to its citizens and their borders is precisely their weakness in a geopolitical conflict between them and the interests of economic blocs with citizens and borders that are oriented much more towards the productive sphere. China and Russia as creditors of the West cannot be subordinated by financial or other economic mechanisms. An economic bloc of Eurasia and other BRICS countries based on productive forces has better chances of coming out of an actual global depression positively. To envision the forthcoming collapse of Western banks, it is necessary to look at what is happening in the City of London and Wall Street. It has become clear that Greece and the euro were two fingers that were pointing at the problem, but they were not the problem itself. The Greek debt reveals in 2010 the infamy of the banks. The survival or not of the euro may be the needle required to burst the bubble of today's financial system.

In 2011, the City of London and Wall Street, along with the mainstream media, blamed the fiscal debt crisis on Greece and the euro, thus throwing up a smokescreen that concealed their impending debacle. One can assess the state of the Western banking system by measuring the evolution of

---

10 See Paul Armstrong *et al.*, 'Germany Riskier than the UK for the First Time since January 2008', www.bloomberg.com, 9 August 2011.

bank personnel, its performance and stockholders. Both Wall Street and the City of London have, since mid-2011, incessantly laid off hundreds of thousands of employees. From 2012 onwards, we may expect the collapse of the global banking system of the City of London and Wall Street. As this succeeds, the time would have arrived to demand the nationalization of banks with audits of the citizens.[11]

In the meantime, the real economy has moved to the emergent countries. According to *The Economist*, in terms of the purchasing power, these emergent countries (defined here as those countries that are not part of the OECD) had already encompassed 54 per cent of the world's GDP by 2011.[12] It is really surprising that 52 per cent of all cars and 82 per cent of all cell phones were sold in these countries. The export sales of these countries together surpassed more than 50 per cent of the world's exports in 2010 against 27 per cent in 1990. Together they held 81 per cent of the international reserves and only 17 per cent of the world's public debt. They consumed 60 per cent of the world's energy, 65 per cent copper, 75 per cent steel and 55 per cent oil. China is the strongest of the emergent countries, with more than 49 per cent of its GDP in investments compared to 16 per cent of that of the US. As Chinese exports reduced and will reduce even more during the Great Depression of the 21st Century, investment in China are being made in huge housing and infrastructure projects, which, sooner or later, will also lead to a new bubble that will burst.

During 2009, spurred on by the government, China's banks increased their lending by almost 1.5 trillion dollars. This is roughly twice the size of the Indian banking system. Much of this lending flowed to some 10,000 investment companies sponsored by local governments, which could not borrow directly in their own name. These companies set about buildings roads, bridges, irrigation works and housing schemes of dubious merit. In 2010, the loans of local governments totalled about 35 per cent of the GDP.[13] An area similar to Manhattan is under construction an hour's train ride from Beijing. Debt accumulated by companies financing local governments is raising the debt disclosed by all 231 local government financing companies that sold bonds, notes or commercial paper through. The total amounted to $622 billion, mostly in bank loans, more than the current size of the European bailout fund.[14] Many of these projects will fail to raise enough revenue to repay their creditors. Defaults have already surfaced in Yunnan province and elsewhere. An undetermined amount

---

11 See Note 8.

12 *The Economist*, 6 August 2011, p. 66.

13 Simon Cox, 'Keynes v Hayek in China', *The Economist*, 17 November 2011, p. 71.

14 Bloomberg News, 'China Debts Dwarf Official Data with Too-Big-to-Finish Alarm', 18 December 2011.

of these projects will be abandoned halfway. The expected bursting of the bubble will impact the economies of particularly Africa and Latin America and thus deepen the Great Depression of the 21st Century.

Latin America has potential even in crisis time, as it will be forced into becoming a more endogenous economy. The continent geographically is bigger than Russia. It is the largest producer of food in the world and possesses the most important biodiversity reserves and water resources of the world. The South American territories have the largest reserves not only of fossil fuels and agro-fuels, but also of minerals in the world. As these resources become scarcer and strategic to their own economies, a more unified continent can channel them to a more endogenous use and even preserve them for future generations. In the context of the Great Depression, a politics of self-reliance or relative autarchy becomes not only a possibility, but it will be, from then on, a necessity. All these elements build a solid base for a proper real economy in emergent countries in the context of the crisis.

Capitalism cannot survive without economic growth, independent of whether this occurs in the metropolis or the emergent countries. The increasing relative or even absolute scarcity of natural resources compromises the economic rationality of capitalism. A politics of preservation or of reduction of the exploitation of natural resources, as espoused by the indigenous communities and organized peasants, like 'Los Sin Tierra' in Brazil, will only increase the scarcity. The demand of a political project that is more endogenous in the periphery during the Great Depression of 21st Century means that fewer natural resources will be available in the world market. Sooner or later, the rationality of capitalism will fail against this extra-economic factor, as this recession looks to be one that lasts for decades. There will be an excellent opportunity, and also no other way out than, to expand the lifespan of products and/or collectivize their consumption.

Doing so, use value will start winning over exchange value. The prolongation of the lifetime of use values will decrease the effective demand in terms of its value in the same way as more collective use values will do. The consequence will be an era of negative growth at a global scale. This seems to be a must, and it announces a new civilization. To satisfy the same collective need would demand less time and resources. According to the social accountability of the content, labour productivity would increase. From the perspective of the form, it will be the contrary, as we will experience negative growth in terms of value. To be able to manage one's own natural resources more is becoming a subject of discussion in the periphery, claim social movements and even governments (China). This may change the global rationality of capitalism in a profound way. Here is where we envision the beginning of a new civilization.

References

Dierckxsens, Wim. 2000. *The Limits of Capitalism*. London: Zed Books.

Formento, Walter and Gabriel Merino. 2011. *The Struggle for the Reconfiguration of the World Order*. Buenos Aires: Peña Lillo/Ediciones Continente.

Marín, Emilio. 2011. 'Goldman Sachs, dueño de parte de Europa, EE UU y algo más', www.rebelion.org, 11 December.

Mayer, J.D., Trace. 2009. *The Great Credit Contraction*. Ebook. Premier Ark LLC.

Vitali, Stefania, James B. Glattfelder and Stefano Battison. 2011. 'The Network of Global Corporate Control', ETH, Zurich.

Wolfe, John Truman. 2011. 'A Greek Tragedy, Part III', www.johntrumanwolfe.com, 4 April.

CHAPTER 2

A Critique of the Hegemonic Ideology and its Roots

Paulo CAMPANARIO

Centro Latinoamericano de Demografía, Brazil

Introduction

Apparently indestructible, a single power system has commanded humanity for more than two centuries. Control of this power, once shared among the colonial empires, has been in the hands of the United States since World War II. Nearly all the socialisms have gone and those surviving are no longer threatening.

But, after so much time to polish its advantages, this power system demonstrates its inability to resolve basic known and persistent problems: unemployment, hunger, inequality, environmental destruction, expulsive migratory flows, personal neuroses and insecurity. In addition, economic crises break out repeatedly and currently they are breaking out at the core, that is, in the 'first world.' There are also geopolitical weaknesses; the most recent ones include: the fiascos in Iraq and Afghanistan, the unpredictability of the Arab spring, the endless Palestinian-Israeli conflict, the growing weakness of the dollar as a universal currency, and the rise of China and India as emerging powers. From these disturbances emerge strong anti-systemic movements, many of international scope.

This essay affirms that despite its problems, weaknesses and challenges, this global power will continue to survive, mainly thanks to a powerful ideology that supports it, justifies it and has many followers.

This ideology, in turn, is based on solid logical principles that were formalized in ancient Greece and then assimilated first in the West and now throughout the world. This structure of principles has the ability to maintain constant harmony in any theoretical system, smoothing its edges and contradictions, and making it appear coherent and balanced. The ideology transfers this harmony to concrete systems – a country, a company, an NGO, a university.

Despite its age, this structural root remains alive, free from threats, currently fulfilling its role as the foundation of the ideology in question, of science, of the systems of power, that is, of the civilization in which we find ourselves submerged. In the past, it conferred reason and honour to ideologies and societies as unjust as the slavocratic, the monarchy and the feudal.

The solidity and prestige of this matrix of thinking impedes the rise of a true alternative capable of substituting it. It will probably continue to give breaths of life to the ideology of the global system as long as an alternative does not appear that would substitute its static, simplifying and conformist rules with others that are more totalizing and appropriate to the complex challenges to come and to the interests of the majority of the population.

The Neighbours Iland and Weland

In the early 17th century, the feudal monarchy Regaland, located on an island in the North Atlantic, was divided after a dispute between two princes who were brothers to succeed their father, who was in a coma. The dispute led to the creation of two countries: West Regaland and East Regaland. Capitalism gradually took root in the second half of the 18th century, primarily in East Regaland. A monoculture – cotton – produced in the two countries throughout the 19th century, caused progressive desertification of the land. Growing poverty and widespread hunger led to the death of tens of thousands of peasants. This period was known throughout the island as the 'Hunger Years'. As an epilogue, the two monarchies were overthrown, giving rise to two nations with representative democracies, Iland and Weland. Today, their small populations live in peace and have similar sizes and structures. The two countries have oil, discovered at the beginning of the last century, which is the only export item produced with foreign capital. Hunger has been eliminated and this fuel, which accounts for the largest portion of the GNP, is sufficient for the per capita income to be equal to that of a European nation. Because there are no arid lands, there is no agriculture and food is imported. Due to the abundance of the black gold, there are distinct services – although the industrial sector in the two countries is limited to goods whose import price is prohibitive – as well as civil construction and infrastructure (roads, ports and sanitation systems). There is a railroad line, built by the English, joining the two capitals since the late 19th century.

Despite a history and many other characteristics in common, the two countries have significant economic, social, ideological and political differences.

An Overview of the Iland Economy

A revolt led by Grygor defeated the absolute monarchy of West Regaland in 1899. The constitution, inspired by that of the United States, a country where this rebel was exiled for 10 years, emphasized the French motto of 'Liberty, Equality, Fraternity', which was included in the charter because of Grygor's personal wish. To terminate the nation's association with the seductive royal family, he also proposed to the parliament a new denomination for the country, with the justification:

> I believe in individualism and respect it, because each citizen, based on personal initiatives, within the law and seeking to not harm the other, generates a virtuous cycle for him or herself and, as a result, for the group. Our motto can be summarized as follows: 'The sum of the good citizens results in a good society'. And for this idea to last as a sign of our character, I propose this new name for our homeland: The Libertarian Republic of Iland.

The proposal was approved nearly unanimously and, since then, Grygor has been known as 'The Libertarian'.

After two decades of coalition governments that did not establish a clear direction, in the 1920s, the opposition, represented by the Social Democratic Party of Iland (SDPI) and led by The Libertarian, won an absolute majority in parliament. Successive victories led to a near total control of the government. In the 1930s, with the flight of capital from the country, the bankruptcy of many private companies and their complete lack of initiative to attenuate the negative and prolonged effects of the Great Depression of 1929, the government exercised a broad state takeover of companies (schools, ports, roads, banks and even large commerce). Only companies with 10 or fewer employees or family-owned companies had a legal license to operate as private property. Behind these measures was the idea that small firms absorb, thanks to their low technologies, a large quantity of workers, allowing the new and large state sphere to become an advanced segment of the economy. Despite the country's small population, the strategy was expected to generate an extensive domestic market, which would be difficult to achieve in the previous situation of chaos. Something similar to what Scandinavian Social Democratic parties implemented with good results.

To avoid the real threat of excessive bureaucratization, the managers of the state companies came to enjoy complete autonomy, but had to follow two basic rules: first, to gain profit by only legal means and, second, to make decisions about what, where and how much to produce without government interference. To reinforce the autonomy of the managers, there was flexibilization of labour legislation and everything produced and imported was free of bureaucratic intervention. The government facilitated the proliferation of companies, both state and private, financing them and simplifying the process to establish new ones. The free market became an essential mediator of the entire Iland economy.

Under these conditions, development came to depend not only on the decisions of managers, who were constantly competing with each other to obtain the highest possible profit, but also on the desires of consumers (individual desires). Together, managers and consumers generated a virtuous development cycle, mediated by the market. The unemployment rate, which before state takeovers was around 20 per cent, decreased gradually, reaching 5 per cent in the 1950s. The country came to be proud of achieving a high average productivity rate and its citizens enjoyed a high standard of living.

SDPI's power grew in the society as a whole, blending with the government between 1920 and 1930 and merging with the state since the 1930s, mainly because of the state control of the economy.

Over time, in a process similar to Darwinian selection, some companies became stronger and influential, others less so. Because of their economies of scale and due to the passion of the Ilander people for vehicles, automobile importers became the strongest economic sector after the 1950s. Istban, the manager of the largest state-run automobile importer in the country, rose to the position of general secretary of the central committee of the SDPI in 1959 and was elected federal deputy and then prime minister in 1960.

State-owned and with sovereign management, banks gave priority to financing automobile purchases, which was an excellent business. To facilitate the traffic of cars, state-owned construction companies arose, also financed by the banks. And from this emerged a strong cartel – state-run – with common interests of its members and used its power in defense of these interests and its own survival, because over time the managers and administrators covertly granted themselves advantages and privileges. The cartel came to exist informally in 1949, led by Istban, and was denominated by its members as 'The Circle', possibly an unconscious allusion to car wheels. Of its five members, two represented the automobile importers, two the builders and one the financial sector. They met at least twice a year to analyse the current situation and define strategies to defend their interests.

Because of its great power, this group forged a new society in the image of and in keeping with its interests, between 1945 and 1990, a period known in Iland as the 'Golden Years'. Automobiles were associated with this opulence. Approved by parliament and proposed by Istban, the 'Savings Law' changed how oil royalties were allocated. Half of the annual total of these royalties was deposited monthly in savings accounts opened for each citizen upon birth. Upon reaching adulthood, when the banks liberated the accounts, everyone had accumulated enough money to purchase a high cost product. According to a 1990 study, 90 per cent of the young adults purchased automobiles with these savings. Another law obliged each new resident to have at least one covered garage. In the 1970s, when there was a rise in the international price of oil, the government kept the domestic price unchanged to maintain the stimulus for this sector. In 1980, another decree released automobiles from import tariffs – but did not include vehicles for mass transportation, whose rates remained unchanged, though no one cared about this detail.

The economy remained robust and despite the control of society by the cartel, the citizens trusted that this minority represented them and defended their interests. After all, these elites were democratically elected with the votes of the majority and were able to satisfy the desires of the majority, manifesting to everyone the strength of their representative democracy.

The Ilanders paid for their own cars, often with financing, and cared for them, but had no knowledge or awareness of their high indirect costs. Vehicles could only circulate with bridges, roads, parking spaces, increased residential spaces to shelter them, gas stations, etc. The powerful cartel forced urban structures and the size of the cities of Iland to adapt to the basic needs of the automobiles, leaving the population to work and live practically in the remaining empty spaces. Even so, these machines often clogged and damaged the roads and caused environmental pollution, which also involved costs.

The Circle transformed the government and even the state into mere appendixes. In 1990, an average Ilander came to consume 10 per cent of the per capita GNP to own and maintain a car. When considering the indirect and invisible costs mentioned earlier, the amount reached 50 per cent.[1] This raises the question: is it prudent for someone to dedicate half of their work time to keep these rolling quadrupeds in their garages and use them for an average of only one hour per day? This irrational consumption, derived from the interests of the cartel as well as the citizens' individualist desire to consume, led to 90 per cent of the GNP getting represented as consumption and only 10 per cent as investment in that year.

With the transformations that took place in the Golden Years, there was a rapid decrease in mortality after 1950 and in fertility after 1960. The number of children per woman reached one and a half in 1980, provoking, in addition to low growth, a strong aging of the population. In 1990, 30 per cent of the citizens were more than 60 years old, intensifying

1 Calculated by a consulting company contracted by the government, which attempted to hide the result, but a journalist published it anonymously in a periodical in neighbouring Weland.

the demand for healthcare.[2] Individual transportation, which squandered a large portion of the purchasing power, led Iland to a dilemma. To resolve the costly healthcare problem, there were two options: either radically change this profile of consumption, which would imply sweeping bankruptcy of the cartel of companies that were linked to individual transportation and responsible for 50 per cent of the GNP, or cut spending on education, decrease salaries, retirement pay, etc., which were very unpopular measures. The cartel fought bitterly to have nothing changed. Moreover, the government itself, not by desire but need, decided to reduce salaries and retirement pay. Istban defended the measure alleging that 'the other option, to change our profile of consumption, would bring a very serious crisis to Iland; it's the lesser of the two evils.'

On the other hand, despite laws and decrees favourable to their sale and commercialization, automobile sales started stagnating in 1990 due to the increasingly slow population expansion in general and the absolute decrease each year in the number of youths reaching adulthood, all aggravated by sluggish economic growth.

The government was able to lower the salaries of active workers and retirees by 10 per cent, thanks to the support of the National Public Employees Union, dominated by the SDPI. Despite the criticisms of its affiliates, the union received broad support from the cartel, with whom it signed an agreement to build a large headquarters on prime real estate in the capital to substitute the current one, which was very small and on the periphery and a 'disgrace', according to the union president. Annual GNP growth had been decreasing since the early 1990s and stabilized near zero in 2000. The salary reductions were not enough to resolve the deficit and there was an increase in the morbidity and mortality of the population, including infant mortality, because of the degradation in the state healthcare system, which had once been efficient. The Golden Years had come to an end.

After 1990, the banks began to finance an increasing number of residential and commercial properties. Since 2000, the list of priorities came to include countless domestic and business electronics, led by computers. Automobile financing gradually fell to a secondary plane. In a meeting of The Circle in early 2001, Istban questioned Jos, a federal deputy and representative of the financial sector:

> Today, to buy and sell real estate and these electronic games for adolescents, you offer better interest rates than those offered to buy cars, the best transportation system in existence. We have realized that this policy has generated a crisis in

2 In Japan today, 32 per cent of the population is more than 60 years old. In 2050, the UN predicts, it will reach 41 per cent and we are all heading down the same path.

our cartel because the situation has become critical for many of us. Our profits have dropped and some importers have gone bankrupt. You practically broke our pact, which has existed since the 1950s. It brought notable and recognized progress to the country. I would like to hear my young friend Jos explain what has led our cartel to be ostracized by the financial system.

With his known sincerity, Jos replied:

Neither you nor I are the owners of the state-run companies, but for administering them we gain privileges and, at the same time, an obligation: we must earn more and more profits. Without this, the capital and our employees disappear, our enemies get ahead, our machines and installations deteriorate; we could not purchase new raw materials or renovate ourselves, we would collapse and lose our prerogatives. This kind of 'free initiative' should be called 'forced initiative'! Until now our thoughts and acts were equal. Now put yourself in my place: you have most of your capital located in the specific sector in which you operate (warehouses, trucks, stores, stock) while we, on the contrary, are required to invest them where we receive the highest return, without regard for the sector; by need we are omnipresent. We are light; our raw material is called money, which today is largely virtual. And it is precisely this lightness that is simultaneously our greatest strength and our greatest weakness. We are omnipotent because in a short time, with intelligent strategies, we can expand our wealth and make it equal to a large country, but we are weak because we can disappear overnight if we make an error in our specialties of speculation and market forecasts. The true reason that led us to give secondary attention to automobile sales was the low population increase and the growing proportion of elderly people in Iland, in addition to new, more attractive businesses. When the opportunity arose to finance the multimillion dollar Air Force project to purchase a fleet of fighter-bombers and earn high interest rates, guaranteeing our survival in coming years, we participated in the bid, formed a consortium with other state banks to present our financial proposal and we won. Wasn't this a good reason to give our pact secondary importance? These planes are worth ten times more than all the automobiles sold in a year. Pacts are like etiquette, ceremonial rules between parties; they only exist while there is mutual interest of the participants and do not guarantee to that they will be kept alive otherwise.

Istban interrupted Jos: 'But the automobiles are useful to the citizens and the military planes are useless. We are what we are because of cars!'

Jos retorted:

With respect to the planes, I agree. Is the country under any threat from its neighbours? No! Our peaceful neighbour Weland has no heavy arms or planes. So, these fighter planes will never drop bombs; they will sit like parasites in the hangers of military airports, insolently displaying their cost and uselessness to the people. Nevertheless, for the manufacturers and for us, the financers, these planes have inestimable utility because with their high costs, capital multiplies and generates profit. For us, the more they cost, the more useful they are. For us, utility depends on price, money, profit and value. Now, with respect to the automobiles, don't be shocked, but I sincerely believe that they will be as or more useless to the citizens as the planes. We were the ones who defined their usefulness for the Ilanders. We sold them and financed them after discovering they offered good profits. The automobile became useful for consumers because of our not confessable profit motivations. They are useful, that is, in a manner of speaking; look at our Weland neighbours, satisfied with their buses and trolleys and their economy without crisis. The Golden Years could well be called The Automotive Years because the return from the sale and financing of cars was excellent. Unfortunately, the flower has wilted. For this reason, depending on the circumstances, from our perspective, fighter bombers, cars, homes and computers are all the same because in the final analysis they multiply capital. The lack of financing for residential and commercial construction in recent decades, precisely because our cartel preferred to finance cars, created a housing deficit that makes the sector more attractive today, but, within a decade, its ability to expand will be limited by the nearly zero population growth. Fighter-bombers do not depend on population growth. Nor do electronics, our rising star, because they have incredibly short lifespans and for this reason their sales never dry up – or so we hope, knocking three times on the wooden meeting table. For these reasons, we have not betrayed the cartel, we are simply following the route of survival imposed by capital. I propose to keep it alive, but expand its objects. Remember *The Leopard*: 'if we want everything to stay the same, everything must change'.[3] I thus suggest the diversification of its activities, because the automobile sector has limited opportunity for future growth and cannot continue to absorb all the capital you have accumulated. We recently released a new kind of investment fund called a derivative, invented by some geniuses on Wall Street. It is based on the profit from financing housing and there are no better interest rates in the market. I invite you to invest your excess capital in these funds. It's profits earning profits! Changing the subject, given the current importance of my sector, I propose that we have a second representative on The Circle to make it more representative.

The meeting ended with doses of single malt scotch. The next year, 2002, Jos came to lead The Circle. His group in the national congress had 15 deputies. These, added to those from construction and other opportunists, made up 55 per cent of the house. He was elected prime minister.

Despite the critical situation after 1990, with expanded unemployment and GNP growth close to zero, the Ilanders still didn't perceive the inestimable help given by them to implant, without wanting to and as useful innocents, a country for the minority of the cartel. The Ilanders were

---

3 Line from the novel *The Leopard* by Tomasi di Lampedusa (1960), made into a movie by Visconti in 1963 with Burt Lancaster, Claudia Cardinale and Alain Delon.

highly qualified, responsible and efficient at work. But unfortunately, the efficiency and the productivity of the autonomous enterprises in supplying the market with specific goods or services was not enough to conveniently supply the population with essential and costly goods and services, such as healthcare. The type of structure of consumption, imposed by the interests of the minority of The Circle, together with the desires of the individualistic consumption of the population, none of which considers the needs of society as a whole, led to a situation in which the companies openly displayed efficiency individually, but society as a whole suffered from a hidden inefficiency. In neighbouring Weland, this situation of apparent contradiction, with micro-efficiency and macroeconomic inefficiency, is known as the Iland Paradox. And there is no hope of overcoming it. Since the 1990s, the financial sector has dictated the rules of the game and simply changed the profile of consumption, moving from autos to homes and then to electronics and derivatives, in addition to a large business in fighter-bombers. This paradox always exists in modern political systems, which are controlled by the wishes of a minority, but the majority almost never perceives its effects and even adopts the same wishes and thinking as the minority.

The average lifespan of products has grown shorter since the second half of the previous century and this has increased global inefficiency in society. In the producing countries, competition among capitalists provoked a growing advance in technology, explained by the objective of the owner or controller of capital to maintain profits and not be crushed by the competition. This process promoted continuous renovation of technology, making goods rapidly obsolete. At first sight, this appears to be advantageous because it stimulates capital growth. Nevertheless, this process is controlled only by blind market forces, and in the long run, this premature aging becomes undesirable because it becomes increasingly costly to dispose of relatively new machines, which are still in operating condition but are discarded simply because the competing neighbour does the same. Thus, there is a decrease in the rate of profit. This was demonstrated in Japan two decades ago. This process also winds up shortening the average life of the final products produced, as can be seen with electronics. For importing countries, like Iland, the shorter average lifespan condemns them to progressively higher expenses on imports, deteriorating their standards of consumption and, therefore, living.[4]

This macroeconomic inefficiency is aggravated even more because of oil, a non-renewable resource. In Iland, the production of many wells is already declining and the discovery of new ones decreasing. Total

---

4 For a more detailed analysis of the average life of products and the growing scarcity of natural resources, see Dierckxsens (2007).

production has remained flat since 2000, and in a few years, it will begin to decrease. The government embarrassingly recognized, after consulting an independent institution, that the country's oil reserves in 2002 were in reality 50 per cent lower than the previous estimate made by the oil companies. The companies simply lied because, for them, what was important was the profit, and being foreigners, they wanted to produce as much as possible, defending, as could be expected, only their own interests and not those of Iland. The simple ignorance about the situation of the oil reserves and the consequent lack of suitable policies for overcoming this problem could lead the country to a more aggravated crisis. This can also be considered a type of macroeconomic inefficiency because the oil companies boast efficiency and profit, but society benefits increasingly less from this commodity, which in theory belongs to it.

In sum, Iland suffers from macroeconomic inefficiency because it gave priority to the automobile without seriously considering other more important social needs. This inefficiency is worsened by the limits of oil production, which has reached its peak and will soon begin to decline. On the other hand, imports are increasing as though oil royalties, which are the source of financing this consumption, were infinite, aggravating this inefficiency even more. Finally, the average lifetime of products has decreased, deteriorating the country's purchasing power. In the medium term, these events will provoke a collapse of the economy. The act of producing for the sake of producing is causing environmental disequilibrium by poisoning, depleting and destroying natural resources, including flora and fauna, water and the atmosphere. Finally, to make things worse, there is still the currently dominant financial sector in Iland, which is shaping the country in its interests and aggravating all of this inefficiency. But the government and the Ilanders still do not realize the importance of this reality because they consider this only as a slow growth situation, not a crisis.

Who has power in Iland? It had been the automobile cartels, today it is the financial cartels. There is no democracy despite democratic elections. There is no liberty or equality or fraternity.

An Overview of the Weland Economy

In Weland, previously Eastern Regaland, a liberal party controls the parliament, having won all democratic elections since the 1920s. The economy developed through the initiative and talent of private entrepreneurs and minimal government interference. Despite this radical liberalism, the Welanders historically had a strong social conscience. They considered the influence of social factors on individual and family life transcendental, contrary to the neighbouring, excessively individualistic llanders. The social awareness of the Welanders is manifested in a tradition of struggle and, as a consequence, in the art of pressuring the government and private groups to conquer advantages and improvements in the standard of living and of simple measures to favour happiness and well-being.

Many history scholars from Weland attribute the well-known fighting spirit of its people to a few unique factors. First, there is the Buddhist religion, the most popular in the country, which is unprecedented in the West. In the 18th century, the Catholic king wanted to marry another woman because the queen was infertile and could not provide an heir. But the Pope repeatedly denied the monarch's request, all in the name of God. The king had always declared himself an enemy of the Protestants and thus could not adopt their religion. As a result of the dispute with the Pope and after secret agreements with Chinese monks, the first and only Buddhist monarchy was established in the West. The eradication of illiteracy in the country was one of the positive effects of Buddhism because after entering the country, the monks, due to their discipline and influence, were soon able to teach a good portion of the population to read, earning support and respect from the Welanders. This was also a catalyst for the substitution of feudalism by capitalism, leading to the modernizing of the country.

Feudalism dominated in Weland until the mid-18th century when the country embraced Buddhism. The country had been controlled by the minority feudal lords, including the royal family and the Church. Serfs, small merchants and craftsmen owned their own land and the tools of their trade and, in exchange for the right to live on the fief with their families, they paid taxes and a tithe or worked part-time for the feudal lords, generating a surplus, which was transformed into luxury goods and services and an army, all of them separated from the productive process. For this reason, the economy grew very slowly and misery ruled.

Due to the introduction of Buddhism in Weland, the Church, which owned one-third of the land in the country, could no longer charge the tithe and went bankrupt. Serfs, craftsmen and merchants in the feudal system comprised the embryonic capitalist class because they controlled the means of production, wanted a steady increase in production and were not disturbed if they were required to hire labour to sustain their business (in fact, if they did not have children to serve as labourers, they hired someone from the village). Thus, in the latter half of the 18th century, some merchants and artisans, who had saved some money, purchased a part of the land from the Church and began to plant cotton for export, using former serfs as salaried workers who lost their hereditary rights to land, mainly those belonging to the Church.

This monoculture provided good profits and turned out to be a more advantageous activity than that of accumulating jewels and palaces. Soon many feudal lords also began to do the same. In brief, the fiefs disappeared and banks appeared. There was a process of concentration and capitalism came to command the country. At the beginning of the 19th century, cotton dominated the rural landscape.

In sum, a minority of the former small merchants, artisans, serfs and feudal lords became farmers, bankers, industrialists and great traders, and the rest, the majority, became salaried workers. The royal family allied itself to these new capitalist lords; they retained some land for leisure and hunting and began to receive a share of the taxes so they could vegetate in their routine of luxury and pomp. Almost contagiously, the neighbouring Western Regaland also transformed and came to live under capitalism, with the same mono-cultivation of cotton. The most important difference between the two countries was that in Eastern Regaland, because of the introduction of Buddhism, the Church lost its power and thus its conservative ideological influence, a fact that did not occur in the neighbouring country. The future Welanders had more open and critical minds, which explained their fighting spirit.

Another reason for this fighting spirit was the influence of Yavie, a leader in the struggle against the monarchy, a founder and inspirer of the republic and of democracy. His father worked for the crown in East Regaland's embassy in Beijing, which had strategic importance because of the historic ties established with China after the introduction of Buddhism. Yavie was born in Beijing in the mid-19th century. In addition to Mandarin, he studied Chinese philosophy and learned to use the I Ching, the Book of Changes, and was an expert in the concepts of Yin-Yang. He was 20 years old when his father was promoted to ambassador and transferred to Paris. Yavie went with his family to France, where he studied philosophy and was highly influenced by leftist thinking, which was respected and in fashion in some circles there. At the age of 25 he returned secretly to his country and came to lead the struggle against the monarchy.

Yavie never accepted the position of prime minister despite the insistence of the local elite. But his responsibility as leader led him to propose and win approval on the principles inspired by his philosophical convictions. These commandments, eight in all, were the backbone of the Weland Constitution, which also guaranteed a fixed part of the national budget to education, the 'priority priority', according to the leader. The country's new name was approved by his suggestion:

> The we, the collective will have priority, but with unconditional respect for the individual and his or her specificities, inalienable longings and rights. But exaggerated individualism degenerates in selfishness and injustice. To

> keep this ideal alive, I propose that our country call itself The Parliamentary Republic of Weland.

Because of this request, Yavie became known as The Balanced One, since he proposed a balance between the collective and the individual. Buddhism, with its deep collective roots and its Eastern dialectical thinking, a religion contrary to the individualism typical of capitalism, combined with the ideas of Yavie, who had deep knowledge of the Welander soul. This also helped to explain the fighting spirit of the people, according to other scholars.

The Welanders always remember Yavie's collectivist vision:

> A single book can elevate the minds of many citizens if it is protected and distributed in a public, private or state library. Why then do many prefer, after buying and reading them, to retire them uselessly on a shelf in their home for many years? Everything should be socially enjoyed to the degree possible. If every teacher would only teach one student, there would only be teachers for the elite and nearly the entire population would be illiterate. The efficiency of a society is crucially measured by the quantity of collective goods and services that it is able to provide the population.

The Welanders like collective transportation, and due to well-organized pressure, the municipal governments in the country's cities were required to install an efficient network of exclusive lanes for buses and trolleys, all built by private contractors. Thanks to this, the middle- and lower-class citizens consider cars useless. The upper classes use them only on the weekends and many prefer to rent them when necessary. The cost of cars in Weland, considering all the indirect costs, corresponds to 12.5 per cent of the GNP (in Iland it is four times as much or 50 per cent). The cities, which are more hospitable, are smaller and less polluted than those of the neighbour. Weland receives many tourists from Iland. They come by train and get around using the efficient mass transit system. But hardly any Welander goes to Iland because of the high cost of travel there, which always has to be in cars or taxis.

Since they import a high proportion of consumer goods, the Welanders are concerned about their durability. For example, they discovered that under pressure, the bus and trolley manufacturers deliver more durable products for a relatively small extra cost, substantially improving the cost-benefit ratio of these means of transportation. This problem exists in Iland too, but they don't do anything about it. In Weland, a certain degree of control is possible.

Since the Welanders dedicate a small percentage of the GNP to cars and their accessories, and not the extravagant 50 per cent like the Ilanders, they have many more possibilities and flexibility to invest in other goods and services like culture, healthcare, education, entertainment and leisure.

Under pressure from various and countless citizen groups, who represent the true power of the majority, the parliament frequently approves measures to improve control over the private economy of the country. It gives priority to the importation and production of goods that are useful for society as a whole, which are called social utilities. The country has a 40-year plan to eliminate unclean energy sources. There is a law requiring importers to consider the durability of a product as much as its price because durability should be an integral and important part of the utility of any merchandise or service. Another recent law subsidizes collective transportation to decrease the number of private vehicles even more. In a decade, this mode of transportation will be 100 per cent subsidized and in 2050, individual transportation will account for only 5 per cent of the GNP.

The law on housing promises to modify the structure of cities. Basically, it establishes that any item of residential or commercial construction of a collective nature can receive financing at low interest rates and even be subsidized. There are already neighbourhoods with very few family-owned facilities and maximum number of collective facilities. Laundries, libraries, televisions, etc., are publicly available in these neighbourhoods, decreasing the private built area of the houses and increasing the collective space. There are few vehicles on the streets, except at times one sees an ambulance, a garbage truck or a taxi. In addition, garages have been eliminated, allowing narrower streets, wider sidewalks and lanes for bicycles and pedestrians. The buildings are no more than three storeys tall, with enough space between them for the sun to come in. In addition to schools, there are small shops on the ground floor. The neighbourhoods have a circular format to reduce the distances and in the centre there is commerce, public squares, sporting facilities, universities, cinemas and theatres.

A polemical Individual Spending Law was also approved in parliament. Today, the proportion of salaries in the GNP has touched 50 per cent (in Iland, it is 90 per cent), with the other 50 per cent allocated to social utilities and investments. In 20 years it should reach 30 per cent. The objective is to condition the profile of supply and consumption to adapt to a form of production and consumption that gives priority to social utilities. Individual salaries will account for a very small percentage of the GNP in the future. The neighbouring Ilanders consider the Welanders to be eccentric.

Inspired by guerrilla tactics, the army in Weland adopted a defensive strategy. Trained by the military at the end of their adolescence, male and female citizens are taught to use light weapons and are organized by blocks throughout the country. According to the military's calculations, an invading army would need 10 soldiers for every armed Welander, making any invasion unviable. For this reason, they do not need fighter bombers, tanks or heavy weapons. Military spending is no more than 1 per cent of the GNP compared to 5 per cent in Iland.

Weland today, with all its measures adopted to make the country's economy more efficient and the emphasis on social utilities, has managed to avoid the Iland Paradox. The oil exports here are only 30 per cent of that of Iland, yet the two countries have a similar standard of living. But, considering some factors that are difficult to measure, such as the more peaceful lifestyle of the Welanders, cleaner air, better distribution of wealth, less delinquency, better healthcare and lower mortality, it can be concluded that the Welanders have a superior sense of well-being.

Concerning the strategic use of oil, important differences are found between the countries. In both countries, oil is extracted by foreign companies, but in Weland, production is strictly controlled to prolong the usefulness of the reserves as much as possible. Aware of oil being a non-renewable resource, Welanders conducted various studies to calculate the size of reserves, always contracting institutes of recognized competence. Correcting the over-estimated reserves of its neighbours and making a retrospective projection, the studies concluded that in around 1950, the countries had very similar reserves. However, Weland now has double the reserves and still does not suffer any threat of decrease in production. And, since it has plenty of wind and the capacity for investment in new projects, it is gradually installing wind turbines to produce electrical energy. There is a 30-year plan to stop using oil for electricity generation. In Iland, no wind turbines have been installed.

In Weland there are more restrictive financing rules. The banking sector is by law required to adapt to the population's desired consumption profile. For example, since plans necessitate the participation of cars in the GNP to reach 5 per cent, the banks can finance cars, roads, gas stations, etc., but with higher interest rates, properly specified by law. If there is interest in increasing the relative participation of an economic sector, as in the case of mass transportation and wind turbines, the interest rates for these items are lower or the cost of the products subsidized. Thus, the financial sector there, although it is private, acts according to the interests of the majority. Additionally, since financing is only approved for production or consumption of goods as per a previously established structure, there is no possibility of a crisis or financial bubble. Different tax rates are part of a mechanism much utilized to adjust consumption to the desired standard and defined by the majority of the population.

To address the issue of aging of the population in Weland, the people decided by plebiscite to increase that portion of the GNP that goes towards healthcare from 10 per cent to 15 per cent. The crisis helped to shape the country even more in its own image, that is, a society for the majority. The people have power and are aware of this. The liberals, despite controlling the government (parliament and other state agencies), in fact, do not have significant power and the people elect them not for their liberalism, but because they have considerable technical and administrative knowledge. The majority of highly qualified technicians are educated in liberal England because of an old tradition from the country's monarchical past, when sons from influential families were sent there to study. They lost their privileges, but now contribute to the well-being of the country and are more satisfied in comparison with their parents or grandparents. So, in reality, the majority of citizens command the society in Weland. Is there democracy? Yes, but not because of elections!

Divide to Explain: Iland versus Weland

The two countries are imaginary. Their current situation is of interest to us here more than the past and the description of some of their historic processes were provided only to better understand the present.

Despite their imaginary existence, their characteristics can be found in actually existing countries. Iland of today represents the authoritarianism of a minority that controls values, a situation that is dominant in any real country today. That is, it personifies a concrete reality in a pure and extreme form. Weland represents the dreams and interests of the majority of citizens, a self-realized prophecy, existing only in a latent state in any real country today. That is, it personifies a utopia in an equally pure and extreme form.

In Iland, the domination of value over utility is completely developed and tends to continue this way in a conservative manner. A cartel with minority interests predominates without impediments or opposition because the majority thinks like the minority. Contrary to this, in Weland, the interests of the majority of the population dominate, there are collective utilities and there is also no opposition because the minority thinks like the majority.

The two together embody a real society with different amounts of Iland and Weland, but with a predominance of Iland, which is representative of the more fully developed and real portion of any modern country. Chile and Denmark, which are both capitalist, have the dominant characteristics of Iland. But Chile, with its extreme neoliberal capitalism, has a greater proportion of the characteristics of Iland than Denmark.

In any real and modern political system, a minority, represented by Iland, always impedes the development of the qualities of the dominated majority, represented by Weland – in other words, it impedes the development of the potential of this majority. This is because the interests of Iland and Weland are at odds. As long as Weland is unable to influence society, there is alienation – or estrangement and unease – something remains 'stolen' from Weland, blocking its full realization. Development of countries is due precisely to the continuous attempts to overcome alienation, to have authenticity and liberty, and to realize the repressed potential. Today, the Weland portion of a real country, although dominated and unable to eliminate the dominant Iland portion, symbolizes hope and the future. This alienation has always existed and will continue to exist because contradictions inevitably exist and a minority always dominates.

By attributing to Weland a grade of 10 and Iland a grade of 0, any real country can be located at any point between these two extremes depending on the amount of characteristics of Weland or Iland they have. Denmark, for example, has a higher grade compared to Chile. If, over time, any country acquires some qualities of Weland, it takes one route and its grade increases. If it acquires some qualities of Iland, it takes the opposite route and its grade decreases. No real country will be equal either to Weland or Iland, but the direction taken is of great importance. With the predominance of neoliberalism, the world today is heading in the direction of Iland, and after the crisis that erupted in 2008, this trend has increased, mainly in Europe.

Personal value judgments determine whether Weland or Iland is considered better or worse. Here, Weland is considered the country model to be followed.

Until now Weland and Iland were analysed mainly from an economic perspective. We will now analyse how they think and how power is exercised in each one of them.

Ideology, Labour and Power

> A spider conducts operations that resemble those of a weaver, and a bee puts to shame many an architect in the construction of her cells. But what distinguishes the worst architect from the best of bees is this, that the architect raises his structure in imagination before he erects it in reality. At the end of every labour-process, we get a result that already existed in the imagination of the labourer at its commencement. He not only effects a change of form in the material on which he works, but he also realises a purpose of his own that gives the law to his modus operandi, and to which he must subordinate his will. (Marx, 1887: 124)

In the second-last sentence, Marx affirms that the idea exists before the result, or, in other words, the mental construction of ideas pre-exists the real construction. This process has a *purpose*, which is revealed in the final sentence. Let us look at this in greater detail.

Let's imagine the construction of a house. The builder designs it and plans all the steps needed for it to be built properly. Then, the builder gets into action and begins the work. During the execution of this activity, the builder confronts certain difficulties, which require adaptations both to the initial design and to the planning of the steps, and thus the work process ends up being modified. This, in turn, presents setbacks that require further modifications to the design and planning, and so on, interactively. By the time construction is completed, both the initial design and the steps first identified to execute the actions have undergone changes. This interaction between thinking and action (or the work process) is called 'praxis'.

The praxis of the builder produces a real object – the house, an object of wealth, which will be analysed in the next chapter. Thus, praxis is defined as a human effort that has the ability to transform nature and construct wealth with a purpose, that is, material and non-material goods and services. *This is praxis, a constructive force, the result of the interaction between thinking and action.* Contrarily, instinct commands the bee and the spider because they have no thoughts nor objectives and the results present fixed and repetitive standards.

The difficulties suffered by the builder show the limitations of the social, historic and even natural character through which both thinking and action pass. The builder, for example, constructs with a technology that is characteristic of a certain historic development that limits his praxis. There are also limitations dictated by nature: the selection of the material used in construction is based on what is available locally (wood, cement, stone, mud, straw). Thus, historic development and nature also impose limits on thinking and action and, as a result, on praxis. And if a real object is produced later, exemplified by the house, it also winds up being subject to these limitations.

Leonardo da Vinci (1452-1519) designed a helicopter, but the technological backwardness of his time impeded its possible realization. The ideal elaboration of the flying machine conducted in the mind of the Florentine required a love for the art of designing, curiosity, an awareness, his dream of flying and his intuitions, all of which were beyond intelligence and technical reasoning. *Imaginary* contains all of this and adapts more to the complexity of the human brain than *thinking*, which is the word that has been used in this chapter till now and is merely the concept that is better identified with reason.

Imaginary and action are applied to individuals, families, groups, institutions and society. But here, we are mainly interested in the latter because of the sociological character of this chapter. In society, imaginary is transformed into ideology, action is transformed into work and the interaction between the two – praxis – is transformed into politics (or simply power). Ideology, work and power develop over time as processes. Processes with a purpose.

Imaginary × *action* = *praxis*
Ideology × *work* = *politics (power)*

Ideology is considered here as a system of coherent ideas adopted collectively and adapted to a certain historic moment. Within it fits everything that fits in the brain, that is, dreams, intuitions and reasoning.

For example, in a democratic country in the 21st century, a deputy in a party that supports the government votes on a law. Thus, the deputy *works* or executes something. And, upon voting in parliament, the deputy accepts a series of Ilander rules and ways of thinking, namely, the norms of the democratic system in vigour, type of remuneration, participation in a party, agreement with its statutes and support to the status quo. Thus, the deputy assimilates an *ideology* coherent with a deputy's *work*. A free citizen of ancient Greece, if out of the blue placed in the parliament of this country, could only work as a deputy after assimilating its ideology. Thus, each moment in history has a peculiar ideology and peculiar form of work, each coherent with the other and mutually interactive. If each epoch has its peculiarity, so does politics because it depends on the ideology and work.

The deputy making laws, when working with a certain ideology, gives life to the society in which he or she lives, transforms it, conducts politics in it and exercises power on it. This power can be limited or extensive, it does not matter; it is power.

The ideology can reflect reality either falsely or truly because free will and creativity exist and can propose or imagine infinite ideologies. A deputy in the opposition in a real country, for example, can have an ideology closer to that of Weland.

Weland and Iland form systems of power – or political systems – because they originate in specific forms of work and from specific ideologies, giving sustainability and meaning to this type of work. They cannot be understood – nor can any other power system – without understanding their ideologies and types of work. The type of work defines the form of producing, and the economy is defined here as a specific form of producing or working (capitalist, for example, as in Iland). Until now Iland and Weland have been analysed mainly from an economic perspective, that is, from each one's form of working. It is thus necessary to analyse them from their ideological perspectives to understand their politics and thus have a more complete understanding of their characteristics.

From what has been said, it can also be concluded that any change in a real society can only take place with a substitution of its ideology and form of working from Ilander to Welander. In this substitution, the Welander ideology precedes and dominates the Welander work because the imaginary always precedes action. But this precedence is restricted by the level of social development and by nature; if not, we would be omnipotent.

Dual Dimensionality of Goods

We have seen that the interaction between work and ideology, that is, the power (or politics), is a social activity that produces goods to satisfy human needs in some way. Thus, a product needs work, ideology as well as a purpose to be developed, given that all ideologies have a purpose. Work, and more specifically the time of work, determines the value of this product, an idea that in this chapter is considered a postulate and, hence, will not be discussed. But there is another aspect to a product that is generally forgotten, which is that ideology and purpose determine its utility. In any case, any product always has two simultaneous qualities, use value and value:[5]

> Beforehand, in relation to use value: prior to elaborating goods, either material, such as a shirt, or non-material, such as listening to music at the theater, human imagination, in concocting it gives it an end and consequently, a use value or utility. Now, in relation to value: in principle, before concocting these goods, that same imagination estimates the time it takes to produce given goods with a certain quality, that is, the imagination estimates their value.[6]

This 'dual personality' or dual dimensionality of goods, despite being indissoluble, suffers important historic transformations, which largely explain the differences between societies, and specifically between Iland and Weland.

> In spite of being inseparable, the link between use value and value has a history and has undergone profound transformations, related to the historical evolution of societies. Hunter-gatherer peoples, in making an arrow, did so to make hunting more efficient. The time it took to make it, recognizing certain limits, was irrelevant. Thus, the real, or dominant qualities attributed to the arrow were mainly associated to its use value, and not to its value, which only existed in potential. (Campanario, 2011a)

In these pre-mercantile societies, value or price existed, but in a potential and less than real form. There have been countless societies with this characteristic throughout history. The few existing today are confined to remote and isolated spaces.

With the appearance of commerce, value passed from an embryonic state into its adult life. All because of a growing division of labour,

5 Use value here is considered to be synonymous with utility and value with price.

6 Campanario (2011a) with French, Portuguese and Italian translations. Also published in Diercksens *et al.* (2009).

requiring increasing accounting to make possible the exchange of goods. Value thus originated from an essential practical need – to facilitate exchange – but also remained as a *means* for the exchange of utilities. All great civilizations prior to the modern era, in all continents, were mercantile. Since then, this unity of contradictions is known as a product.

Around 1500, with the appearance of mercantilism and the first banks in the European City-States, there was a clear tendency towards an increase in domination of value over utility of a product, which culminated in the society of consumption and in the current globalization. The terms have been inverted: value became an end in itself and utility became a simple means at the service of value to multiply values (prices, capitals), as took place with cars in Iland. In these modern societies, while creating a product, priority is not given to the utilities needed by the greater part of the population or to ecological sustainability or average lifespan and other factors. And the work process continues under the control of minority groups, but with a different and dominant ideology that was revolutionary at the time of its appearance. In addition to an inversion of the parties, this process concludes with the preponderance of financial capital, the most pure and essential form of this new phase, thanks to its omnipresence, speed, levity and omnipotence. The primacy of value over utility has reached absurd extremes, by generating an oversized financial system:

> The current size of the inverted pyramid of securities reveals the magnitude of fictitious capital and its profits of an equal nature. The Bank for International Settlements (BIS), until December 2010, reported US$ 601 billion in derivatives issued, an amount that is more than 10 times gross global production, although according to some estimates these derivatives have a value of 30 times global production. ... The more this pyramid grows, the more it appears difficult for capital to connect with the real sector of the economy and return to the productive sphere with an attractive rate of return. The giant and apparently insane inverted pyramid constructs leverages to seize a greater amount of the global wealth generated. (Dierckxsens, 2011)[7]

In sum, utility and value form a unity, the product, which simultaneously embodies two different and opposing parts. In the modern era, value dominates utility, with financial capital as the predominant form of value.

Iland and its cartel, The Circle, exemplify how value imposes the type and form of the product without considering its social utility. Many other examples would be possible and even exist simultaneously: the location of residential neighbourhoods and commercial centres, defined according to the interests of builders and real estate agents; wars and atomic and

[7] About fictitious capital, see Carcanholo (2011).

offensive weapons; advertising, which generates new, totally dispensable needs based on luxury, ostentation, etc.

This modern and relatively recent supremacy of values, with its elevated microeconomic productivity, led Iland to a higher macroeconomic inefficiency, generating injustices, inequalities, crisis, environmental pollution, etc. This phenomenon, called Iland Paradox, is caused by the consumption of socially less advantageous goods (cars) or simply useless ones (fighter bombers), by the rapid obsolescence of machines and goods and, finally, by the lack of control over non-renewable resources (oil).

All of these factors have the same origin: the supremacy of value over utility, which is only possible when a minority controls value and capital. Nevertheless, this inefficiency does not exist from the perspective of the owners or controllers of capital because, as long as capital is able to multiply, they consider the system to be efficient, as they are only and exclusively interested in the increased return on capital. Therefore, the Iland Paradox exists in the minds of the Welanders, but does not exist for the Ilanders because they are not aware of this phenomenon. There is, however, one unquestionable fact due to this paradox: the majority of Ilanders work a lot in exchange for nothing and the owners of capital are very content while this ignorance lasts.

Companies in Iland are state-owned, but run with a capitalist logic based on profit and the independence of the managers. In Weland, companies are privately owned and owners have profits, but with a non-capitalist logic because they are subordinated to the interests of the majority. This democratically imposes what, where and how much a company produces. For this reason, the essential difference between the two societies does not depend on the state or private ownership of the businesses or of the means of production, but on the composition or structure of goods and services consumed by the population. The divergence depends on the object of each one: corporate profitability in Iland versus the control of production of goods according to a profile determined by the majority of the population in Weland.

In Iland, with the acceptance of consumers, a minority enjoys the profits, which are the objective of the entire system and as a consequence define its operational logic. Profits are necessary for the good progress of any modern country. But, in this case, the production of profit is made possible by the work of a minority – labour – which, moreover, is not remunerated. This is a form of exploitation baptized by Marx as surplus value and is part of a more specific category of that previously mentioned alienation.

Meanwhile, in Weland, private companies dominate the scenario, make profit and do not function without it. But, the quantity they produce and where is decided by the population and not by the minority owner or controller of the companies. In this utopia, profit is nothing more than an instrument to measure the efficiency of the business, an accounting issue, abandoning its primordial objective. In this case, profit no longer means surplus value and there is no exploitation because, in fact, the workers control it, despite the predominance of private companies.

Thus, what is important is the de facto and not the de jure control of property and surplus by a majority to define exploitation. This emphasizes the fact that there are no scientific criteria whatsoever to consider the perspective of the majority or the minority as correct. The option for a perspective of the majority is conducted by making choices based on value judgments. But this does not invalidate the fact that the majority does not defend the interests of the minorities that control power, except when they may make mistakes.

The deputy, used as an example earlier but now inserted in a real modern country, represents the Iland part of this country. Nevertheless, there is the Weland portion: deputies from the opposition, the ecology movement, the pacifist movement, etc., representatives of minority groups and those belonging to the dominated majority. Other types of ideology and work also exist: craft, cooperatives, independent professionals, religious, etc. The hegemonic ideology and labour processes thus coexist with many other ideologies and forms of work that are subordinated or subsumed, many of which are survivors of previous forms of production regimes.

In the countries with a socialist past, such as the former Soviet Union, companies also produced with the aim of making a profit or surplus, but there were economic goals with a global five-year planning to avoid the chaos of the market, and this was accomplished to a certain extent. The achievement of profit was left to the administrators, as takes place in Iland or any capitalist country, but the decisions about who, where and how much to produce remained with isolated planners, who made their decisions in isolated offices removed from the people. This was the most extensive and deepest attempt to eliminate the market and substitute it with planning. And it was a failure despite the unquestionable initial success with a few items. Surplus value also reigned in countries with these systems.

This difference between actually existing socialism and capitalism, observed over a long-term historical perspective, is nothing more than a detail because in both cases, a minority always took decisions separately from the interests of the majority of the citizens. From this perspective, and from a long-term perspective, capitalism is equal to the countries of true socialism because in the final moment, producing to create or accumulate value became the object of both. The defenders of capitalism believed that the perfect market was the best way to achieve this objective, while the socialists believed in perfect planning. Different tactics, identical objectives: the accumulation of values. Who decides the profile of consumption of these societies? Always a minority. Both China and the United States are dominated by Iland qualities and this identity joins them strategically since the agreement signed during Kissinger's secret visit to the Asian giant more than four decades ago, gratifying capitalism with an extended lifespan to demonstrate its exceptionalities.

Aristotelian Thinking

With the identity principle, Aristotle (384-322 AC) assured that anything is identical to itself and not equal to any other. A can only be A; it cannot be B. Thus, according to this perspective, reality is composed of different, isolated things added up, as in a collage. In addition to this principle, Aristotle also proposed principles of non-contradiction and the excluded third.

The West completely assimilated these principles, which spread across Europe through the Roman Empire and spread throughout the world due to capitalism. For more than 2,000 years, they have conditioned our daily lives. They became transformed into a logical structure upon which is based everything that is thought, spoken, written, felt, intuited, desired. And as a consequence, everything worked. We do everything under the straightjacket of this structure. It was adopted by both medieval scholastics and modern science.

This logical structure formed by these postulates wound up defining a specific and standardized form of thinking. If we adopt them, two affirmations that are contradictory cannot be called truths. In summary, the relations between things (like Socrates and man) are based on propositions or judgments that are united (Socrates is a man). These judgments are articulated, in turn, in syllogisms, forming a theory, or a coherent set of judgments and syllogisms, without contradictions, explaining a certain reality. Thus, for example, the many affirmations made to explain an aspect of real society cannot present among them any contradiction. If any affirmation about it cannot be contradictory, it follows that society itself and everything that composes it cannot be contradictory either, and for this reason society has a coherent structure and all its individuals are in *harmony*, exactly like the theoretical structure that describes it. This structure can be called ideology or religion, but if it also intends to acquire scientific merit, it should be coherent with the facts.

In addition to not presenting contradictions, the general form of these theoretical structures, whether scientific or not, ranges from the particular to the general, from the concrete to the abstract, and thus is similar to a pyramid where there is an implicit hierarchy. If the theories that explain reality have this form, the people wind up seeing reality itself in this way. Based on this, the world moves under orders from above, in line with the interests of the minority that controls power. This form of seeing things becomes a suitable means not only to 'eliminate' contradictions, but also to generate an authoritarian leader or, alternatively, to idolize one. It is not an accident that the pharaohs built the pyramids. Aristotle considered the monarchy the ideal government, and modern democratic societies accept a state that concentrates power in the hands of the minority. There is, therefore, an authoritarianism implicit in this thinking, which is disguised by simple principles accepted by all.

It is important to indicate the flexibility of dialectic thinking, which accepts the Aristotelian thinking as a part of it, while the latter does not accept the dialectic. For the latter, judgments are articulated according to Aristotelian rules (from things to judgments, from the articulation of judgments to theories). In addition, the dialectic thinking has the form of a pyramid. That is, the dialectic also understands that affirmations about a given aspect of a society cannot contradict each other. But, contrarily, in dialectical thinking, things have, within themselves, contradictions, an idea that is not accepted by Aristotelian logic because of the identity principle.

For the dialectic, Iland and Weland are present, together and inseparable, in a real country. They are opposites and have opposing qualities; Iland dominates Weland, which cannot realize its potential; and in this struggle for authenticity, the world changes. These developments are located at the interior of things and not at the tip of the pyramid. Reality can be considered a continuum running from a point closest to Iland to a point closest to Weland. The world thus becomes diverse, complex, colourful and contradictory. Consequently, the two forms of thinking become equal only when the differences between Iland and Weland are equalized, in a moment of abstraction. In an analogous framework, Einstein's relativity theory encompasses Newton's theory. However, this does not mean that Newton's theory or the Aristotelian way of thinking must be abandoned. They interpret the world in a more specific manner and have their usefulness depending on the level of abstraction used in the analysis.

With its requirement for non-contradiction, the Aristotelian logic necessarily opts for Iland because it conforms to the real part of the country, that is, the visible and the dominant. This logic thus attributes to Weland the qualities of Iland, seeing the two countries as identical. In one way or another, this vision eliminates differences and winds up discarding Weland by simplifying reality and speaking half-truths. We will see here how this form of thinking transforms the already seen dual dimensionality of goods into a single entity, transforming values into utilities.

An expert in the Aristotelian form of thinking, upon observing a real country, only sees harmony by exclusively discerning its real and dominant characteristics, that is, its Ilander characteristics. An expert in dialectical thinking always strives to find the dominated and hidden portion and ends up discovering discontented workers and their protest movements, that is, the country's *critics*. Aristotle was a defender of slavery but recommended that to maintain social peace, masters not ill-treat or belittle their slaves. Implicit in this recommendation is the idea that possible social disturbances or contradictions are caused by incompetent masters or subversive slaves, never by the slave system, which is considered balanced and coherent by its very nature. Other 'scapegoats' may be human error, poorly prepared leaders, fortuitousness or misfortune, laziness of the population, tropical climate, topography, etc. There is no better formula to justify and give continuity to unjust social systems, including the current one, which is also controlled by minorities and their interests.

This logic defines the rules and the limits of our thought, that is, all thinking is subordinated to it. Different forms of thinking lead to different forms of work. The current world functions primordially as it does in Iland because we think in an Aristotelian manner and not any other. This logic is transformed into the backdrop for thought in the world and is, therefore, found behind the ideology, giving it logical sustenance. The ideology, in turn precedes the labour process. For this reason our European origin civilization was already in a certain way implicit and predestined to exist in its current form based on the adoption of this thinking; it just lacked favourable historical conditions and the time to mature. The world does not proceed without conflicts, but this thinking conditions reality to move with fewer conflicts and achieves this goal at least partially. This logic, by imposing itself on the current world, is somewhat able to shape it according to its own non-contradictory structure and nearly able to transform it into a self-realizing prophecy.

Dialectical Thinking

After the defeat of the monarchy in 1895, The Balanced One proposed a new republican constitution, which was approved by the Weland parliament. To assume the post of prime minister, impose his ideas from this position and enjoy the prerogatives of its power would have been an option for him due to his leadership and good reputation. But he never wanted to participate in parliament and used this as a strategy to win over his compatriots with the imaginary of bringing about an extensive revolution in his country, offering them the eight principles mentioned earlier.

At first the intellectuals did not give much importance to these postulates, but gradually they began to understand them, especially when they realized that the Welanders, who were traditionally free of prejudice, were organizing themselves independent of the traditional networks of government power, such as the congress and the courts, and putting the principles in practice one by one. Most of these ideas were inspired by the dialectical vision of The Balanced One, assimilated primarily in Beijing and later in Paris. Since his main concern was social justice, he stated the principles or commandments in the simplest way possible. The last three were actually value judgments and related more to The Balanced One's political choice in favour of the majority and moral issues:

1. The country always changes
2. Changes occur due to oppositions, dissent or resistance
3. Oppositions together form the nation
4. Principal opposition is realized internally
5. One group always dominates
6. The majority must fight to dominate
7. Power must dilute itself
8. Do not do to other groups what you would not want them to do to you

At the time of the creation of the parliamentary republic, the country had already been capitalist for more than a century and the loss of power of the Church, the adoption of the Buddhist religion, the enormous influence of the leader and the high educational level of the Welanders shaped the population's ideology, and this explains its current peculiarities.

The Balanced One strongly believed in a more flexible and truthful ideology than the dominant one that was based on Aristotelian thinking and represented a rigid and simplified reality. This ideology would assimilate both the western and eastern dialectics. With it, citizens would live more happily because this way of thinking would generate, in perhaps a not very distant future, an appropriate method for shaping a more just society and one with respect for oppressed minority groups, which was more realistic and critical and had less Manichaeisms.

In relation to the first principle, whose meaning was equal to 'everything flows' (Heraclites, 535-484 AC), he said:

> One who profoundly adopts or assimilates the idea 'the country always changes' is part of the majority because the elites of societies of minorities always praise their systems as flourishing with harmony, equilibrium, eternity, perfection and immutability. By agreeing with this idea, the citizen comes to observe the world in a different manner, because, from that moment on, the political system will be considered conflict-ridden and ephemeral and this

> will demystify the defenders of minority systems, the populism and the false leaders who remain eternally in power. And when a magic quantity of citizens adopt this idea, they themselves will feel its collective strength and begin to intervene to change things according to their majority interests. This wave of activism will attract the undecided, and an indestructible political force will thus be established.[8]

The Welanders began to adopt the first commandment, and no one knows how much critical mass was necessary, but things began to advance according to the desires of The Balanced One, who had already passed away. In Iland this precept was obviously not accepted. Its corresponding principle, coherent with Aristotelian thinking, was different: "the country never changes, it is always perfected." Thus, in a supposedly harmonious society, as the Ilanders considered their country to be, there were no internal contradictions and things could not truly change but be improved. Change had a more qualitative connotation, deeper if compared with perfection.

If 'changes occur due to oppositions', as the second principle indicated, the Welanders, upon adopting them, acquired awareness of the inequality inherent in society and struggled against it. The Ilanders, on the other hand, supposed that their country was free of contradictions and defended a struggle for better salaries and for the perfection of companies through market forces. That is, in Iland, everything depended on the rivalry between the citizens, but all within laws that maintained the status quo apt for a republic. The corresponding principle from them was: 'improvement will only occur if there is competition within the legal rules defended by the state', that is, everything would happen without questioning the status quo. Evidently, if the group of citizens assimilated this, the dominant minority benefited because everything would take place according to the rules dictated by this very minority.

The Welanders became more realistic and critical after growing aware of the theme 'oppositions together form the nation' because they assimilated that both they as well as other opposing groups, inevitably, were an intrinsic part of society. The acceptance and, as a consequence, the confrontation of diverging interests were the starting point for decreased inequality and of a more mature and tolerant vision concerning differences. On the other hand, for the Ilanders, experts of the identity principle, which, as we saw earlier, defends totality as the sum of the parts of individuals, the corresponding principle would be: 'individuals combined are the nation'. Or, as The Libertarian said: 'the sum of the good citizens results in a good society'.

---

8 Today, 'magic quantity' would be called 'critical mass' because of the influence of nuclear weapons in the imaginary of people. Critical mass is the minimum quantity of fissionable material needed to trigger a nuclear reaction.

Since 'principal opposition is realized internally', the Welanders did not lose time looking for it externally. Joining this idea with the previous ones, they concluded that the engine of change is always found within society. There are no scapegoats. According to The Balanced One, 'we are essentially responsible for our own success and failure; to blame other leads to inaction.' On the other hand, since the Ilanders essentially considered society to be harmonious, any crisis that disturbed this harmony could only have as a cause some element that was independent or outside of it. Thus, for them the principle was: 'the main cause of conflicts is external'.

By considering oppositions as a need and an inevitability and not as a contingency, the Welanders remained more understanding and created a democracy in which there were always important conflicts. For this reason, and inspired by the principle, 'one group always dominates', they began to ask the question, 'which group?' They discovered that in an economy with private companies, like Weland, the main and almost only objective of owners and managers is profit. And they, the simple workers, have an opposite interest, which is that the work must be conducted for their own benefit and not to make profits for these owners and managers. After the establishment of the republic decades ago, the Welanders gradually began to perceive that a simple minority made all the decisions and, therefore, dominated and, with the goal of defending their minority interests, this minority subjected the state and concentrated its power in this apparatus to defend its interests. In other words, the majority became aware of its alienation or exploitation and began to struggle to impose its interests as a majority. It became critical. In contrast, the state companies in Iland had tremendous power, but the Ilanders said that this power was justified by competition adjusted by the invisible hand of the market. The Ilanders believed that the most powerful were a minority, but they knew more, they ruled the country because they deserved to, and they had greater wealth because they controlled and managed capital. In any case, in the end there were elections that prevented any form of abuse. Therefore, 'the dominant groups represent the majority' was the Ilander principle that corresponded to 'one group always dominates' of the Welanders. For this reason, no one in Iland struggled to become a majority because they considered themselves to be part of it.

'The majority must fight to dominate.' With this value judgment and moral code, The Balanced One made clear his favoured choice to the people and his hope for a better future for them. He said: 'the majority may be mistaken, but the society it engenders can never favour the minorities that control power precisely because it constitutes as majority.' There was no corresponding principle for the Ilanders because they already considered themselves to be within the majority.

So, if 'the majority must fight to dominate,' this majority decided to come together from every corner of the country and make explicit its desires and define its priorities by vote. First, it applied the Buddhist Middle Path: there will inevitably be profit, but it will be controlled so that only goods that interest the majority will be produced. The majority affirmed that: 'we concede to them the profit, but they compensate us with the goods defined by us, the majority.' There was also no corresponding idea among the Ilanders for this.

The Welanders quickly discovered that these goods almost always had a public nature, such as collective transportation, health care and education – in other words, the collective utilities. In addition, they had the characteristics of requiring much less labour effort compared with goods for individual use. In Iland, in contrast, since everyone faced things in isolation and individually, they only wanted better salaries, which was the main struggle of the unions. But the result, as we saw earlier, was discouraging.

Since 'power must dilute itself', the Welanders decided that to achieve this goal, they had to transform the state into only an administrator of the decisions taken by the majority. And they remained 'outside' the state. The Ilanders considered it normal and desirable to have the dominant groups control the state and make all the decisions because they represented everyone by merit. For them, 'power should be concentrated in the state'. Those who win elections in Iland supposedly represent the majority and for this reason, there, nothing changes, but seems to change.

The Welanders came to defend their points of view in an organized manner and ended up being able to adopt a policy that was always favourable to the collective utilities, with legislation to protect these interests. The final motto, 'do not do to other groups what you would not want them to do to you', showed the importance of respect for minority groups and was designed to avoid violence. It was inspired by the moral rule of most religions, probably formulated first by Confucius (551-479 AC). Today, the Welanders are proud to belong to a nation where minorities are respected. If there is ever a competition for the country with most diversity, they would win: they have diversity of cultures, races, businesses and minorities. For the Ilanders, this norm has no importance because democracy resolves this problem by attending to the interests of all by means of their elected representatives.

Over time, the Welanders concluded that a single practical rule encompassed all the previous ones and put it forward as the country's motto: 'for the predominance of advanced social utilities over values.' They did this to reaffirm the defence of the collective (social) and advanced utilities, that is, they saw it positive to control technology so that it did not generate either unemployment or a consumerist society, like that of the Ilanders, or lead to the depletion of natural resources. In other words, the concept of 'advanced' implied the durability of goods and controlled consumption, without waste. With the use of the word 'predominance' they clarified that they did not want to eliminate value but control it to act according to their interests. In keeping with their motto, the last labour union in Weland recently closed its doors because of a lack of members; they no longer believed in salaries to resolve their problems of material and mental well-being. In the final analysis, they considered a society without wage-earners as ideal. The Ilanders thought that the Welanders were very critical. And they were right.

The Iland Ideology

In Iland, as in any modern country, power produces goods with the purpose of accumulating value. This purpose is an integral part of the Ilanders' ideology and has a close connection with it. Ideology is considered here as a system of coherent ideas, constituted by countless judgments, from the most general to the most specific. The most general judgment of all is called the 'mother idea' here. What is this idea in Iland?

The search for profit as a purpose, without concern for the social utility of what is produced or for the negative consequences already illustrated in Iland, generates a fixed idea in the minds of company owners and managers. For them, the utility of what they sell simply consists of multiplying their money because without it, they cannot gain profit. The more they sell, the more money they obtain and, therefore, the more profit they gain, which qualifies as greater utility. Their mind, hence, absorbs the idea that the quantity of values sold increases in direct proportion to the quantity of utilities produced.

The representative from Iland's financial sector, Jos's explanation has already been mentioned before:

> Is the country under any threat from its neighbours? No! ... So, these fighter planes will never drop bombs; they will sit like parasites in the hangers of the country's military airports, insolently displaying their cost and uselessness to the people. Nevertheless, for the manufacturers and for us, the financiers, these planes have inestimable utility because with their high costs, capital multiplies and generates profit. For us, the more they cost, the more useful they are. For us, utility depends on price, money, profit, value.

It is not worthwhile asking Jos the reason for this. From his perspective, whether it's a fixed idea or an illusion, the final conclusion cannot be refuted: 'utility depends on price, money, profit and value' or, simply put, utility is value. There is a generalized acceptance in the world today of this one-dimensional vision of goods. Here 'utility is value' is considered the basic principle of contemporary societies.

It is worth reiterating what was established earlier: the duality of utility and value together compose a unity, that is a good, within which two different and opposite entities, utility and value, coexist simultaneously. Consequently, to equate value and utility, like the basic principle 'utility is value' does, is the same as affirming a half-truth, because utility is both value and not value simultaneously.

To survive, workers must purchase goods in the market with money from their individual salaries, as individuals or as part of a family. Having high salaries or income is thus an unquestionable objective because the workers do not have any other option and cannot even imagine one. This leads them to the false conclusion that with higher salaries they can obtain higher quantities of utilities and, hence, greater well-being and, finally, happiness. Therefore, 'utility is salary' or 'utility is value' also becomes the basic principle of the workers of Iland, the same as their bosses. Their strong workers' union, which calls itself leftist, supports and encourages this way of looking at things because increased salaries has always been the paramount struggle for the union, as affirmed by its by-laws.

Accepting support of the union does not mean the workers have made the wisest choice, as their vision falsifies reality. As we saw earlier, capitalist production, with the pre-eminence of a product – the car – preferred in an individual manner led Iland to the hegemony of the financial sector and a dead end. The struggle of the unions for better salaries is only able to increase the consumer market and stimulate the financial sector. We live in a world of illusions shared by those who have diverging interests, but who behave like siblings because they have adopted the same ideology.

This basic principle sprouted and gave life to modern societies and now dominates the labour process. This domination nearly leads us automatically to overestimate its power. Thus, the conviction of the possibility of ad infinitum growth of values, profit and capital remains implicit, as if there were a magic wand and the owner simply needed to wave it to multiply wealth. But in reality, this capacity depends on work processes, which, as advanced as they may be today, defend and confront the Iland Paradox and cause it great damage, mainly because of the fragility of nature and its limited capacity to offer us air, water, raw materials, land, etc. forever. These impediments only became clear in the second half of the 20th century, which gave rise to environmental movements. But the main factor in overcoming this illusion depends on the rise of a dominant ideology coherent with the interests of the majority of the citizens, who are truly interested in the sustainability of the world and nature. For now, these citizens do not feel either exploited or manipulated and are not aware of their alienation. Perhaps one day it will happen, as it happened in the utopian Weland.

It is undeniable from the perspective of this chapter that goods have two simultaneous qualities: value and utility. But the Aristotelian logic considers this dual dimensionality of goods incoherent, that is, the affirmation that values and utilities differ and are equal at the same time contradicts the Identity Principle. There is only one solution for an economist adept at this logic to confront this dual character of goods: to simplify reality and consider utility and value as identical things, that is, 'utility is value'. And once again, by another route, the basic principle is reached. This shows that when the unity utility-value is defined and simplified in this way, it has quantitative purity and practicality because of its reduced scope. It can be transformed into numbers (value = price = X dollars), which facilitates the calculation of profit, commercial transactions, the measurement of well-being with per capita GNP, etc. The relationship obtained based on these numbers can generate different theories of economic science. Though these theories arise with a logically coherent structure of complex numeric relations, they all have a common starting point that simplifies things: the basic principle of 'utility is value'. As a result, these theories lead to false conclusions about social and economic reality. If a purely quantitative analysis were conducted based on value, 'forgetting' the utility of goods, Iland and Weland would be identical because both produce surplus. The inequality between them is in the utility produced, namely, social utility as defined by the majority in Weland versus individual utility as defined by the minority in Iland but with the support of everyone.

Going back to the basic principle of 'utility is value', we realize that both the bosses and the wage-earners as well as the Aristotelian logic adopt it. For this reason, this basic principle becomes a type of foundational idea, which best represents the status quo. From this arise many judgments or principles of the ideology of our society that are in keeping with this basic principle. They establish a coherent ideological system that is not contradictory. In practice, all ideas that contradict the basic principle are rejected by the Aristotelian logic and all ideas coherent with it are accepted, and this process of selection is transformed into the architect of this ideological structure.

The following affirmations can be deduced from this basic principle and in their pure form are part of the ideology of the Ilanders. By agreeing with these affirmations, the Ilanders give sustenance to and justify the regime. If 'utility is value', everything that has utility has value and something simply has to have utility to have value or price. Pleasure, love, happiness, etc., obviously 'useful' human qualities, are transformed into goods in the minds of people and are purchased and sold. In sum, 'everything that has utility has a price'. Some other general affirmations are: 'happiness is obtained with greater income', 'knowledge and abilities serve to increase income', 'the value of an individual is based on his or her income, on what they receive, what they consume or what they appear to be able to buy', 'personal relations serve to maximize income', 'labour time should be expanded and that of leisure and consumption curtailed, 'goods should be consumed individually', 'individualism allows greater happiness', 'society is the sum of its individuals', etc.[9]

These few ideas are enough to identify the extreme individualism of the modern world's ideology, derived from the basic principle of 'utility is value'. Consequently, it becomes honourable to receive individual salaries, to individually consume goods and services, to manage independent companies, etc. Everything is individualized and this form of seeing and acting is considered morally positive and efficient. The set of these ideas form the ideology of modern societies, and in Iland it appears in its pure and ideal form.

On the other hand, the ideology of Iland is totally coherent with the Aristotelian idea of isolated things, derived from the identity principle. Combined, these things produce a harmonious whole, an idea that is similar to Smith's invisible hand of the market, which 'resolves' everything and any conflict and harmonizes society by force. In socialism, planning presupposes a world without contradictions, where the five-year plan substitutes the market. But, even supposing that managers are highly capable, the sum of the results of all proves to be counterproductive, as was exemplified in Iland. But the Aristotelian logic insists on the veracity of this way of seeing and confronting reality without contradictions.

In sum, the current system is supported by an ideology. This ideology, in turn, is sustained by the Aristotelian structural logic, which implies a harmony of things. As a result, it is necessary to first shift this structure of thinking to be able to shift the ideology that sustains our civilization, and then transcend it. But what logical structure could substitute it?

The Weland Ideology

We have already seen that the Welanders simplified and embraced all of Yavie's eight commandments into one practical rule and presented it as the country's motto 'for the predominance of advanced social utilities over values', in which social or collective utility clearly gets priority. Because of its generality and its opposition to Iland's basic principle, it will be considered the basic principle of Weland. Other ideas, some of which are presented here, can be extracted from this one, which together form a coherent and non-contradictory structure. As mentioned earlier, dialectical thinking has greater flexibility and embraces Aristotelian thinking.

9 For a more detailed presentation of these judgments, see Campanario (2011a).

Implicit in Weland's basic principle is the determination of value by labour, utility by ideology and the existence of an objective. Consequently, that which is not produced by human labour cannot be considered a product and, therefore, does not have value, but it can have utility. In Weland, the Ilander norm 'everything that has utility has a price' is not accepted because there are utilities not produced by labour. Thus, the corresponding motto in Weland is the opposite: 'not everything that has utility has a price'. This new norm eliminates one of the most absurd ideas currently prevalent that intrinsically associates human values, such as love and friendship, with prices, and transforms everything into a commodity.

Money and income become a means to satisfy basic individual needs because most goods should have a social function and not be tied to salary or personal income; in other words, 'happiness is not obtained with greater income'. Hence, the Welander unions disappeared. In this new situation, knowledge and qualification become a means for the advancement of new potentials. These, now free, expand, reviving what is most essential in humanity: the ability to think, feel and invent, qualities that currently face obstacles and are repressed. The Welanders have a strong inventive capacity. They participate in daily decision-making to modify their reality (or improve it). Contrary to this, the Ilanders do not at all imagine the possibility of proposing and struggling for a better society for themselves. They waste their time inventing ways to 'maximize' their salaries and fantasizing about what new car they will buy in the coming year.

Ostentation disappears and thus subverts the concepts of fashion, luxury and aesthetics, liberating the route to our infinite creativity: 'social utility should be maximized'. This motto was successfully applied in Weland in mass transportation. In Iland, the opposite idea, 'goods should be consumed individually', resulted in an alienated country controlled by minorities. If people's objectives are no longer limited to their personal income, it is not necessary to increase the time of work. Free time and rest will dominate work: 'time for leisure and consumption should be expanded and that for working curtailed.' The Welanders work less and the Ilanders naively think that this is the reason that the Welanders do not have cars.[10] Favourite goods are consumed socially. This practice has eliminated selfish individualism from Weland and has enormously reduced waste during working hours. Solidarity has become an ethical value that is good for everyone: 'altruism allows greater happiness'.

Once this is accepted, each person does not feel exclusively responsible for their successes and failures – which is characteristic of selfish

10 A law recently established a limit of a maximum work week of four seven-hour days for all citizens of the country. Half of the neighbouring Ilanders classify the Welanders as lazy; the others envy them.

individualism – but does feel responsible for the successes and failures of others and of society in general. In place of individualism, where isolation is equivalent to happiness, there are certain intrinsic values of humanity, such as solidarity, love, friendship, cooperation, support and happiness. Architecture emphasizes public spaces and is designed to increase personal contact. It is simple but practical, economizing the time taken on construction. Upon comparing Welanders with Ilanders, the differences are striking. The latter are more sympathetic, communicative and happy.

In ethical terms, it is important to emphasize the precept, 'do not do to other groups what you would not want them to do to you', which is a logical derivative of the basic principle. Implicit in this principle is unlimited respect for all and any group or minority, whether social, behavioural or economic, and as a consequence, unlimited respect for differences between people. For this reason, they will all have greater opportunities for developing their unequal potential. The Welanders practise diversity and tolerance with individuals and with groups and forms of production, that is, democracy reigns there. Elections, as they exist today, are no more than a farce because they do not unseat the minorities who remain eternally in power.

In Iland, the ideology presupposes the functioning of the country based on individual initiatives ('goods should be consumed individually', 'individualism allows greater happiness', etc.). Moreover, labour processes are also individual because citizens have their own jobs, they buy their goods personally and individually administer companies. This ideology and these personal initiatives create the illusion that the individual dominates society and within it enjoys greater diversity and liberty because each individual acts independently ('society is the sum of its individuals'). But in reality, a minority dominates, through its ideology and its labour processes, which derive from the interests of this minority and not from the interests of the majority of individuals. Thus, Iland does not have diversity or liberty but a homogeneous thinking, like that of a flock, which is controlled by a minority and is, therefore, collective and crushes the individual. Iland produces citizens who are ideologically very similar and everyone likes to buy cars.[11] The Ilanders are proud of their individualism. However, this can only be seen and justified through human qualities that are non-essential, such as the way of dressing, eating, consuming and entertaining, or through undesirable qualities, such as egoism and aloofness. The Ilanders are more homogeneous and collectivist than they think and consider themselves individualists without

11 Some modern democracies have for decades alternated between two parties in the government, which take great pains to demonstrate that they have sharp differences, but in reality they are insignificant.

being so. They live in a dictatorship accepted by all because of an ideology that sustains it. In contrast, in Weland, the motto 'for the predominance of advanced social utilities over values', gives the impression of a collective dictatorship at first, where the individual is worth nothing and has no voice. The Welanders admit contradictions in their society, the existence of interest groups etc., that is, they admit the limitations imposed by historic development and by nature. But since the majority rules and respects inevitable disagreements, in reality the individual there has more power than in Iland, despite the contrary impression. The Welanders do live in a democracy. Thus, in terms of real countries, when grading them on a scale of 0 to 10, the higher the grade obtained by a country, the more they enjoy democracy and more respect there is for the individual.

Divide the Enemy and Join the Ally to Govern in a Minority

From the perspective of this chapter, power is defined as a constructive force, which is the result of the interaction between ideology and work and is found dispersed throughout society, where everyone has power, and some more than others. In a real country, power exists in its Welander portion and is found dispersed or diffused in factory workers, union leaders, opposition parties, alternative newspapers, organizations of various types struggling against the dominant power, etc. This non-hegemonic power is asphyxiated by real power that is in the hands of the minority that controls values. Thus, in addition to being dispersed, this power is practically invisible because it is utopian and because it is found more in a potential than real state. The hegemonic power is also dispersed because it is composed of groups represented in cartels, organizations, newspapers, company unions, ruling parties, owners and managers of companies, banks, etc. But, because it is already developed and real, this power manifests its characteristics in a clear and visible manner.

On the other hand, these minority groups that control power come together, due to a need to survive, making themselves the nerve centre of a complex network, strongly bonding with each other, concentrating on some institutions needed to maintain this power, like the army and the courts. In sum, this power is dispersed because it is composed of different groups, but it is concentrated because these groups have the state as the locus of the union between them. For this reason, the state appears as the incarnation of total power in society. It is in the interest of those who create the hegemony of power that the state is seen in this way because it creates the impression of having more strength than the state really has. This impression is generally reinforced through inaugural ceremonies, military parades, patriotic anthems, etc., creating a sense of respect, fear and impeding the appearance of oppositions. This ability to simulate strength can be called the 'mimicry of power', analogous to Batesian mimicry, in which an inoffensive animal species disguises itself as a dangerous one, thus increasing its opportunities for survival.

Machiavelli (1469-1527) created a modern and secular concept of the state that distanced the divine or religious attributions from the medieval state. In short, the state can be considered

> an organized and institutionalized force with supreme power over a certain population and a territory, which adopts measures for self-preservation and strengthening with respect to other states and that has the function of imposing, in a monopolistic manner if necessary, the coercion and or strength needed to maintain the social order and the territory that it controls (Campanario, 2011b).

This definition supposes a legitimate and concentrated power, with a certain independence from society and with a supposed representation of all the citizens. In this concept, power is located and concentrated in the state, blending with the state itself.

We have already seen that the theories that explain the world based on Aristotelian thought and on the ideology derived from the basic principle 'utility is value' have a hierarchical form, conditioning people to see reality in a pyramidal, vertical and, consequently, authoritarian form, or according to the circumstances and the perspective, as docile. Machiavelli's concept of the state and power is perfectly adapted to this thinking and ideology and, therefore, involves an inherently authoritarian concept, in which power is concentrated at the top.

This need for concentration and authoritarianism occurs when a minority holds power. Machiavelli proposed the motto 'divide and rule.'[12] But divide whom? Clearly, the enemy. 'Divide the enemy to rule', thus, better particularizes the maxim. In addition, if there is a need to divide, this means there is a ruling minority; if not, it would not be necessary to divide the enemy. 'Divide the enemy to rule in minority', therefore, particularizes this motto even further. 'Unite to rule', the corollary of Machiavelli's precept, can be joined to this phrase. But unite with whom? With the ally. Combining these, we have 'divide the enemy and unite with the ally to rule in minority'. Machiavelli's motto is now clear. The minority follows it religiously to maintain its concentrated and authoritarian power. It is able to control power in Iland with alliances with other minorities and buying – dividing – workers through the Single Public Employees Union.

This concentration, paradoxically, tends to grow. Thus, the complexity and the heterogeneity of the modern world, despite demanding increasingly more flexible, rapid and efficient management, also requires a growing

[12] In fact, variations to this motto were found prior to Christ, both in the West and the East.

concentration of financial, military and industrial power to protect its minority interests. In addition, this power is threatened by economic crises, wars, conquest of territories, unproductivity at a global level, environmental, ethical and other problems. There is also growing opposition from groups that, although small, represent the interests of the majority and are potentially dangerous to the minority.

This concentration is principally maintained by oversized institutions – security forces, laws, the legislative and executive systems – and a strong hegemonic ideology, with the objective of maintaining order and avoiding anarchy. All routes lead the hegemonic power in the direction of the state, an intrinsic and structural need in modern societies. In socialist countries, the concentration is imposed even more because, additionally, the mostly state-owned means of production require an enormous bureaucracy to control the system and execute development plans.

On the other hand, the concentration of power in the state without acceptance from the citizens would put in check the entire system. As we saw, the logical-formal thinking interprets the world in a coherent, hierarchical and vertical form, free of conflicts. Thus, this form of interpreting the world, once again, eternalizes the status quo because this verticality coincides with the need for a state that centralizes power and hovers above everything. Once again, Aristotelian thinking sustains modern societies.

The nuclear powers accumulate thousands of nuclear weapons; some can destroy entire countries or even wipe out humanity. Why so many weapons? By adopting the basic principle 'utility is value', as in Iland, they accept that 'everything that has use-value has a price', as has been discussed earlier. Thus, logically, everything produced and spent by the state, by the simple fact of possessing a value, comes to have utility. Since these weapons cost billions of dollars, it apparently makes them necessary, resulting in deceiving the population. We can understand the costs of the exaggerated size of the legislative, judicial and executive powers in an analogous manner, as well as military costs, war costs, etc. All of them, in principle, have utility because they have costs and the more they cost the more utility they have. Evidently, there is a limit to spending and there can be corruption, but this is controlled by including the internal costs of a budget and arresting those who are corrupt. This false vision supports the idea of utility of the state and its concentration and, of course, helps maintain the hegemony of the minority.

Modern democracy also legitimates and justifies the state as a concentrator of power. It presupposes that common citizens, through periodic elections, directly or indirectly, control the high bureaucracy of the state apparatus. Those elected will represent these citizens and, if they do not meet expectations, can be substituted with better ones in the next elections.

The assumption of the state as the main source of power is implicit in this concept of representative democracy and no one proposes elections for the managers of companies, institutions or any enterprise outside the state. In reality, this falsity is very useful to the hegemonic block because the people believe that the state represents them. But, in reality, the state can be considered, as we saw, as a product of power and not the cause of it. Inevitably, in our modern societies, power is concentrated in the state and everyone accepts this and it is part of the hegemonic ideology.

It can be concluded that the power concentrated in the state exists in complex societies, where a minority of the population exercises hegemonic power, whether it is capitalist or socialist. We have already defended the idea that any social change can only take place if there is a substitution of ideology and in the way of working and that in this substitution, the ideology precedes the way of working. The current centralizing state, however, is sustained ideologically, as we saw, by the hierarchical and vertical Aristotelian thinking, then by Machiavelli's concept of the state, followed by the basic principle and finally by the idea of democratic elections. It is a mistake to think that the substitution of one political party with another in a democratic election can lead to a real change in power. The centralizing power in the state will not change if the hegemonic ideology that sustains it does not change. A large portion of the Chilean left, in the 1970s, conceived of power concentrated in the state. When they won the elections in 1970 and began to govern and administer the state institutions, because of this mistaken concept, they believed that they had conquered power or at least an important part of it. The result was tragic.

Diffuse Power to Govern in a Majority

Hegel (1770-1831) and mainly Marx (1818-1883) conceived of the state in a more totalizing and historic manner than Machiavelli. For Marx, the state did not hover above society, it did not legitimately represent the citizens and it did not necessarily resolve conflicts. This was because it had strong ties with companies, culture, ideas and other social institutions. Gramsci (1891-1937) perfected and expanded this concept of power. According to him, the state apparatus represents only a fraction of the power, the others who hold power include the organizations that control capital and knowledge, the communication media, the unions, religions, social movements, international and non-governmental organizations and political parties. Gramsci affirmed that the controlling or hegemonic block of these organizations and institutions has the capacity to effectively defend its specific and strategic interests. Each one has its share of power, even if it is not necessarily part of the hegemonic block. For this reason, there is no sovereignty of the state as Machiavelli maintained. The perspective adopted in this chapter is similar to Gramsci's because he also affirmed that all social organizations are permeated by power. Nevertheless, for us, power results from the interaction between ideology and labour, and has various implications, one of them being that there is a concentration of hegemonic power in the state.

The complexity of Weland goes beyond that of any modern capitalist or social country, requiring increasingly flexible and decentralized administration, but it presents a specificity, which is the non-requirement of the concentration found in the modern world. The Balanced One said, '...the majority does not need to concentrate power in the state to represent nearly the entire population. But be on your guard to avoid the state being controlled by a minority group.' In Iland, the need for a centralized power in the state is due to the fact that power is found in the hands of a minority. In Weland, there is diffused power, which is contrary to the situation in current societies, where there is intrinsic and structural concentration. On the scale mentioned earlier, the closer a country is to Weland, the less the concentration of power in the state.

It has already been concluded that by adopting the postulate 'utility is value', automatically everything produced by the state, by the simple fact of having value, has utility. In contrast, by adopting the maxim, 'for the predominance of advanced social utilities over values', which is Weland's motto, the work of the legislative, judicial and executive powers as well as the armies with their bombs, planes and rockets automatically come to be critically examined to determine if they have utility or not for the majority of the workers; if not, they are discarded. The Welanders have effective control over the state and its activities and are not fooled by affirmations such as 'everything that has utility has a price', which justify spending in the countries dominated by minorities. One practical consequence of this is that the army has a defensive strategy, the citizens participate in it and do not possess heavy weapons.

Since any organism tends to sustain and perpetuate itself, a hegemonic power of majorities is not interested in defending the state as producer of goods and services, with rare exceptions (strategic goods and services). Thus, the executive and legislative powers and the military remain in the hands of this state, and the technical coordination of strategic sectors, such as energy and transportation. The state, in these conditions, becomes a mere administrator of the decisions taken by the majority and not a repressive apparatus and defender of a minority, nor inventor and amplifier of expenses in the interest of minority producers. Paradoxically, this involves a minimum possible state. For this reason, in Weland, the majority can have the luxury of leaving the apparatus of the state in the hands of a liberal technocracy. It does not dominate, but is under control.

The motto in Weland about power could be 'Diffuse power to rule in a majority.'

Conclusion

To create Christianity as we know it today, St Paul modified the utopia of Christ, which had a moral foundation, and created a religion based on power, controlled by an elite. In the Middle Ages, this elite caste tried to bring heaven to earth and in the process transformed Europe into a concrete hell, with prisons, bonfires and instruments of torture. We are not questioning Dante's brilliance, but since he lived in this dark time, we can suspect that he only needed to conduct an inverted chronicle to invent the paradise described in *The Divine Comedy*.

The same is true in Iland. A hegemonic power, resulting from a form of production based on the control of capital by independent managers, who compete with their companies in a free market of buyers and consumers, together with an ideology that sustains this form of production, imposes on Iland the entire profile of production and consumption. It also condemns to ostracism or prison those who dare to not pay homage to 'free initiative'.

The same is true under socialism. When the Russians, Chinese and others with a Marxist utopia tried to impose this utopia by force, they created a dictatorship of a minority because everyone was required to adapt to the structure that was determined, designed and implemented by a small group of 'thinkers', who quickly broke with the principles and ideals of this utopia. The decisions remained in the hands of the minority that controlled this structure, while the rest of the population was alienated and had no power to realize their dreams.

Therefore, to avoid falling into explicit or disguised dictatorships, utopia can only be considered as a far-off goal, and not be imposed on reality in its totality and all at once. We never reached equality with Weland, but it is there inspiring us. Thus, the route is flexible, creative and democratic, adapting to the circumstances without losing its way. Here it is worth remembering Antonio Machado (1912): '… traveller, there is no path, the path is formed by walking.'

The focus of the future is on a path, a process, and not on a prefabricated structural solution, whether it is of the free or planned market. The attempts to change the foundations of society through the simple taking of the 'power of the state', even democratically through elections, are only able to change appearances, while nothing really changes.

In society, ideology precedes labour. As a consequence, any deep change in society only exists when there are primordial changes in ideology, which are responsible for placing a priority and emphasis on utopia. The more we come closer to the ideology of Weland, and its golden rule 'for the predominance of advanced social utilities over values', the more our realities also come closer to it, increasing the grade in the direction of honour. These changes necessarily require long time periods and are limited by given social and natural conditions.

There is an inevitability of the state because it alone can undertake certain functions in a complex society. But the minority sectors have hegemony over it. In Weland, this state differs from the current one. Its employees fulfil the functions determined by the majority, and these functions are determined by Weland's principles, regardless of whether it is under property that is private, state-owned, mixed, artisanal, individual, without salaries, etc. What is important is that production should be adequate for the interests of the majority.

The utopia defended here is simply summarized in a policy increasingly commanded by the majorities. The pacifist and ecology movements, the Indignant Movement, Occupy Wall Street, internet activism and many other struggles that are becoming increasingly widespread are the embryo of a future that is already under full gestation in the womb of the present one. These are symptoms of the unease of the majorities, who want to create a world for themselves and no longer want to be subject to the manipulation of the minorities. As these ideas become concretized and universalized free of the interests of the minorities, there will be an approximation to Weland. Little by little countries will no longer be socialist or capitalist. None of these movements put faith in the state, they always act in a horizontal and diffused form.

Nevertheless, without changing the foundational formal logic upon which our ideology and thoughts depend, one cannot arrive at a hegemonic ideology of the majorities because this, as we have concluded, must be done on a dialectical basis. Fortunately, this way of perceiving the world includes within it logical-formal thinking and, as a consequence, this change can be gradually realized by aggregation.

References

Campanario, Paulo. 2011a. 'The Hegemony of Advanced Social Use Value: A Key to Surpassing Present Societies', Observatorio Internacional de la Crisis (www.observatoriodelacrisis.org).

———. 2011b. 'Hegemonía del Poder Social Difuso', in Andrés Piqueras and Wim Dierckxsens (eds.), *El Colapso de la Globalización, La Humanidad frente a la Gran Transición*. Barcelona: El Viejo Topo.

Carcanholo, Reinaldo. 2011. 'Interpretaciones sobre el capitalismo actual, crisis económica y gastos militares', in Andrés Piqueras and Wim Dierckxsens (eds.), *El Colapso de la Globalización, La Humanidad frente a la Gran Transición*. Barcelona: El Viejo Topo, p. 71-113.

Dierckxsens, Wim. 2011. 'La gran depresión del siglo XXI ¿Hacia un Estado Global?' *Le Monde Diplomatique de Colombia*, 105, October.

———. 2007. *La transición hacia el poscapitalismo: El socialismo del siglo XXI*. San José: DEI-Ruth Casa Editoral (3rd ed.).

Diercksens, Wim, Antonio Jarquín *et al.* 2009. *La gran Depresión del Siglo XXI: Causas, carácter, perspectivas*. San José: DEI y Observatorio Internacional de la Crisis.

Machado, Antonio. 1912. *Campos de Castilla*. Madrid: Renacimiento.

Marx, Karl. 1887. *Capital: A Critique of Political Economy*, Vol. I, Book One: *The Process of Prodution of Capital*. Moscow: Progress Publishers. Accessed at: http://www.marxists.org/archive/marx/works/download/pdf/Capital-Volume-I.pdf.

Tomasi di Lampedusa, Giuseppe. 1960. *The Leopard*. London: Collins and Harvill Press.

Part II

Global Problems

CHAPTER 3

The Great Depression of the 21st Century and the Military-Industrial Complex

Antonio JARQUÍN & Wim DIERCKXSENS

International Physicians for the Prevention of Nuclear War, Nicaragua

and

International Observatory of the Crisis (IOC), The Netherlands and Costa Rica

Productive and Non-Productive Labour and the Military-Industrial Complex

To understand actual geopolitics, we think it is important to take a brief look at the economics of war. This leads us to understand the war economy in times of a new Great Depression. Let us define first of all the basic ideas of productive and non-productive labour in relation to the military-industrial complex. We want to be brief but clear. Those interested in going into further details and data may refer to our study *The Post Cold War Era* (Dierckxsens, 1994b).

In terms of its content, the production of armaments and the means of destruction will in general permit, in a given economic cycle, the creation of destructive products that have surplus value and create profits. During this cycle, merchandise will have been produced that counts as national monetary wealth. Its consumption leads to the destruction of the environment, human lives and material goods produced in the sector of the real economy. But even when these destructive products are not consumed – that is, when they do not destroy lives, the environment or material goods – they are not contributing to an enlarged reproduction of capital in a future cycle. Labour carried out for the production of armaments and destructive goods, even when these goods are not used, appears at the social-global level as non-productive labour. It seems as though the productive forces have not developed as much as they could have.

Why is there non-productive consumption of weaponry even when weapons are not used? The answer is simple. In a future cycle of production, weaponry figures neither amongst the means of production necessary to renovate or enlarge the productive forces, nor amongst the means of consumption necessary to contract the same, or more, labour forces in the reproduction process. The circulation of this merchandise tends to increase the amount of money, but does not increase the amount of consumption goods (private or otherwise), all of which contributes to more or less permanent inflation. In other words, although the selling of merchandise and the realization of surplus value does not affect the overall economy in a given cycle, nor even in the next cycle when the process is still going on in the military-industrial complex, the creation of destructive products, in the long run, leads to a reduced reproduction of capital that may even turn into negative growth. Negative growth eventually endangers not only the civilian economy but also the total economy, and so, the military-industrial complex itself. In this way, one can envisage the internal limits of a war economy in a capitalist system.

In a closed economy, the redistribution of defence spending is done via the tax system or by government debt. Its payment in the latter case is transferred to the future, so to speak. The monopolies linked to the military-industrial complex can make their profits (usually above the average profit level) and continue their individual accumulation process. In some of the subsequent cycles, the purchaser of destructive materials hands these over to the army, thereby taking the materials out of the spiral, which then do not appear as a means of enlarged reproduction. It is in this context that we have to understand why countries that have had reduced levels of defence spending in the post-war period (Japan, Sweden, Switzerland) have had relatively higher economic growth rates than countries that have had relatively high defence expenditures, such as the US, the former Soviet Union, France and the UK.

Arms Exports as a Transfer of Non-Productive Expenditures

In an open economy, there is a method of transferring non-productive expenditures to other nations: via arms exports. For the producing country, the export of weapons means the realization of merchandise and value produced by the military-industrial complex without the state having to absorb the non-productive effects and transfer it to the taxpayer. By buying the destructive materials, the importing countries also receive the negative effects of limited reproduction, while the exporting country, by transferring the non-productive expenses to these countries, receives the income necessary to import the means of production and/or consumption that are necessary to enlarge its reproduction. The more a country monopolizes the production of destructive materials (as is nowadays the case with the US), the more that country will have an interest in fomenting war as the best guarantee to sell them. The Cold War formed a perfect way of internationally redistributing military spending, predominantly subsidizing the military-industrial complex of the USA. During the Cold War, more than 2,000 low intensity military conflicts in the third world, with the direct or indirect participation of the US, granted constant effective demand for weapons. The amount of human lives lost exceeded 20 million. Damages to the ecosystems and the economies of the attacked countries are still incalculable. Vietnam and Nicaragua are just examples. The latter suffered damages equivalent to 84 years of its gross domestic product during the 10 years of US-led war in the 1980s (Medipaz, 1994).

The end of the Cold War introduced a new chapter in the history of the USA: looking for new enemies in the world. It was primarily in the so-called third world that the competition to sell arms took place and, thus, war. It was necessary to seek new conflicts there so as to transfer the non-productive costs to those nations. The Gulf War opened a new way to transfer the costs of war to those nations. If nations in the UN approved of this conflict, they had to co-finance it. The war against terror since 2001 may be better understood in this context: permanent conflicts in the Middle East increased and the policy was that other (third world) countries had to contribute. We can also better understand the 'drugs war' that began at the end of the 1980s. In the places where this war is most successful, drug trafficking, corruption, criminalization and, last but not least, money laundering in the North are rampant. It shows how decadent capital accumulation in core countries has become. A drugs war generates huge funds for money laundering. The drugs war in Colombia is just an example. The US military presence in Colombia for decades caused the development of the biggest cocaine market in the US. An open war of the drug cartels against the Mexican government, where 50,000 people die every year, is a more recent example. The war in Afghanistan re-established the opium industry and its market generates huge funds for money laundering.

After World War II the ruling elite, in one or another, transferred the costs of war to other countries, and especially to the peripheral ones. They didn't take into consideration or care about the damage and long-term effects of the Cold War, nor about the more recent conflicts and wars in the South. Military production and militarization of the planet on a global scale have consequences not only for the economic system but also for human and natural life. Planetary capacity to absorb waste cannot be taken for granted and the damage caused by a war economy to nature cannot be underestimated. This is what we called the 'boomerang effect' in our book '*The Nicaraguan War: Low Intensity Warfare*' (Jarquin *et al.*, 1994).

US Defence Spending in the 21st Century

During the first decade of the 21st century, civil industrial production in the US decreased by 19 per cent. It took around four years for the manufacturing sector to recover and again reach the levels that existed before the 2001 recession. All these profits have completely vanished in the current recession. The military-industrial complex, however, has increased by 83 per cent from levels reached in 2000. It expanded severely at the time when the domestic economy shrank. Growing military spending indicates that the government generates artificial demand for military products, and it does so when the civil economy contracts in the area of equipment or so-called capital goods. In the short run, as we argued earlier, this investment may represent a sustained demand. In the middle term, however, defence spending is a drain on the economy, reducing efficiency, slowing growth and costing jobs. A loss in the pattern of growth occurs with previously collected taxes. However, military investments are made with growing public external debt and, most recently, with quantitative easing a way of uncontrolled printing money.[1]

The announced military budget of the US was 707 billion dollars for 2010 and around 1 trillion for 2011. As a matter of fact, asserted Rick Rozoff,[2] an expert on the matter, this represented half of the real military spending of the US, as there were indirect suppliers. With this, military spending reached 9 per cent of the GDP of the US. In comparative terms, it was the highest budget since 1945, the last year of World War II. The official military budget of the US actually represents about 45 per cent of the world's military spending. It is six times larger than that of China, which holds the second place. It is even ten times larger than that of Russia, which at present has to settle for a modest fifth place, behind France and the UK.[3]

Even if there are economic arguments to support accumulation of capital goods, this trend in the development of the military-industrial complex cannot be explained without arguments of the geopolitical

1 See Washington's Blog, 'The Military-Industrial Complex is Ruining the Economy', www.globalresearch.ca, 9 January 2010.

2 Rick Rozoff, 'Nobel Committee Celebrates War As Peace', http://www.rickrozoff.wordpress.com, 8 December 2009.

3 *The Economist*, 'The World in 2010', November 2009, p. 113.

order. The United States, or at least a conservative section of its leaders, is prepared to unleash a greater war. In our opinion this is to ensure that the US maintains, or does not lose, its hegemonic place in the world. The consequence of an arms race and a more dangerous world is that other countries are forced into becoming a part of this logic as net buyers. This might become the case with some Latin-American countries, like Venezuela and Brazil, which may feel threatened and aspire to set up their own military-industrial complex. The consequences for a country's economy, where the country practises this type of unproductive spending without any control, will be negative. With or without a great war, an arms race means a decline in the civil economy, due to a great unproductive consumption of wealth by new armaments. It may increase profits of bigger capital in the military-industrial complex, which is officially supposed to exist to enable the stability of the system itself.

Military spending is once again considered the recipe to face the current crisis. It was also supposed to be a way out of the crisis in the 1930s, which ended in World War II. 'Military Keynesianism' is sometimes used to refer to the crisis of 1929 in the United States and to its dominant economic situation during World War II. It is true that this war assured the US its definitive world hegemony. There are, however, some differences between that scenario and the current situation. During most of World War II, the US was benefited by being the world's factory of weapons and civilian products for the powers in dispute. It was not in the US' interest to get involved in the conflict early. It entered the war towards the end and also became the winning power and the absolute leader of the world economy. The US was benefited even more as its territory did not suffer the destructive consequences of the war, unlike Eurasia.

Map 3.1: Regional Military Expenditure, 2010

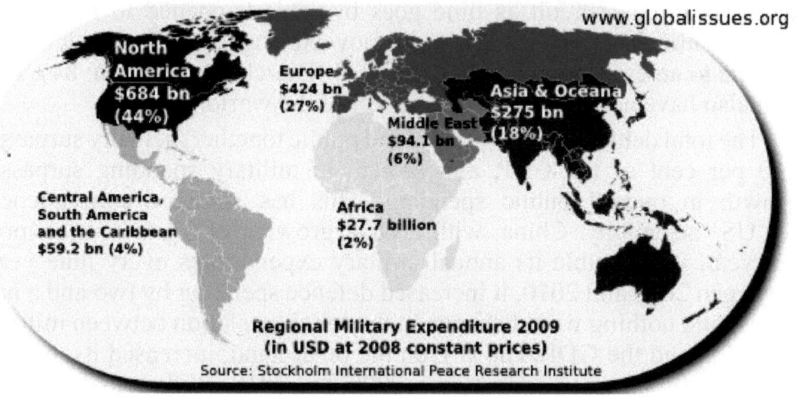

It was, however, not until the 1950s that markets became stable after the Great Depression. World War II secured US hegemony in the world and it is likely that the country's conservative elite think that it will sustain this power during the current crisis as well. The Great Depression had left a huge debt, and the US is confronted with an even larger debt now, which will only grow with the increasing defence spending. This will lead directly to default. General Eisenhower had already forewarned in the 1950s that 'we might lose control over the military-industrial complex'. Today, military spending appears to be completely out of control, as it is the most important factor leading to indebtedness. By the 1950s, the total indebtedness of the US was already 150 per cent of its national income. This gap has only become wider since then, surpassing 350 per cent now. It is clear that with one dollar as income, one cannot continue to spend three or five dollars.

Military Spending, Economic Growth and Hegemony

A strong investment in the military-industrial complex tends to generate, in the short run, employment, products and growth. It will also demonstrate expansion of technology and knowledge. However, we must not forget the essence of all this: this investment generates extraordinary profits for the big capital active in this sector. Military spending may give a boost to growth in the short term; in the middle and long terms, things are quite different. It has been one of the main causes of the breakdown and disintegration of the Soviet Union. This might also be applicable to some arms manufacturing countries in Europe, but most of all, it relates to the United States. In our opinion, the US with a sustained arms race is at risk of spurring its own collapse. A policy that encourages a sustained arms race implies a loss of dynamism in real economic growth. A growing proportion of the installed capacity of the industrial park becomes more unproductive. Reconversion of the military industry into a civil one becomes more difficult as time goes by. This happened to the former Soviet Union two decades ago and is now endangering some countries in Europe to an extent and definitely the US (Dierckxsens, 1994a: 84). This will also have consequences for the rest of the world.

The total debt of the US (private and public together) actually surpasses 350 per cent of the GDP, and growth in military spending surpasses growth in overall public spending. This has strategic consequences for US' hegemony. China, with a GDP growing at 8 per cent or more per year, may double its annual military expenditures every nine years (between 2000 and 2010, it increased defence spending by two and a half times) and nothing would change in the relative relation between military spending and the GDP. The US, on the other hand, increased its military spending by 83 per cent between 2000 and 2010. With actual negative

GDP real growth, the US will see how this unproductive spending will impact negatively on its civil economy. By focusing its economy on productive sectors and thus generating sustained growth, China can afford to go deeper into this arms race. The sustained race for the US, however, means an ever-deeper economic crisis, as it was for the former USSR. When an economy shows negative growth, increasing defence spending by pure credit sooner or later leads to default. Growing debt in a time of a new Great Depression will undoubtedly lead to a default. The US, in other words, is digging its own grave, just as the Soviet Union did a few decades ago.

The real difference between the economies of the US and China is that for several decades, the latter has invested mainly in the real economy and, hence, in enlarged reproduction. In the last decades, China has become the world's manufacturer par excellence. With a vigorous civil economy, it shows high rates of sustained economic growth. This is the economic basis that permits an arms race. The US has, however, not only participated in a permanent arms race since World War II, but has also squandered much of its investment in the last decades in financial and speculative areas. In other words, it has developed particularly fictitious capital accumulation. This is not a basis for military spending as it concerns, by its content, another unproductive investment. Together they will lead to the end of US' hegemony. High non-productive investments by its content affect both capitalist and socialist countries negatively. They have already affected the existence of historic socialism, which collapsed two decades ago. We may be close now to the collapse of the US economy, which is already in full crisis, and with it, there is a profound crisis of capitalism as a whole.

Perestroika Revisited

In the 1980s, the US spent more on defence related matters, in absolute terms, than the USSR. The defence expenditure as a percentage of the GDP in the Soviet Union was more than twice as high as that in the US, more than four times that in Western Europe and more than fifteen times that in Japan. With an economy two or three times smaller, military spending (as a proportion of the Soviet GDP) reached 14 per cent in 1984. Other estimates peg it as high as 17 per cent. This is almost three times the proportion of the US' invested expenditures, as we showed in our former study (Dierckxsens, 1994: 82-84). During the 1980s, the US accelerated its defence spending and the USSR joined the arms race. This meant that the Soviet Union accelerated the arms race at an even higher rate than the US did, although its capacity to transfer these non-productive expenses to other (third world) nations via exports was simultaneously reduced, as illustrated by Aguirre and Taibo (1989: 288-97).

The more a country spends of its GDP on defence (non-productive spending), the less its investments in the civilian economy will be (which includes consumption), and, therefore, the less the spending on generating the means of production will be that are necessary to make an economy run dynamically. When a higher percentage of the GDP is assigned to defence spending, it means there is a further obstacle for the civilian economy to grow. The result for the USSR was that its economic growth became negative. Abel Aganbeguian, principal economic advisor to the Gorbachev administration, concluded that the physical volume of industrial production had decreased by 40 per cent (Mandel, 1991: 26). That is to say that a good loss of industrial products was observed in the civil economy. Hence, consumption per capita showed negative growth. An increase in military spending in a decreasing economy represents an ever-increasing negative growth in a nation's economy as time goes by. The Soviet economy was in a vicious circle moving towards its collapse. The conversion of the military-based economy into a civil economy became necessary. President Mikhail Gorbachev was thus forced to introduce the policy known as 'Perestroika'.

Bolstering of the civil economy of the USSR required a bigger decentralization. That meant a higher degree of autonomy and democratization for the Union of Republics. An economy based on a heavy military-industrial complex implied strong centralization. It sacrificed the republic's civil development plans. 'Perestroika' led to unexpected nationalist feelings. This strengthened local powers in the republics, which resulted in separation from the central power. It was a clear phenomenon of disconnection or disengagement with existing socialism. The fall of the Berlin Wall symbolizes this breakdown of the socialist bloc and, with it, the fall of the existing or so-called historic socialism. This breakdown opened a new path to understand the big problems, errors and contradictions accumulated by the Soviet Union since Stalin. These contradictions had rotted away the foundations of historic socialism, in both Soviet society and the Warsaw Pact. In a trice this alternative project to capitalism, proposed in a historic period, thus collapsed.

At the end of the 1980s, everyone observed that capitalism seemed to be the only possible system for humanity. It was presented to be eternal by nature. This perspective was promoted by Francis Fukuyama. It meant that any alternative project for countries of the South was closed. The consequence was their virtual subordination to the globalizing finance capital during the era of neoliberalism. These powers as a whole, but mainly the US, displayed themselves as glorious winners of the Cold War. This interpretation is marred by a serious error, as capitalism was already at the edge of its own collapse, as we predicted in 1994 in our study (Dierckxsens, 1994: 115) and as reality now demonstrates. As a matter of fact, no one won the Cold War and everyone lost it. The Soviet Union was the first power to fall and now the US and even the Western civilization may be at risk. Both are victims mostly of non-productive activities, such as fictitious capital, corruption, wastefulness and, last but not the least, massive military spending. At the end of the 20th century, socialism failed and, today, at the beginning of the 21st century, capitalism appears to follow. In the 21st century, no other clear options are left except for the good and bad experiences from the past. With this inheritance we think that reconstructing the world in a different and fairer manner may soon become a reality.

The Necessity for a 'Perestroika' in the West

Times of crisis mean decrease in exports of most industrialized countries and thus imply a decrease in capital goods, such as machinery tools. Reduced civil demand of capital goods is substituted by an increase in defence spending. A consequence is the enlargement of the military-industrial complex. This apparent solution will, sooner or later, intensify the existing economic crisis. The only way to avoid negative growth is to transfer more military spending to third countries. Effective demand of weaponry supposes wars. The military-industrial complex in general, and particularly in times of crisis, leads to more intensive search for – a long – war. This war, first of all, will be directed to countries with payment possibilities, that is, countries with huge energy and natural resources that the whole world needs and consumes. However, one may be risking a 'great war', that is, a war between core countries. It will be perpetrated especially against those powers that could represent a threat to the current established order. In our opinion, this most surely means a US military conflict with China and probably Russia.

Due to the growing difficulties of selling its capital goods in times of crisis, the state has to guarantee the demand of those final products. That is why states favour actively unproductive capital in the military-industrial complex. Since the last few decades, defence spending is no longer largely funded by annual taxes collected from US citizens. In 2009, 44 per cent of the US taxes, however, were still allocated to defence spending. The US government funds war increasingly by credit and a lot of it is obtained from abroad. This means that foreign countries are increasingly financing the US military-industrial complex without the US needing to export its final products. This becomes more and more doubtful as the acquired credit has been mainly from the US' direct rivals: China and Russia. Today, it has become harder for the US to obtain those credits. Quantitative easing or money printing has since become the ultimate solution. The US is printing money without any real support. As long as this money is accepted worldwide the show might go on. However, a default increasingly becomes a real risk.

More military exports might appear to be a solution. A country's capacity to transfer unproductive military spending is measured in weapons export. Numbers indicate that weapons export of the US increased only 12 per cent in the last decade. Stockholm International Peace Research Institute (SIPRI) informed further that the two biggest importers of armaments over 2006-2010, India and China, bought over 80 per cent of their weapons from Russia. To the displeasure of the US, even its own European allies did better with weapons export. In 2009, six European Union countries (Germany, France, UK, Netherlands, Spain and Italy) together had larger weapons export (7.376 million dollar) than the US (6.658 million dollar). Russia and China together, with 6.575 million dollars, almost equalled the US' arms export in 2009. The European Union has its own more limited military-industrial complex as its defence spending is about 50 per cent of the US' military spending. As European military exports equal those of the US, this means that they have better possibilities to transfer the unproductive military spending to other countries. We believe, together with Sara Flounders, that this time the economic crisis of the US is so large and its military spending so unbearable that the possibilities of transfer to other nations have become insignificant.[4] A growing debt is the consequence of huge military spending, which will unavoidably, sooner or later, lead to default. This means that someday the US will have to declare a payment cessation to its creditors.

Curiously, the US obtained huge credits from its direct opponents (especially China). As credit becomes even more difficult to obtain and actual quantitative easing heads towards default, the US might consider transferring the effects of this unproductive-destructive expense by eventual non-payment of its debt in general, and to China and Russia, specifically. It is not that the US cannot pay its debt, unlike Greece, but that it is in the exceptional condition to deny payment. This, however, requires special conditions. We are already witnessing a growing currency war between China and the US. Economic wars historically lead to more direct conflicts. A direct conflict between these nations might be an argument to stop debt payments. A great war, in other words, is no abstraction. Historically we have seen that these scenarios contradictorily create a favourable scenario for the disconnection of the peripheral countries and to change the economic rationale, as was the case during World War I with Russia and in World War II with China.

---

4 Sara Flounders, 'The Pentagon Budget: Largest Ever and Growing', www.globalresearch.ca, 7 November 2009.

We have to reiterate that it is not just defence spending that leads to unsustainable debt and default. Fictitious capital accumulation in general is financed basically by growing debt and leads to an economic depression, that is, generates negative growth rates for years. In early November 2009, during the celebrations of the 20th anniversary of the fall of the Berlin Wall, the former Soviet president Mikhail Gorbachev referred to the fall of another wall, this time in New York (Wall Street). He mentioned the systemic crisis of capitalism. He stated that the United States 'needs its own Perestroika', as we predicted in our 1994 study (Dierckxsens, 1994: 115). In another book, *The Great Depression of the 21st Century* (2009), we referred to the possibility of a Perestroika in the West as prospects of non-productive cost transfers become very hard during a new Great Depression. This implies that, first of all, the US needs to convert its military economy into a civil one. Chronic negative growth rates will demonstrate this need. Reconversion is neither easy nor can it be done quickly.

The former Soviet president added that there are signs of change favouring the whole world. He referred to the process of decentralization and independence in peripheral economies. Gorbachev asked for 'more transparency and more openness' (glasnost). Finally, he wished President Barack Obama good luck. We think he suggested that Obama prepare himself for an eventual disintegration of the US empire and even of the United States of America. It seems that the eventual disintegration of the European Union is not the only danger, as was hot news in 2010 and 2011, but even the American Union may be at risk.

During the Cold War, it was stated that the ideology and political system of historical socialism in a specific country would drag its neighbours into the same system. This statement, better known in geopolitics as the Domino Theory, is attributed to John Foster Dulles and President Truman. More recently, it was advocated by Henry Kissinger, among others, to justify US' military intervention in Vietnam and Southeast Asia. Apparently this theory worked, not as its advocates foretold, but the other way around. Nowadays, we are observing a 'boomerang' effect (Medipaz, 1994) of accumulating contradictions among the core countries. It seems that the power that dared to practise such a theory ended up as its own 'victim', paying a high price. First, a disintegration process was observed in the USSR, recently we have seen the EU at risk, and now, the next station seems to be the US.

Geostrategy of the Financial Elite in the Past

> *'Permit me to issue and control the money of a nation, and I care not who makes its laws.'*
>
> — Baron of Rothschild (British banker)

'The money power preys upon the nation in times of peace and conspires against it in times of adversity. It is more despotic than monarchy, more insolent than autocracy, more selfish than bureaucracy. It denounces, as public enemies, all who question its methods or throw light upon its crimes. I have two great enemies, the Southern army in front of me and the bankers in the rear. And of the two, the bankers are my greatest foe.'

— President Abraham Lincoln, 1866 (assassinated)

'Whoever controls the volume of money in any country is absolute master of all industry and commerce.'

— President James A. Garfield, 1881 (assassinated)

'I am a most unhappy man. I have unwittingly ruined my country. A great industrial nation is controlled by its system of credit. Our system of credit is concentrated. The growth of the Nation and all our activities are in the hands of a few men. We have come to be one of the worst ruled, one of the most completely controlled and dominated Governments in the civilized world, no longer a government by free opinion, no longer a government by conviction and the vote of the majority, but a government by the opinion and duress of a small group of dominant men.'

— President Woodrow Wilson (1856-1924)

'The high office of the President has been used to foment a plot to destroy America's freedom and before I leave office, I must inform the citizens of their plight.'

— President John F. Kennedy (10 days before assassination)

These presidents were assassinated apparently because they defended interests that were contrary to those of the financial elite. In our book, *The Great Depression of the 21st Century*, written when Barack Obama was being elected president, we pointed out that he would have few options of implementing his own policy faced with the banking elite, unless he took a big risk. Bankers and transnational corporations have probably not been absent from any modern war of some importance. They have financed one side of the conflict, often both sides, destroying entire countries, dragging millions of human beings to their death and deciding on the winner at the end of the conflict. They financed both sides during the American Civil War and the Russian Tsar while they supported the Bolshevik Revolution. They supported both sides during World War II, Hitler's National Socialism as well as the Allied Forces who defeated it. This is true in almost every war of the 19th and 20th centuries. They are the main element of the elite of powerful agents who decide the present and future of humankind.[5]

5 R.K. Moore, 'Prognosis 2012: Towards a New World Social Order', www.globalresearch.ca, 27 February 2010.

Map 3.2: Eurasia – Heartland and Rimland

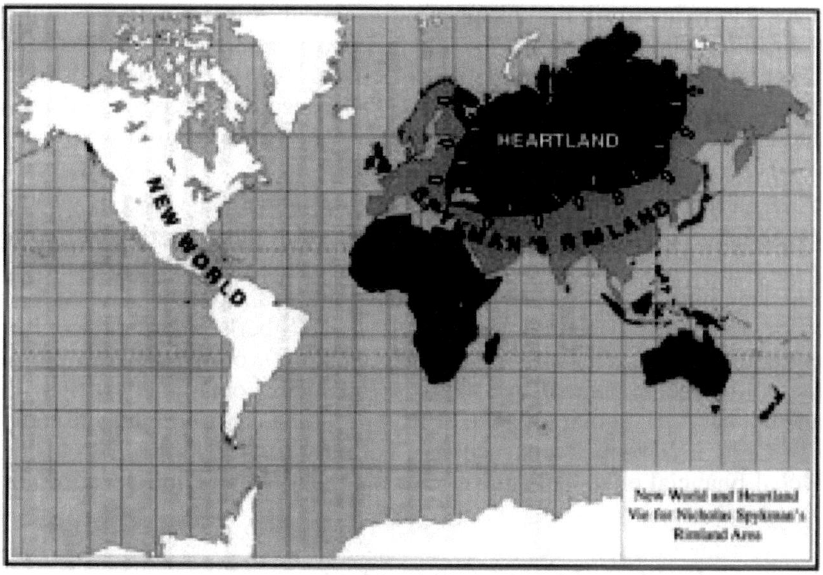

Throughout the 20th century, a whole theoretical and geostrategic theory was developed to justify and spur on, on a global scale, the concentration of wealth and power in the hands of a few. Halford John Mackinder, an Englishman and the father of geopolitics (1861-1947) established the link between geography, human beings and their surroundings as the basis of geopolitics. In his 1904 essay, '*The Geographical Pivot of History*', he describes the world as a politically closed system where nations cannot ignore incidents in any part of the globe. It is an idea that is a precursor of globalization and that established a policy of permanent war as a system of international relations. Mackinder asserted:

> Whoever controls Eastern Europe (Russia), will rule the centre of the World (the 'Heartland'), whoever controls the centre of the world will rule the 'World Island' (Eurasia) and, whoever controls the World Island will rule the world.

American-Dutch geo-politician, Nicholas Spykman, would later provide the concepts of 'contention' and 'Rimland'. He did so by referring to the ring of countries, which by their proximity, size, importance, population and wealth, might be susceptible to an alliance with the Soviet Union, or later with Russia and China. The policy of contention would be developed further by George F. Kennan and used as the basis for the defeat of the USSR. Mackinder's ideas became a key part of British foreign policy during the first half of the 20th century and the two world wars. These ideas did not disappear after World War II. On the contrary, the United States strengthened them. One of its keen advocates was Zbigniew Brzezinski, who is the current advisor to President Obama. Brzezinski announced the use of NATO as a spearhead to besiege Russia and China. On this basis, the Cold War and the fear of communism were its justifications.

With the elimination of this ideological pretext since the collapse of the socialist system, it has become clearer what the objective of a new great war might be. It is to prevent the expansion of or alliances among Russia, China and Iran, and other Asian countries. A further objective is to secure entry into Central Asia, all the way to Siberia, in order to control mineral and energy resources in this region of the world. As stated before, the policy recommended by Brzezinski includes containment of Russia and China. A triangular alliance of Russia, China and Iran – maybe India and Germany, too – is unacceptable not only to the US but also to the global financial elite. This makes Eurasia the most probable location for a new great war.

Financial Elite's Present Geostrategy

Global Perspective

Bankers and transnational corporations are the main component of the powerful elite who decide humanity's present and future. They topple and install new governments, destroy and rescue nations, start and finish wars, build and demolish institutions, and manipulate laws according to their own interests; they pay for the services of the best scientists, intellectuals and universities; they control the means and technology of mass communication and, thus, define the 'good guy' and the 'bad guy'; they divide and/or confront nations; and so on.[6]

Zbigniew Brzezinski (1997) describes Russia and China as countries whose interests threaten those of the US in Central Asia. In this context, Russia would be the more serious threat. He describes Ukraine, Azerbaijan, Iran and Kazakhstan as essential 'second category nations' that must be controlled by the US as buffers or counterweights to Russian and Chinese influences to control the exploitation of oil, gas and minerals of the Central Asian republics (Turkmenistan, Uzbekistan, Tajikistan and Kyrgyzstan). He also notes that any nation that might become influential in Central Asia would directly threaten the current US control of oil resources in the Persian Gulf (*Ibid.*: 53). He states that 'America is now the only global superpower, and Eurasia is the globe's central arena'. In a

6 *Ibid.*

clear reference to defend the US' unipolar domination, he states that 'The Eurasian continent will be of decisive importance to America's global primacy and to America's historical legacy... A power that dominates Eurasia would control two of the world's three most advanced and economically productive regions.' An obvious difference between the ideas of Mackinder in 1905 and Brzezinski in 1997 is that, at that time, there were neither nuclear weapons nor intercontinental missiles.

The rich fields of Siberia and Central Asia are a clear objective for the corporate capital concentrated in the West. In our opinion, it is not just a US strategy that aims to separate Russia and China. The global financial elite, with their centre in Wall Street and the City of London, also aim to prevent the economic and military integration of Eurasia and its possible alliances with European countries, as currently appears to happen. The objective of a new 'cold war' is undoubtedly to prevent the expansion of Eurasia with alliances among Russia, China and Iran, as well as with Europe. A second important objective is to force an entry into Central Asia and Siberia to assure access to the rich mineral and energy resources of this region. Developments in recent years increasingly show not just the US, but also NATO as the new 'policeman of the world'. The United Nations has become the instrument to give legitimacy to this global 'policeman'.

With the catastrophic tsunami in Japan in 2011, when its nuclear plants suffered huge damage in Fukushima, the country's confidence to use nuclear energy, as a substitute for oil, for civil purposes was lost. The incident showed Japan's people once again how dangerous the use of nuclear energy could be. As a consequence, Japan's dependency on oil has suddenly become very great. The rich oilfields in Siberia and the peninsula of Kamchatka as well as the fields in Central Asia and South Asia, from where oil is imported, now have enormous strategic importance. In this context, Japan will have to turn towards NATO's strategy of a possible military adventure with Russia and China.

The actual policy of 'contention' established, in fact, a 'permanent war status' in the world and constituted a pretext for interventions in internal matters of other countries and even declare 'pre-emptive wars'. NATO installs armaments as close as possible to the borders of Russia and China. This has to increase the capability to launch a surprising 'first nuclear strike'. This concept of modern war means that we are talking about 'total war' and even a 'global war'. A total war does not exclude any means of devastation, including weapons of mass destruction. This strategy has extremely dangerous variants. This re-installation of a new cold war demands to be supported by massive deliveries of weapons and plans for the setting up of supposedly 'interceptor' missiles. Apparently it would mean that the only winner would be NATO, but it could imply the beginning of something worse as well: A total thermonuclear war. A question we might want to ask is, how does one finance this war with the bankruptcies in the Western world? Are we talking not about a bank of last resort, but a bang of last resort?

This strategy has dangerous implications. It means provoking states like Russia and China that have the capacity to retaliate to a nuclear attack. In this context, Iran is at risk of becoming the test case of these plans of the US and NATO. For years public opinion is being regularly informed about this possible pre-emptive nuclear strike in the context of Israel. Iran has the capacity to defend itself and retaliate against Israel, the US or NATO with conventional weapons, but not with nuclear ones. The US recently announced the withdrawal of its troops from Iraq. This is not necessarily good news, as, in our opinion, a nuclear strike has become a very real possibility. The US and NATO would have needed to withdraw their troops from the region before such a nuclear strike can be executed.

The provocation of conflicts with neighbouring countries has already caused strong reactions. Moscow demonstrated its concern with regard to NATO's expansion with moving its military blocs closer to the Russian border. It was known that NATO had not only placed anti-missile shields in Eastern Europe, but also installed 480 B61 thermonuclear bombs in five 'non-nuclear' nations: Belgium, Germany, Italy, the Netherlands and Turkey.[7] Based on this, Russia announced in February 2010 that it would make use of atomic weapons if it felt threatened and would respond militarily to any of NATO's allies. Furthermore, it stated that the use of its army outside its borders in order to defend its vital interests was 'legitimate'. Russia also criticized the move that was being considered to provide NATO with global military functions, as this would be in violation of international law.[8]

A reaction could be expected. Russia threatened to install nuclear missiles in Kalingrad, close to the European Union border. On the other hand, *Rossiyskaya Gazeta* informed about a regiment of anti-aircraft defence established recently on the outskirts of Moscow and showed journalists the real masterpiece of Russian armament, the S-400 anti-aircraft system.[9] Europe obviously became nervous, as this continent is not looking for another great war within its own borders. Pascal Mallet reported that the European NATO allies were pressing President Obama to withdraw nuclear weapons from the European territory.[10] Furthermore, Belgium,

---

7 M. Chossudovsky, 'Europe's Five Undeclared Nuclear Weapons States', *www.globalresearch.ca*, 23 February 2010.

8 Source: *Agencia EFE*.

9 RIA Novosti, Moscow, 19 February.

10 Source: *Agence AFP*.

Germany, Luxembourg, Holland and Norway would soon also demand the withdrawal of nuclear heads installed mainly in Italy and Turkey.

The aforementioned threats at the geopolitical and military levels are the most dangerous aspects of the actual crisis of the Western civilization. We have integrated different crises and dangers for the present, one of them is the possibility that in this complex and multiple crisis, the dominant elite may cause a bigger military conflict – not just a new cold war, but an even more dangerous great war. It will be much more destructive than previous ones because the current advances in military technology and armaments exhibit a destructive capacity without any precedent. The most valuable thing that we have as humanity is life itself and the possibility to live in peace, with freedom, justice and dignity. In contradiction with it and at its very extremity is the logic of anti-life based on profits at any cost, which may finally lead to a new great war. It may mean the end of life not just of uncountable people, but also of life in general. To save the people, we have to stop the global bankers as those elite who are most responsible for this global destruction of life.

The Strategic Location and Role of Latin America and the Caribbean

Today, Latin America and the Caribbean are of great strategic importance to the United States, as they were during World War II, and especially so for the more conservative and unilateral section of its elite. This is not necessarily the case with the global financial elite, which means there is a contradiction in the USA between the nationalist unipolar elite and the global financial elite, which is played out in Wall Street and the City of London. In any case, the region is the secure, main strategic reserve vis-à-vis the large military adventures planned in Eurasia. Latin America has all varieties of weather needed to cultivate all kinds of food. It has large reserves of hydrocarbons, minerals, water and biodiversity. Since the beginning of 2008, the United States' Fourth Fleet controls Latin American seas. This action is undoubtedly to guarantee its access to the region's natural resources. Latin American governments responded to this with the procurement of new war equipment and investments in military technology. This implied redirecting valuable productive resources necessary for their civil economy and population to non-productive equipment. And in so doing, they willy-nilly supported the US' military-industrial complex.

In response to this situation, it is important to have a strategic policy so that Latin American people and governments are able to preserve this region as a zone of peace, isolated from military conflicts of the United States and other nations. For this reason, their main struggle should be oriented toward preventing the militarization and intervention of the

United States in the region. This is a policy for the survival of all, without distinctions of political thinking, religious beliefs and social position. UNASUR (Union of South American Nations) and, more recently, CELAC (Community of Latin American and Caribbean States) are the regional institutions created to prevent Latin America from foreign interventions. The prevention of a new era of authoritarianism must be the cornerstone of this policy, which enables countries to move forward in the construction of a more sovereign system based on liberty, peace, democracy and social justice. These days, Latin American social forces are building a process of unity in diversity, creating regional integration with the mechanisms this involves, in all spheres, economical, political and military.

There have been clear advances towards unity and integration in the last few years to restore the sovereignty lost during the neoliberal era. There is unanimous opposition to the Fourth Fleet in Latin American waters; there is also complete agreement among governments on rejecting the coup d'état in Honduras and Paraguay; and there is a growing undivided condemnation of US military bases in Latin America. The proposals of CELAC – created in Cancun, Mexico, which excludes the United States and Canada – represent, from our point of view, a remarkable move towards a more sovereign integration. And these efforts are supported by more than just the progressive social and political forces in the region. They have to disconnect from the neoliberal policy of subordination of whole countries to foreign corporative and financial interests and reconnect with internal and regional sovereign interests that will lead to self-determination. This would allow, yet still does not guarantee, a reconnection to the people's interests of the Latin American countries.

It is highly recommended that the continent avoid falling into the trap of an arms race. What is needed to deal with conflicts is a defence with low investment in armament, accompanied by continental unity and non-conventional methods. With this in mind it is possible to respond properly to any aggression. The vastness of the territory facilitates its self-defence, and a military strategy to control a territory only with planes, ships and bombs has not been invented yet. This was already proved in Vietnam and Nicaragua and can be seen today in Iraq and Afghanistan. Any military presence of the United States in Latin American territories and seas is highly dangerous and must be rejected. This is not only because it diminishes the strength of self-determination, but also because in the case of a new great war, those Latin American countries that hold US military bases might become the target of an eventual attack. This attack might be with nuclear weapons, from either the enemies of the US or NATO or even international terrorists. This is why it is necessary to strengthen the sustained and united struggle against all US military bases in the region and all foreign intervention in Latin American domestic issues. It is urgent to demand the withdrawal of foreign fleets from the Latin American seas and it is necessary to respond as a region to any external aggression, threat or intervention. For this, it is appropriate to create regional mechanisms and define possible conflict resolving policies without extra-regional interventions.

We encourage Latin American and Caribbean leaders to gain full consciousness of this historic moment. They must avoid the temptation of rhetoric or unnecessary confrontations or fall into the hands of ambitious or authoritarian leaders. Liberty, justice and more integral and participative democracy are not negotiable because they represent a precious heritage conquered by the people. This struggle of all the people is for life itself, which implies, first of all, the right of survival of everyone.

Disconnections and Reconnections in Crisis Time

We recommended in the past the reconversion of the military-industrial complex into a civil economy in the context of international cooperation towards peace. We cannot expect this reconversion to be promoted by the conservative elite in the world, and especially in the United States. Such a process anyway will take quite a long time, probably even decades. A new Great Depression and the eventual collapse of the capitalist system itself might create more objective conditions in this direction. This collapse will provoke the disconnection of wide regions of the world and even the US is at risk of disintegration. Similar to the disintegration of the Soviet Bloc, we believe that a process of disconnection of wide regions may suddenly get accelerated during the actual new Great Depression and will be even more radical with a great war.

We have not paid much attention to a possible crisis in China. An economic crisis in China is not implausible. It will not so much be due to overproduction of goods and equipment at home, but particularly due to the reduction in export possibilities to the West because of the latter's economic depression and the consequent probable protectionist measures. As the export of consumer goods made in China may really go down, the country will have to concentrate on how to substitute huge losses in external demand with fomenting internal demand. This substitution process may work, but it won't be easy. It could involve an economic slowdown and even a crisis in China. As a consequence, the export of raw materials from the South, especially Latin America, to China will fall. It will mean lower growth rates in the South, and thus the new Great Depression will become a worldwide phenomenon. This will be the moment that the Great Depression of the 21st Century will be announced officially. From then on, substitution of imports will become a general policy in these peripheral economies. This will mean a progressive disconnection from neoliberal policies and possible South-South reconnections. It will also open possibilities of reconnections with class struggles. In times of crisis, it can also be argued that China will be forced to increase its defence spending. This will obviously contribute to an even more dangerous world. This may be countered with a third alternative: an intensified commerce between China and Russia and China and Germany. The consolidation of a Eurasian bloc will make the world particularly insecure, as this is not in the interest of the actual ruling elite.

Capital accumulation is becoming decadent, as it is progressively leading to worldwide corruption. It is true that corruption has always existed, but actual capital accumulation goes together increasingly with war, drugs, criminalization and corruption of the political systems, institutions and states. With the invasion of Iraq, and more recently, the attack on Libya, Syria and Mali in 2011, another modality of capitalist accumulation was reborn: classic old piracy, which existed during the first historic period of capitalism, has been reinvented and even legalized by the United Nations. The expropriation of the international reserves, investments or property of any country has become an institutionalized practice. In this way, the neoliberal process of globalization is ending up becoming a more corrupt and criminal form of accumulation. Possibly new wars will foment this practice even more with highly destructive consequences for the majorities. It is incredible that it is a practice supported by the United Nations. After Libya, no periphery country will feel secure anymore to keep funds or foreign reserves in Europe or in the US. From now on, any country in the South could eventually expect the same treatment. A country that has already withdrawn its foreign reserves is Venezuela. Nowadays, even a core country like Germany is trying to withdraw its foreign reserves from the US, but not without difficulties. The action of repatriation signifies the acknowledgement of credit risk and the Bundesbank's concern about the possibility that gold held at the Fed may be over-pledged in some manner.[11]

Millions of people respond with growing indignation to this actual decadent phase of the capitalist system, with demonstrations taking place in the streets of a thousand cities in more than a hundred countries around the world, against bankers and with demands for a life of dignity. The rebellion started in 2011 in Tunisia and Egypt and is rapidly spreading around the world. The movement reached southern European countries and even the UK and the USA and nobody can say that it won't take place here. The 'Occupy Wall Street' movement in the United States rapidly

[11] Peter Krauth, *The Real Reason Germany Wants its Gold Back*, http://www.marketoracle.co.uk, 29 January 2013.

spread beyond New York to all over the country. It is notorious that the movement converged on Wall Street, the epicentre (together with the City of London) of the Anglo-American global financial business. The protestors shouted, 'Save the people, not the banks'. Indignant unemployed people in Spain and excluded people anywhere who feel like victims of a corrupt financial, economic and political system simply demand a life of dignity. A prolonged struggle will create higher levels of consciousness, political position and organization. At that stage majorities may even question existing society as such and struggle for another civilization that has respect for life and a place for all of us, including nature. This demands not only a stop to wars, but also dismantling the military-industrial complex and relocating all military investments to the civil sector to improve the well-being of the people, stopping waste and repairing the damage done to the planet, life in general and the environment.

References

Aguirre, Mariano and Carlos Taibo. 1989. *Anuario del Centro de Investigaciones para la paz, 1988-1989*. Madrid: Editorial IEPALA, pp. 288-97.

Brzezinski, Zbigniew. 1997. *The Grand Chessboard: American Primacy and it's Geostrategic Imperatives*. New York: Basic Books.

Dierckxsens, Wim. 1994a. *De la globalización a la perestroika occidental*. San José: DEI, p. 84.

———. 1994b. *The Post Cold War Era: Unsustainable Economic Development*. Tilburg University, Holland: IVO.

Diercksens, Wim, Antonio Jarquín *et al*. 2009. 'La gran Depresión del Siglo XXI: Causas, carácter, perspectivas'. San José: DEI y Observatorio Internacional de la Crisis.

Mackinder, Halford John. 1904. 'The Geographical Pivot of History', *The Geographical Journal*, 23: 421-37.

Mandel, Ernst. 1991. *¿Hacia donde va la URSS de Gorbachev?*. Mexico: Editorial Fontamara, p. 26.

MEDIPAZ. 1994. *Guerra de baja intensidad, efectos y consecuencias en un país subdesarrollado*. Managua: MEDIPAZ.

CHAPTER 4

Is a 'New Green Deal' an Alternative?

Paulo CAMPANARIO, Antonio JARQUÍN,
Wim DIERCKXSENS

Centro Latinoamericano de Demografía, Brazil

International Physicians for the Prevention of Nuclear War, Nicaragua

and

International Observatory of the Crisis (IOC), The Netherlands and Costa Rica

Control oil and you control nations,
control food and you control the people.

Henry Kissinger (1970)

Sustainable Growth: A Myth or Reality?

For the elite in power, 'military Keynesianism' is not at all an option for meeting the current crisis, as was the case in 1929. The previous chapter is quite clear about this subject. The next question is: is there a possibility of another 'New Deal' in order to rescue the capitalist economy? All conventional ways out of the crisis point to a tacit condition and a sine qua non: the necessity of sustained economic growth. Capitalist society clings to the myth of economic growth. Without it sustainable accumulation is impossible. Myth holds that growth would be a necessary condition for people's welfare. Although economic growth may be and has been throughout history an important vehicle to create greater welfare, it is not a necessary condition for it. At certain degrees of capitalistic development, according to authors like Daly (1996), it is more likely to obstruct welfare and to even lose it.

Economic growth, however, is a very necessary condition to make profits in the long run. Sustainable capital accumulation requires investments in productive labour by its content. It is simply not possible to sustain productive labour based on its form (making profits) without it being based on its content. Only then when sustainable growth is guaranteed as permanent real economic growth, sustainable capital accumulation will be assured. Without real economic growth, it is only possible to accumulate capital temporarily. In which case, it is based on a more unequal distribution of income and existing wealth, mortgaging the future, as it has become clear today. Another way to do so is by means of fictitious capital accumulation. This way to accumulate however, sooner or later, reaches a limit and hence produces a deep economic crisis. This evidences the impossibility of creating profits without creating real wealth based on real value in a sustainable way.

Nowadays the world economy is five times greater than it was half a century ago. The world is in danger. Although no one could imagine it 50 years ago, today energy resources and natural resources cannot supply enough to sustain capital development and its perspectives of growth. Global warming is an immediate threat. CO_2 pollution and other forms of contamination represent a threat to the life of ever-expanding number of species and to natural life in general on our planet. If hypothetically the world economy continues to grow by 3 per cent annually, the way it has grown in the past half a century, in the next 50 years the world economy will have a volume 5 times larger than its current size, and in a century, it will be 10 times. Every 10 years we would need to occupy another planet to maintain this current rate of growth. This is simply impossible.

Today our planet is more than saturated. In other words, there is already a need for another planet. Humanity, however, will have to manage with only one. If we do not stop global economic growth, nature will destroy us due to our destruction of the natural resources. So it is absurd to maintain the myth of sustainable growth. We are facing a deep crisis derived from the Western lifestyle. Its logic of practical, ideological and political performance rules the world today. Thus, this crisis is not only of this mode of production, but also of the very Western 'civilization' itself.

The Limits of Growth

As Western model of development is based on economic growth, energy resources are the very basis for this process. They represent the most strategic resource to maintain the engine of growth of the current economy. Therefore, with continuous shortage of such resources, this development paradigm is reaching the limits of its possibilities. Oil is the main energy resource today, which, together with natural gas, covers more than 90 per cent of all the energy used on a global scale. According to the Energy Information Administration of the US (EIA), oil production has not met world demand since 2005.

We are currently facing the so-called peak oil. Peak exists when the difference between demand and possible supply becomes negative. In other words, peak exists when new discoveries and development (supply) do not meet the ever-rising demand. In which case, price tends towards a permanent increase. Peak oil, thus, is a worldwide phenomenon. For many years, authors forewarned its arrival. Even if estimated dates vary, it is generally accepted that if we have not encountered the peak yet, we will do so in a few years. Authors also agree that we will soon be witnessing the 'natural gas peak', an energy resource whose supply depends heavily on oil discoveries. When oil is relatively scarce, its price tends to rise, as we have seen in recent years. Due to the current crisis, oil prices may decrease temporarily, but the trend is they will increase more or less rapidly again. This demonstrates the relative shortage of this energy resource. Superpowers, including the US, are net oil importers. The difference between oil imports and domestic supply is growing larger.

Energy resources represent the engine of economic growth on a global scale. When those resources become scarcer, growth is in danger. We, however, should not underestimate the relative shortage of other minerals. Besides peak oil, other minerals have already reached their limits. Almost 20 per cent, that is, 11 out of 57 minerals have been stretched to their extraction limit: mercury (1962), tellurium (1984), lead (1986), cadmium (1989), potassium (1989), phosphate (1989), thallium (1995), selenium (1994), zirconium (1994), rhenium (1998) and gallium (2002). More than half the minerals will reach their extraction limit in the next 30 years.[1] Mineral coal, a still much used energy resource today, will also have its 'peak coal' somewhat later. The Energy Watch Group (EWG) estimates this peak in 2025, while the EIA projects that mineral coal production may increase until 2030. On the other hand, B. Kavalov and S.D. Peteves from the Institute for Energy Technology do not make estimations of concrete dates. They conclude, however, that coal in the future may not be plentiful and widely available. Growing dependence on this energy resource has no future. Besides nearing its peak, mineral coal contaminates the atmosphere and the environment and intensifies global warming. These are important reasons why it will be questioned as an energy resource as time passes by.

As 'peak gas' approaches, new dangerous processes of exploitation are being introduced. The process of hydraulic fracturing of natural gas involves the injection of fluid into wells under high pressure to create cracks in the rock formation. The fluid is forced under high pressure and consists of water, chemical additives, and a propping (opening) agent. As the well goes into production, there is a 'flowback' of fracturing

1 See 'Industry Database', 2003 IHS, 'Peak Oil', www.en.wikipedia.org.

fluid from the well head that is very salty and contains a variety of other contaminants (IOGCC and ALL, 2006). Identified water-related concerns include: (*i*) water withdrawals; (*ii*) groundwater contamination associated with well drilling and production; (*iii*) wastewater management; (*iv*) truck traffic and its impacts on water quality; (*v*) surface spills and leaks; and (*vi*) storm water management.[2] There were more than 493,000 active natural-gas wells across 31 states in the US in 2009, almost double the number in 1990. Around 90 per cent have used fracking to get more gas flowing, according to the drilling industry. Nationwide, residents living near fracked gas wells have filed over 1,000 complaints regarding tainted water, severe illnesses, livestock deaths and fish kills.[3]

Agro-Fuels: Speculating with Hunger

Substitution of non-renewable energy resources with renewable ones is an immediate necessity. It is not only a relatively slow process, but it also has its limits. It is expected that by 2020, all alternative energy resources together will cover at most 20 per cent of the world's overall energy demand (Middelkoop and Koppelaar, 2008: 108). Furthermore, energy production based on renewable resources (including agro-fuels) will not be enough to properly compensate the non-renewable energy decline (oil, gas and coal). This will be manifested in a permanent oil price rise. Supply of renewable resources will not be able to satisfy the growing demand, which will lead to an increase in prices of such renewable resources as well.

Competition between agro-fuels and food tends to increase the price of the latter. Something similar happens with prices of arable lands, too. They are used more and more in the production of all kinds of agro-fuels, which is detrimental to food production. The outcome of this will be the omnipresence of famine precisely in places where purchasing capacity is lower, affecting the poorest countries. Permanent price rise of all energy resources will imply a constant increase in production costs, the recovery of which will become a chronic difficulty. It will hinder capital to realize profits, creating a more or less chronic crisis. In Middelkoop and Koppelaar's (2008: 166) view, the so-called credit crisis will be an insignificant one compared to the chronic crisis caused by peak oil.

The current world crisis will be more devastating than the Great Depression of the 1930s. It has many more geopolitical implications. Economic dislocations have accompanied the beginning of regional wars,

---

2 Brian Carr, 'Hydraulic Fracturing: Are there Public Health Dangers?' www.lubbockonline.com, 1 October 2012.

3 http://www.sourcewatch.org, 9 January 2013.

the fracture of national societies and, in some cases, the destruction of entire countries. This is, by far, the most severe economic crisis of modern history (Chossudovsky, 2008). Faced with the real estate and financial crisis that hit the United States in August 2007, large speculative investment funds transferred huge amounts of money to control agricultural products (agricultural commodities) in international markets. Once real estate bubbles burst, speculators returned to a former paradise: cereal markets (Halimi, 2008: 40). It is estimated that these funds control 60 per cent of the wheat business and a high percentage of other main grain markets. A greater part of the soy harvest for the next few years has already been purchased as 'futures'. These grains have become another object of speculation. Their changing (rising) prices are the result of speculative ups and downs and not of changing local markets or people's needs.

This mix of speculative increases in food prices has led to a wave of world famines with no precedent due to its scale. Absence of regulations in these speculative markets triggers famine. Volatility in food markets is mostly due to deregulation, lack of control over big agents and lack of necessary state intervention at the international and national levels in order to stabilize markets. Since 2009, speculation with new menaces of hunger was back in the economy. In 2011, commodity food prices were even higher than in 2008. A stop on speculation in staple food markets, taken as an imperative political decision, would immediately contribute to decrease in food prices. There is nothing to prevent this from happening. We cannot foresee, however, a cautious group of measures of this kind being implemented.[4]

The food crisis is occurring despite there being enough food in the world to feed the global population. Famine is not the consequence of the shortage of food but the other way around. In the past, food surpluses in the core countries were used to destabilize production in developing countries. According to the FAO, the world is able to feed up to 12 billion people in the future. World grain production in 2007/2008 was estimated to be 2,108 million tons (a rise by 4.7 per cent in comparison with that in 2006/2007). This surpasses the standard of a 2 per cent increase during the last decade. Even though production remains at a high level, speculators betted on an expected shortage and artificially increased prices. According to FAO reports, price of basic necessity grains rose by 88 per cent since March 2007.[5]

While speculators and large-scale commercial groups profit from the current crisis, most farmers don't get benefits from these high prices. As land becomes more expensive, speculation on agricultural land rises.

---

4 See Chossudovsky (2008).

5 See Ian Angus's (2008) article.

Evictions, sometimes by force, are one of the consequences. Farmers that still 'survive' cultivate their land, but their harvest is frequently already sold either to the lender or a provider or agro-industrial companies or a merchant. Even when prices paid to the farmers have increased in the case of some cereals, the rise is too small compared to both the increase in the world market and consumer taxes.

During the last years, superpowers and multinationals have rapidly developed production of agro-fuels. For this reason subsidies and large investments are being allocated to this growing sector. As a result, land usage is largely being redirected from food production to agro-fuel production. Multinationals and conventional analysts foretell that lands will be increasingly utilized for agro-fuels (corn, but also palm oil, sugarcane, etc.). An important part of the US corn suddenly 'disappeared' because of purchases for ethanol production. This uncontrolled explosion in the agro-fuel sector caused a great crash in already unstable international grain markets. Speculation takes advantage of the relative shortage of food. Sellers keep their stocks off the local market to stimulate price rise in the domestic market, obtaining huge profits. Multinationals aggressively obtain large areas of agricultural land around cities, dislodging farmers, for speculative purposes.

In the last decades, the World Bank and the IMF, together with the WTO, forced peripheral countries into reducing their food production investments and their support to small farmers who are basically responsible for food production. The rules of the game changed dramatically in 1995. Then, the WTO treaty on agriculture came into force. Neoliberal policies undermined domestic food production. They forced farmers to produce commercial crops for multinational companies and to buy their food from multinationals in the world market. Free Trade Areas (FTA) have compelled countries to 'liberalize' their agricultural markets and dismantle their import barriers. At the same time, multinationals dumped their, often transgenic, surpluses in these markets, using direct and indirect export subsidies. As a result, Egypt, the former wheat provider of the Roman Empire, became the principal importer of transgenic wheat. Indonesia, one of the rice cradles, nowadays imports transgenic rice. Mexico, a corn cradle, imports transgenic corn. The US, the European Union, Canada and Australia are major exporters.

Peripheral countries became addicted to cheap food imports. However, as prices increase, famine becomes a global menace. Many countries that till now produced enough food for their own consumption were forced to open their markets to agricultural products from abroad. At the same time, most of state regulations concerning the existence of stocks, prices, production as well as import and export control were gradually dismantled. As a result, small agricultural and cattle raising initiatives all around the world were not able to compete in the international market place and many went broke.[6]

Neoliberal policies from the last decades expelled millions of people from the countryside to the cities, where most of them have ended up in slums, with very precarious lives. They will be the first victims of the current crisis because they are not able to produce their own food. Their number has dramatically increased and they have to spend large amounts of their income on food. According to the FAO, in developing countries, food represents up to 60-80 per cent of consumer expenses. A sharp increase in prices condemns great majorities to famine and even to massive deaths. It is not odd that in recent years many disturbances have erupted all around the world and especially in Sub-Saharan Africa due to rising food prices. A struggle for life itself is at stake.

Towards an Economy in Favour of Life

As we have seen, conventional ways out of the crisis are strategically non-viable. Income and wealth concentration, military Keynesianism, economic growth with rising expenditures of energy, food and natural resources, etc., are also non-viable. On the other hand, it is important to analyse the current huge waste of energy from the perspective of the world's diminishing oil production. In fact, is the much touted modern productivity a phenomenon that comprises the whole society or does it limit itself to products and specific services that reaffirm life? Productivity of a rifle factory, for instance, may be high and even growing in terms of profits for private capital. However, from the point of view of society as a whole, rifles instead of supporting growth are the cause of the opposite, not to mention their effect on well-being. Therefore, all the work involved in this production is a waste and becomes socially useless and even harmful. Furthermore, it is a destructive enterprise in which a death ethic is involved and, thus, is reproachable even from an ethical viewpoint, which stands up for life. Even in the US this is becoming clearer after a lot of tragedies.

Our societies produce increasingly more goods that are useless, dispensable and harmful. In other words, it concerns products and services that do not reaffirm life. Vehicles, weapons, wars, the whole structural system of cities for automobiles, marketing, innumerable merchandise and services of needless consumption, not to mention drugs – all these tend to be produced with growing productivities. They only create more profits, regardless of their real use in people's lives, leave

6 See Henry Saragih, 'La Vía Campesina saluda el reconocimiento preliminar de los derechos de la/os campesinas/os por la ONU', www.ecoportal.net, 18 February 2010.

alone the decreasing lifespan or durability of all that is produced nor their destructive implications. As a matter of fact, the simple change of current emphasis on individual transportation based on vehicles to collective transportation would substantially reduce the size of cities. It would, thus, lower the cost of equipment and urban services needed for people, such as parking lots, highways, bridges, sewers, electricity lines, etc. Hence, cities would become more liveable. By the same token, urban planning based on concepts of local production, taking into account the location of factories, shops and residential neighbourhoods in accord with collective interest, would substantially reduce both the size of cities as well as costs.

The gap between production to support people's lives and production to make profits, taking into account those desires and/or 'necessities' created by capital itself, is growing. In the Western world of the 21st century, 30 per cent more is invested in cosmetics than in reproductive care for all women; barely 10 per cent less is spent on dog and pet food than on finding a solution for famine and malnutrition for all human beings; 300 per cent more is invested in perfumes than in teaching illiterates how to read and write; 30 per cent more is spent on ocean cruises than on drinkable water for all; and 600 per cent more is produced in ice cream in Europe than invested to immunize all children against curable diseases. The West's production and consumption is, in other words, directed far from life itself (International Observatory of the Crisis, 2010: 79 and 80).

In the information presented, there is no mention of weapons. An important decrease, or even the eradication, of the arms race and of all wars in the world would create enormous surpluses in governmental budgets. These might be directed to services really needed by people, such as in the area of health and education as well as other needs that reaffirm people's lives. Increase in lifespan or durability of goods would save energy and raw materials and would reduce a lot of work necessary to produce these goods and services one time and another. This would create more leisure time for workers and their families. If advertising, needed mainly to create 'new indispensable necessities' were restricted to its purely informative aspect, it would reduce the cost of selling products and services and would direct information to the real usage of things. It is clear that productivity of modern societies exists just in the sphere of microeconomics because it is failing and being wasteful and irrational on the level of macroeconomics. Thus, we support the necessity for a zero, or even negative, growth economy in terms of value. A negative growth economy may be the only alternative to overcome the blind alley in which our economies are placed. Individual approach has to be substituted by a more communitarian one. Simple democratic and participative definition of needs and controlling the amount, specifications, localization and durability of goods and services, or, in the case of harmful goods, their pure and simple elimination, would reduce pollution, save energy and natural resources. It would create leisure time for the workers' personal growth. This is the road needed to transform the current economy of constant growth and microeconomic productivity into a stationary zero growth economy and, even better, a negative growth economy. It will show high productivity in terms of satisfaction of real needs not only in the micro world, but primarily also in macroeconomics. Such an economy would substantially improve people's material and spiritual quality of life.

The Transition Moment

Current civilization is based on two basic pillars. The first one is the isolated and vertical decision-making by elite controlling productive and financial processes. The second is the existence of an individualistic, selfish and non-inclusive rationality. Current civilization is derived from a dogma of making free choices – choices supposed to be free from these same controllers, who end up obliterating freedom of all other human beings. Both, the way of exercising power and the ideology of our societies derive from these two pillars. Transition to and the existence and effective performance of a zero growth economy require a new civilization. In this new society, decisions will in fact be democratic and based on as large as possible citizen's participation. It will be in such a way that rationality and the prevailing power will be englobing as well as cooperative.

On the other hand, we can ask ourselves if it is plausible to envisage this transition process. We pose this question in view of the measure and seriousness with which Western civilization, based on the myth of growth, is wearing itself out. Ecological economists, such as Daly (1996), have shown with enough clarity that people's welfare does not depend on economic growth per se. They have pointed out that after reaching a certain level of growth, another increase in a country's GDP is more likely to decrease the material welfare of a nation. These economists, along with us, conceive the promotion on a global scale of at least a stationary or zero growth economy as a necessity. This implies a regulated economy. This kind of economy, however, should not be centralized nor administered by elite, as happens nowadays with bankers, and nor should it be at rich countries' discretion, in particular the US, as they consume, squander and contaminate the most. Nor must it take place under a scheme similar to that of the UN Security Council, where just five members with veto power decide for the rest.

The implementation of a stationary or zero growth economy implies a rearranging of the world economy and society. It supposes an absolutely democratic participation of all countries and regions. This process will require wealth redistribution from rich countries to those of the South in order to eliminate existing imbalances. The basic principle is common good and not the privileging of the strongest. The latter has led nations to the current imbalances and to this actual civilizational crisis, which is just beginning. The cancerous tentacles represented by bankers, corporations and multinationals of the North are spread all around the planet and must be controlled as the first step. They are like an unproductive parasite that sucks all productive wealth and life out of the so-called Third World. They do so in order to reinvest in militarism, warfare, and wasteful and unproductive consumption concentrated in rich countries. Such a regulation does not have to deteriorate the life quality of populations in the richer countries. On the contrary, regulation will improve it through a more rational and efficient use of world resources. In the meantime, food supply problems, which are most indispensable, proper housing, decent public transportation, public health and good quality of public education, among others, need to be solved with immediacy for the poorest populations. We need to begin repairing these fundamental imbalances. In the middle and long terms, reorganization of a new, balanced, stable, fair and democratic world system is a priority.

Emerging countries of the South are net producers of all kinds of natural resources and have recently been claiming these resources for their own endogenous projects, as in the case of China. However, if countries of the South would proceed in accordance with the same rationality as the West, the world economy would soon need several planets in order to sustain itself. We all know we only have one. There is no justification to hinder or block Southern countries in their right to use their own resources. It implies, however, stopping core countries and their elite in their continuous ravishing of peripheral countries. The countries in the South, even China, still keep their consumption and contamination levels within sustainable limits for the planet and nature. If consumption and contamination of India, for instance, would be generalized to the entire planet, less than half the planet would be required to sustain the economy and repair the damage done to nature. If the levels of Latin America and the Caribbean were to be used as a measure, more or less the planet would be required. If those of Africa were to be generalized, less than a quarter of the planet would be required. On the contrary, if we apply the consumption levels of Europe to the world, we would need three planets, and if we apply those of the United States, we would require more than five planets. The problem is that we only have one planet and the countries of the South will demand more resources for themselves.

In order to reduce contamination levels and avoid the depletion of natural resources, Malthusian theses are promoted in the West, which states the need for reduction in population growth in the South. Even though we know that more than 80 per cent of natural resources are consumed by just 20 per cent of the world's population concentrated in the North. This population is responsible for almost 80 per cent of all contamination due to their style of consumption. It is important to point out, on the one hand, that populations not only just consume. They are the real wealth consumers based on productive labour, which is increasingly generated in the South. 'Made in China' is visible worldwide nowadays. Unproductive labour, on the other hand, mostly takes place in the North, as we mentioned earlier.

Contrary to what is happening today, genuine welfare of its citizens should be the objective of any political and socio-economic system. World population in 2010 reached almost 7 billion inhabitants. In 2050, according to United Nations' projections, world population will surpass 9 billion, a growth of almost 30 per cent in 40 years. Global fertility rate, as we can now foresee, will be at that time 2.05 children per woman. This means that from then on population will start to decrease. It is a phenomenon already happening in many countries classified as 'more developed' by the UN. The conclusion of countless investigations is that this historic trend is irreversible. It is mostly caused by a rapid decrease in fertility, since the 1960s, in all countries classified as 'less developed'. The main challenge drawn from the previous facts is that the economy will have to solve the welfare problem of a large poor population, which will still grow by 30 per cent in the near future. On the other hand, these figures show the strategic geopolitical change that occurred in the 20th century. In other words, a huge difference exists between population sizes of less developed countries (85 per cent) against the more developed ones (15 per cent).

A system of stationary or even negative growth economy has to be established in all those countries that consume above the planet's capacities. Countries that consume less will have to grow for a while until a more balanced world system is established. As previously stated, the transformation of the current military-industrial complex into an industrial complex for cooperation and international solidarity would be helpful. It would sever unproductive squander of weapons and wars. It would also favour the establishment of a more equal and coherent world system. This sub-sector would change from being destructive and unproductive to productive and constructive. This would, however, not imply massive unemployment in countries where it is strongly developed, as in the United States.

Another clear example is China. This country opened up to capitalist markets, which allowed its economy to grow spectacularly. China has very recently achieved the second position among the world's largest economies. It is a direct rival of Western economies and competes using the same voracious rationality. Nowadays China is not only the world's second economy, but also holds the first place as a contaminator. India is another emerging country with more than a billion inhabitants. It also follows the same quantitative development. With a generalization of this manner of Western development, we would soon need two more planets in order to maintain a Western lifestyle everywhere.

Positive Growth in the South and Negative in the North

We are facing a real dilemma. We cannot and must not restrain the development of countries of the South. Moreover, peripheral countries will call for it with increasing force. There are several reasons for this. During the last decades, the real economy has been gradually moving towards the South. The highest potential for real economic growth will be there where activities are based on productive labour by its content, as we are observing during the current crisis. Most natural resources necessary for economic growth are right there as well. China is already claiming these resources for its own economic project and other emerging countries will follow. If the emerging countries claim their resources for their own economic projects, there won't be enough resources for the core countries. This transition may occur without an increase – or perhaps a little bit – in energy costs and natural resources, as long as the productivity growth of society as a whole is achieved through participative and democratic mechanisms. It implies various things: a more communitarian definition of the demand for goods and services by giving priority to the collective consumption of goods, etc.; a demand for more durable goods; a reduction of production and/or consumption of weapons and needless spending; changing the structure of the urban system; and changing production profiles.

As for the core countries, apart from measures mentioned earlier, the message is clear. In order to achieve ecological sustainability, a dematerialization of economies in the core countries is required. They will be obliged to do so due to social pressures internally and from the South as the latter will claim more resources for its own project. This means that the demand for energy and natural resources per unit of the GDP should decrease, not only in relative terms (relative dematerialization), but also in absolute terms (absolute dematerialization). Relative dematerialization implies that the impact on the environment is lower by unit of product, as is already the case. Impact continues to grow in absolute terms in a specific time span (a year generally) due to GDP growth. In these analyses, it is very important to segregate results obtained in the consumption sphere from those obtained in the production sphere. We will look at this in more detail.

On a global scale, between 1970 and 1999, energy demand decreased almost 33 per cent to obtain an equivalent GDP. What is not mentioned is that this reduction was made mainly by more conscientious consumers. The battle for a more rational use of energy, which is becoming more aggressive as time goes by, is happening there. We cannot say the same about the production sphere where this battle is not being fought. CO_2 emissions, for instance, increased between 1990 and 2009 by almost 40 per cent in the production sphere. Demand and consumption of large amounts of minerals (iron, copper, nickel and bauxite) increased in the productive area even faster than GDP growth. This happens basically due to shortening the life cycle of produced goods. When everything made is based on a short life cycle, as is increasingly the case, a smaller percentage of material per product or value unit is required. However, a higher volume is produced per time unit, contaminating, therefore, more than before. This implies lower use of material per product unit but an equal contamination as more products with resources and contamination are produced per time unit (a year). This is due to the shortening of the life cycle of all that is produced. In such cases we cannot talk about dematerialization in absolute terms.

Authors consider it impossible to achieve real dematerialization in the ecological economy without a policy of absolute dematerialization. This suggests the necessity for negative growth and involves making more durable, more collective and better quality products. It would indicate a historic triumph of use value over exchange value. A higher percentage of material per product unit will be used producing a much longer lasting product. Only then a process of dematerialization and decontamination per time unit may be achieved. How much dematerialization do ecologists talk about? Ernst von Weisäcker talks about a need of 'Factor 4'. This means a double of the world's wealth should be achieved with half the natural resources in three to five decades. Schmidt-Bleek even talks of a 'Factor 10'.[7] Analysts agree that reaching a 'Factor 4', or even a 'Factor 10', without negative economic growth is a mere illusion. Thus, it is very clear that a 'New Green Deal', that is, continuous economic growth with ecological sustainability is purely a myth. There is no real possibility for capitalism to turn around economic growth with a 'New Green Deal'.

'New Green Deal' promoters, like Al Gore for instance, do not question capitalistic production systems as such. Their solutions basically refer to individual consumptive behaviours. They refer to a reduced use of electric energy by consumers, a more judicious and rational use of automotive transportation and a more moderate and rational consumption of food (less meat mostly). It is a positive result, of course, and everybody will agree with it. However, as energy and natural resources become scarcer

---

7 See Jones and Meyere (2010: 83 and 84).

for productive purposes, this might bring about the imposition of an 'authoritarian green society'. Consumers may be pressed by authoritarian rules to consume less energy and resources (through sky high taxes, for example) just in order to release energy resources and contamination rights for producers. The final result will be a more contaminated world with even less resources.

In this context, it is particularly interesting to mention recent changes proposed in the automotive industry, aiming at the large-scale introduction of a cleaner electric car. Until now, cars with more economical motors for fuel consumption have not succeeded in lower use of fuel due to users' preference for heavy cars and long journeys. On top of that, 'ecological tourism' involves travel by plane to exotic and faraway places. It is not unreal to foresee a future society with high energy taxes on the consumers' side combined with sky high taxes on CO_2. On the production side, it may be a completely different picture with all kinds of subsidies. The alternative presented in the automotive industry is the electric car with an electric motor, which works together with a combustible motor to charge the battery. Such a vehicle is able to run 1,000 kilometres before charging the battery again (Middelkoop and Koppelaar, 2008: 145).

By focusing the issue of contamination and energy use exclusively on the consumers' side, promoters of the 'New Green Deal' support and encourage manufacturing new car models. It is presented as the great solution to the problem. Permanent technological innovation, that is, 'creative destruction' would be the nostrum. By promoting large-scale construction of new, more eco-friendly car models, average life expectancy of these models becomes increasingly shorter as time goes by. From the perspective of automotive manufacturers, this implies an increase in capital rotation. It increases sales and, therefore, profitability for big private capital. Making profits more quickly increases the profit rate, which is the essence of capitalism. For promoters of the 'New Green Deal', permanent innovation must provide the solution for capital. Hence, for instance, Peugeot encouraged consumers to buy new models with the following ad: '20 per cent of the oldest cars are responsible for 60 per cent of automotive contaminating emissions. Replace them!'[8]

From an ecological point of view, car production with shorter useful life, used by individual drivers, means a growing use of raw materials and greater energy consumption. This also causes more contamination. CO_2 emissions in industries are already higher (40 per cent of all emissions) than the mere use of manufactured vehicles (responsible for only 30 per cent of all emissions). The benefits supposed to be obtained in transportation after introducing new car models are lost when producing

8 See Houtart (2009: 93).

them with greater speed and rotation.[9] The lesson is clear: in order to achieve absolute dematerialization, it is not only necessary to produce cars more economical in fuels and cleaner in gas emissions, but, above all, it is necessary to produce more long-lasting and collective means of transportation. It is not about improving vehicles with ever-shorter life expectancy, but progressively substituting them with durable collective transport of good quality and service.

The 'New Green Deal', inspired by the 'New Deal', which was introduced in the second half of the 1930s during President Roosevelt's administration, pretends to be a paradigmatic answer to the current world crisis. It conceives large-scale investment programmes in infrastructure and eco-friendly production. The ultimate purpose is promoting sustainable growth and thus prolonging capital accumulation. In other words, the final goal is sustainable accumulation. By focusing on the consumers' side on how to save energy and reduce contamination, it not only promotes the large-scale introduction of short-lived so-called eco-friendly cars, but it also introduces construction of residential and public buildings that save energy by improving isolation mechanisms. By promoting the replacement of older and less eco-friendly buildings, technological innovation in shorter life construction is encouraged. By promoting buildings that meet the conditions of the newest technology, the existing stock of buildings becomes obsolete ever faster. More and more old buildings do not meet the requirements for energy consumption. We have gone from one extreme to the other. Today, people are already talking about 'sick buildings' due to the lack of ventilation in new construction because of high isolation degrees. In short, technological innovation in construction norms shortens average life expectancy of buildings permanently.

Energy consumption in the construction of new short-life buildings requires more frequent extraction of natural resources (cement, steel, wood, etc.) and energy to manufacture construction materials as well as more frequent transportation. So, they would damage the environment more than the ecological benefits obtained with a more rational use of energy in those new buildings (Jones and Meyere, 2009: 268). We can perform this analysis on durable products in general and the story would be almost the same. The 'New Green Deal' includes then a more generalized tendency towards less lasting products in the area of production. This would imply a larger absolute materialization of the economy. The consequence is a growing shortage and an accelerated depletion of available natural resources and greater contamination. Alternative rationale would be to build longer lasting and cleaner community buildings. Such a measure

9 *Ibid.*: 44.

would, however, suggest the end of economic growth and thus the end of capitalism. To avoid this, the system will seek, through all means possible, an ecological approach on the consumers' side to safeguard growth in the production area. It may even imply ecological dictatorship. This will only guarantee depletion at an ever-increasing rate of natural and energy resources. Sooner or later, absolute limits to growth on a global scale will become evident.

In order to achieve a stationary economy on a global scale, a change of paradigm is needed. It will imply mainly negative growth in the North, with positive growth ideally directed in favour of the common good in the South. Without achieving the first, it will become really difficult to achieve the second. In the first case, the South will find no other alternative but to disconnect from the North in order to survive in a more or less united South-South relation. As we previously stated, it is very clear that there is a shortage of natural resources around the world, which are concentrated mainly in the South. Thus, we consider that negative growth will first take place in the core countries. More warfare may postpone it, but it cannot be avoided. For a determined time period, it will be possible and even necessary to stimulate positive growth in the peripheral countries. However, while capitalism rules on a global scale and imposes its authority, it is really difficult to move past neo-development projects in the South. This is what is happening today in the Southern Cone of Latin America. We may ask, why. Disconnection from neoliberalism is not something that can happen in a day and will demand more integration, as is taking place in Latin America.

Where is the weaker link to break the current economic rationality? A new rationality will involve a change not only in the core country's lifestyle, which focuses more on consumption, but also require a change in the mode of production. A civilization change this suggests must first occur in the core countries. It will be based on their more difficult access to natural resources in the South on the one hand, and internal social movements on the other. It is obvious that current and future wars for natural resources will postpone this situation. However, facing the Great Depression of the 21st Century, the process of disconnection of the South will be sudden and strong. Its reorientation will be more inward and less towards the centre, and the unification among the Southern countries will become strong.

A crucial question remains: How is this change going to occur? Will it be more or less spontaneous? Will it be derived from a profound crisis? Will it be in the middle of a global war? A crisis, without any doubt, will create favourable conditions. We do not believe, however, that this change will occur without social conflict of various kinds and intensities. We will observe both poor people struggling for survival as well as privileged minorities, who seek to maintain their habits of squander, fighting tooth and nail to maintain the status quo. In any case, it is about class struggle. With this, other questions emerge: Who will be the historical actor of change in the 21st century? Where is it likely for advanced social forces to appear to lead this civilizational change? We believe that the main forces will emerge from the necessity for survival. Great majorities in the South, and also growing minorities in the North, are faced with catastrophes in the 21st century.

References

Angus, Ian. 2008. 'Food Crisis: The Greatest Demonstration of the Historical Failure of the Capitalist Model', *Global Research*, April.

Chossudovsky, Michel. 2008. 'Hambre global', *Rebelión*, 12 May.

Daly, Herman E. 1996. *Beyond Growth: The Economics of Sustainable Development*. Boston: Beacon Press.

Halimi, Serge. 2008. 'El FMI y el hambre', *Le Monde Diplomatique*, May.

Houtart, François. 2009. *La agroenergía: solución para el clima o salida de la crisis para el capital*. Panama: Ruth Casa Editorial.

International Observatory of the Crisis. 2010. 'XXI Century: Crisis of a Civilization: The End of History or the Birth of a New Society'. DEI.

Peter Tom Jones and Vicky de Meyere, 2011, *Transisitie naar rechtvaardige duurzaamheiden de rol van het middenveld*, Jan van Arkel.

IOGCC and ALL (Interstate Oil and Gas Compact Commission and ALL Consulting). 2006. 'A Guide to Practical Management of Produced Water from Onshore Oil and Gas Operations in the United States.' Prepared for U.S. Department of Energy, National Energy Technology Laboratory, IOGCC and ALL. October. http://www.all-llc.com/publicdownloads/ALL-PWGuide.pdf

Jones, Peter Tom and Vicky Meyere. 2010. *Terra Reversa*: *De transitie naar* Middelkoop, Willem and Rembrandt Koppelaar. 2008. *De permanente oliecrisis*. Amsterdam: Nieuw Amsterdam.

Part III

Rebuilding Theory

CHAPTER 5

Fictitious Capital and Fictitious Profit

Reinaldo A. CARCANHOLO &
Mauricio DE SOUZA SABADINI

Federal University of Espírito Santo (UFES), Brazil

and

Federal University of Espírito Santo (UFES), Brazil

In this chapter, our central questions are: what are the characteristics of the new stage of world capitalism that began in the late 1970s and early 1980s; which of its perspectives are worth pursuing and developing; and which perspectives are required to overcome such a system? These are extremely important questions today, and the appropriate answers, as we have pointed out in our previous works, are related to the Marxist concept of fictitious capital.[1] This concept, described by Marx in *Capital*, Volume III (Marx, 1887), is not well understood nor accepted by those who owe something to positivist and metaphysical conceptions, whether they are Keynesians or not. Some others tend to accept it due to its obvious existence and prevalence in the present, but they do so 'reluctantly'. Actually, they are not able to correctly grasp the concept from a dialectic point of view, which is a necessary perspective to comprehend the explanation power of the concept. The fact that fictitious capital is, at the same time, fictitious and real, could seem a contradiction in terms. And it is precisely in this real-imaginary dialectic that this concept acquires its complete relevance.

While the concept of fictitious capital is not often assimilated, that of fictitious profit is even less considered from a theoretical point of

[1] See Carcanholo and Nakatani (1999). Also, Carcanholo and Sabadini (2010). Of course, we need to say that our interpretation differs from that of Katz (2002), although we agree with many of his criticisms of what he calls specialists of the 'financial capital' and with several conclusions about the current stage of capitalism, in particular the increment of labour force exploitation and the impact of the likely decreasing profit rate.

view, including by some that call themselves Marxists. First of all, it is not a concept that has been elaborated on by Marx himself, and that can be definitive for many authors. Of course, at that time, the idea of a dominant fictitious capital over substantive or real capital was far from possible.[2] To think that a part of the profit was not derived from surplus value nor even from value in excess from non-salary production forms was a contradiction in terms. However, today, when fictitious capital has turned out to be dominant to such an extent that we need to call it something else (*parasitic speculative capital*), the idea of fictitious profit came to us as something no less than automatic, and as completely inspired by Marx's analyses in various chapters of *Capital*, Volume III. First, let us make an effort to throw light, at least in a summarized form, on the concepts of fictitious capital and parasitic speculative capital, and later explain what fictitious profit consist of.[3]

From Illusory Capital to Parasitic Speculative Capital

First of all, we should clarify that interest-bearing capital, which finances production or circulation processes, is completely different from fictitious capital, although the latter emerges as a consequence of the existence of the former.[4] The first thing we have to consider is that interest-bearing capital produces a social illusion and that fictitious capital is derived from this illusion. In capitalism, the widespread existence of interest-bearing capital apparently shows us that any considerable sum of money generates remuneration. This produces the contrary illusion that all regular remuneration must have as its origin the existence of capital. This capital doesn't have real significance for the functioning of the economic system and it may be called illusory capital (current value of a regular return).

However, when the right to such remuneration is represented by a title or security that may be tradable, that is, it can be sold to a third party, it becomes fictitious capital. The tradable security is the legal representation of that form of capital. Perhaps, the simplest example of the existence of fictitious capital could be a public concession to individuals on the right to negotiate a radio or television frequency, to pay back political or any other kind of favour, and that may be sold to a third party.

In this way, fictitious capital emerges as a consequence of the widespread existence of interest-bearing capital, but it is the result of a

2 For us, substantive capital is productive capital plus commercial or mercantile capital.

3 This matter has been treated in Carcanholo and Nakatani (2001).

4 Several authors have different interpretations. See, for example, Trindade (2006): 'Fictitious capital is, therefore, a specific form of the loan monetary capital and has specific functions, but as loan monetary capital.'

social illusion.[5] And, why should we call it fictitious capital? The reason lies in the fact that there isn't any real substance behind it, as it doesn't contribute towards producing or circulating wealth, or at least it doesn't finance either productive capital or circulating capital.

With respect to interest-bearing capital, capital appears as if it were an autonomous source of value-generation. And this source is presented, according to Marx, in a mystifying way, because the interest is appropriated without productive labour and its existence in the capitalist world appears separated from any connection with the creation of surplus value resulting from labour. Once the credit system is developed, with the primordial objective of financing production, interest-bearing capital acquires great importance and dimension in the capitalist system because it is directly subordinated to the logic of industrial capital. While it appropriates a part of the generated surplus value in the production sector, interest-bearing capital increases the efficiency of surplus-value production as well as the reproduction speed of the cycle of capital.

Marx highlighted the dependent and complementary character of interest-bearing capital vis-à-vis productive capital in the following words:

> Where capitalist production has developed all its manifold forms and has become the dominant mode of production, interest-bearing capital is dominated by industrial capital, and commercial capital becomes merely a form of industrial capital, derived from the circulation process. But both of them must first be destroyed as independent forms and subordinated to industrial capital. (Marx, 1863: 900)

Statements like these assure us that the growing autonomization of the functional forms of capital, represented now by interest-bearing capital, interfere positively in the capitalist system by stimulating growth. Thus, if capital already becomes mystifying with the appearance of interest-bearing capital, it gets even more complex and dematerialized in the form of fictitious capital. Apparently, it develops independent of the dynamics of production:

> With the development of interest-bearing capital and the credit system, all capital seems to double itself, and sometimes treble itself, by the various modes in which the same capital, or perhaps even the same claim on a debt, appears in different forms in different hands. The greater portion of this 'money-capital' is purely fictitious. (Marx, 1894: 324)

Thus, fictitious capital hides the connections with the real process of value generating capital even more, when consolidating the image of a capital that creates value by itself, particularly in the market of speculative

5 Illusion, paradoxically, has a very precise economic reality.

sales and purchases: '... all connection with the real valorization process of capital is lost without a trace, and the conception of capital as an automaton which valorizes itself through itself is reinforced' (Marx, 1968: 439).[6]

After explaining the theoretical emergence of fictitious capital, Marx refers to some forms of its existence. He discusses, among others, the share values corresponding to the real wealth (or 'patrimony') of companies. To facilitate reasoning in this matter, let us think exclusively of production companies.

What reasons take Marx to classify capital shares as fictitious capital, although the total amount of the shares corresponds to the real wealth of a production company? The first reason is that shares make it possible to have an annual return and, moreover, they can be sold in the shares market. But even then, we should realize that they have real substance behind them, that is, they represent the wealth of the company. Actually, shares are fictitious capital because they represent wealth that gets registered twice: first, with the value of the company's wealth and, second, with their own value. The proof that this is true is that both values can be used as guarantees, for example, for bank credits. They can be counted twice or thrice or more, thanks to the existence of holding companies. This means that fictitious capital doesn't emerge only as a result of the previously mentioned illusion, when it becomes a negotiable title. It is also a more direct result of interest-bearing capital, of the credit system, when it seemingly doubles real wealth, as in the case of a company shares.[7] This kind of fictitious capital, which is composed of share capital with a value equal to that of the real wealth of production companies, will be called 'type 1 fictitious capital' here.

However, there is a second reason why shares should be considered fictitious capital: the fact that their value often moves independently of the value of companies' wealth. Thus, a speculative valorization (or rise in value) of the shares means a sudden rise in the total fictitious capital operating in the economy. But that increase in value has a different characteristic from the original value: it isn't an apparent doubling of the real value. In fact, there is no real substance behind it. For that reason, we will consider this kind of increase 'type 2 fictitious capital'. Thus, fictitious capital also appears as a result of speculation, when the latter increases the market value of any type of asset (whether real or not). Obviously, if there is a speculative reduction in the value of assets, there could be a destruction of fictitious capital. As a consequence, and by

6 In this chapter, when the cited work is in a foreign language, it has been translated into English.

7 For Marx, shares are credit instruments. Their remuneration, called dividends, is basically interest.

extension, we can classify any speculative rise of real assets or securities as type 2 fictitious capital.

Marx also highlights that public debt bonds are fictitious capital. But here, we must also distinguish between types 1 and 2. When public bonds are issued to finance real investments, such as highways, ports, bridges, tunnels, railroads and buildings, it is type 1 fictitious capital. On the other hand, when an increase in public debt is caused by unproductive spending or due to current costs or even transfers, we may talk about the creation of a new kind of type 2 fictitious capital because there isn't any substance behind that new debt.[8]

In this context, we can summarize that fictitious capital has three sources of origin: (*i*) the transformation of the illusory capital into negotiable titles, (*ii*) an apparent doubling of the value of interest-bearing capital (in the case of shares and public bonds), and (*iii*) a speculative rise in the value of different assets. These three different forms of fictitious capital have this fact in common that they are fictitious and real at the same time. They are real from the perspective of an individual and isolated act, in the day-to-day market, that is, from the point of view of appearance. This is the fictitious-real dialectic that we will discuss in more detail later on in the chapter.

Nevertheless, there is one more thing to clarify. If public debt in the hands of creditors is fictitious capital, why doesn't the same thing apply to private debt related to credits for industrial capital? Above all, why is there a difference even when private debt can be represented by a transferable title to third parties in the market? This would also mean that even credits to finance productive or real investments in the hands of creditors should be considered fictitious capital. In fact, when credit is directed to the private sector and formalized by means of a transferable title in the market, it must also be considered fictitious capital because apparently the value has doubled. Behind it there is real substance, and so, it is type 1 fictitious capital. Actually, it is the same for shares of a private company with just one difference. A loan to a company implies a debt as counterpart, which is different from the case of shares. Although there is this counterpart to the debt and the sum with the obtained credit is zero,

8 For example, military expenses. It is interesting to point out that the military expenses only differ from luxury expenses because the latter are used to guarantee the bourgeoisie's enjoyment and the former its power, since they are financed by tax revenue. Both these are the destination of a part of the socially produced surplus value that cannot be used for other purposes. However, they differ much more when they are financed by public debt. In which case, their value will appear to be an increase in fictitious capital in the hands of the bourgeoisie. For example, interest payment on existing debt on top of what is available according to a primary surplus.

there is, in fact, an apparent doubling of wealth: the credit instrument in the hands of the borrower and the real goods bought by the creditor.

However, it is essential to highlight that in the case of the aforementioned credit, we deal with two totally different things: interest-bearing capital cannot be confused with the fictitious capital it has generated. Interest-bearing capital corresponds to real wealth produced in the form of surplus, whereas fictitious capital is purely fictitious from a global point of view.[9] Fictitious capital generated in these conditions is like the mirror image of interest-bearing capital. It concerns two different types of capital: one real and the other subjected to the real-fictitious dialectic. Perhaps, the matter may become clearer later on in this text, but the fact is that the amount of interest-bearing capital allocated to, for example, investments in the real economy, can never be bigger than the economic surplus produced after making deductions with respect to consumption.

Here, Corazza is right when pointing out that, in practice, interest-bearing capital tends to be confused with fictitious capital. Thus, in the complexity of the current capitalist finance, it seems difficult to know when capital is real, when it is only financial and when it is purely fictitious, since its movements are intertwined in such a way that productive capital presupposes financial capital, and the latter can finance real capital accumulation (Corazza, 1999). However, Corazza is wrong when he says that fictitious capital is able to finance real capital accumulation.[10] As we have seen, one thing is fictitious capital and the other is interest-bearing capital.

Furthermore, although Harvey is one of the pioneer Marxist authors in the discussion on fictitious capital and has described this category with scientific rigour, he has also suggested the application of fictitious capital in the real economy when he states:

> This (fictitious) capital is defined as capital with a nominal monetary value and paper existence, but has no weight in terms of real productive activity or real physical assets. Fictitious capital may become real capital when invested in useful assets (for example, infrastructure and equipments to be used by productive labour) or useful exchange values (goods and services that may be sold with profits). (Harvey, 1996: 171-72)

With a similar perspective, Paula *et al.* (2001) state, based on Hilferding's ideas, that fictitious capital is directed towards productive

---

9 Once the company earmarks the received credit towards some kind of investment.

10 Katz (2002: 6) also seems to suggest the same thing, although it is not very clear: 'The border between fictitious capital and other modalities of money-capital is quite confusing, since its role in accumulation is not illusory.'

or industrial spheres in different ways: when monetary capital goes to the stock market that turns it into fictitious capital by issuing transferrable shares; in reverse, when the stock market transfers those shares to industrial enterprises; and thanks to the proliferation of financial institutions (for example, pension funds), when these resources may be used as new productive investments. If we consider just these words in themselves, they are right, but they can leave the impression that there is a no difference between fictitious capital and interest-bearing capital.

It is true that any holder of fictitious capital can easily convert it to finance production. But if this is done, that fictitious capital is simply transferred to another holder so that the aggregate value in the economy as a whole is not affected.[11]

We said earlier that illusory capital doesn't have a greater significance for the functioning of the economic system. However, one cannot say the same about fictitious capital, although the latter is derived from the former. This is especially true when, in certain historical circumstances, the amount of fictitious capital reaches significant proportions, as in the case of the current capitalist stage. In this stage, fictitious capital has achieved dominance over real capital and this is the main characteristic of the aforementioned stage.[12] This capital has changed poles: the previously dominated pole has become the dominant pole. This is the reason we now call this capital *parasitic speculative capital* and the current stage of the system *speculative capitalism*. The existence and magnitude of parasitic speculative capital have caused the main contradiction of the current stage of capitalism, that is, the one between appropriation and production of socially produced surplus value.[13]

About Fictitious Profit

What is fictitious profit? How is its existence demonstrated? Why isn't it easy to accept this category? To demonstrate the existence of fictitious profits is not an easy task, and in some senses, it is not even possible. First, to understand the existence of fictitious profit presupposes, according to us, not only the already mentioned dialectical perspective on things, but also an appropriate interpretation of Marx's theory of value – a condition

[11] The truth is that the holder of a certain fictitious capital can change that capital for any other form in the market, whether it is productive (buying a factory, for example) or commercial (acquiring a commercial enterprise). However, the total volume of fictitious capital doesn't change; what happens is that there is a change of hands.

[12] In the contradictory unit called 'capital', fictitious capital dominates real capital.

[13] We use the expression surplus value because it is not only composed of the surplus but also of the produced surplus depending on non-salary relations that are present in contemporary capitalism.

which is rare. Second, to think about an empirical demonstration of the existence of fictitious profit is something completely outside of scientific logic and, within the dialectical perspective, completely meaningless. Perhaps, the best possible thing to do is to describe it and make the different forms of its existence explicit as well as clarify its theoretical dimension and its relation to the other categories of the theory of value.

Let us begin with the simplest way to explain fictitious profit: the speculative rise in the value of physical assets. In order to make use of a didactic method, let us describe the emergence of fictitious profit with regard to something very trivial, that is, the speculative valorization of a property or real estate:

1. Let us suppose that, in normal economic conditions, a lot of land is bought for $100 and a house is built on it by a construction company that requires to be paid the exact value of the construction, neither more nor less. It is assumed that the price in this case matches the value exactly. Let us suppose $300 was paid to the construction company.
2. Of course, the owner is neither poorer nor richer. He/she owned $400 in cash earlier and now continues to have the same amount of wealth, but in the form of a property, that is, a house built on his/her own land.
3. Clearly, there was production of surplus value while building the house, but it was appropriated by the construction company or other companies that provided inputs or lent money. However, it's not important now.
4. The value of the owner's wealth has not been affected, but the global wealth of society has increased by a value corresponding to $300 (minus the value corresponding to the constant capital consumed during the production process).
5. Now let us suppose that, for special reasons, there is a speculative valuation of properties in society and that the house can be sold for $1,000 and in fact the owner does so.
6. Let us suppose that average prices of the economy didn't change, or, put another way, the $1,000 is a real value rather than a nominal one.
7. Should the individual who sold his/her real estate consider himself/herself richer than before? Yes, of course. Earlier, his/her wealth was $400, now it is $1,000 in cash. The buyer of the house won't feel poorer than before the purchase because he/she has invested $1,000 and now possesses a house that costs $1,000, which can be sold when he/she wants to, as long as the market conditions remain the same.

8. Let us calculate the wealth of society as a whole by simply adding up every member's wealth. Speculation has caused society to possess greater wealth now. The seller of the house had $400 and now has $1,000. And the buyer of the same house has $1,000 and he/she keeps the $1,000 in a different form.
9. The seller doesn't exactly know how to define the increase in his/her wealth. Is it profit? Perhaps, it doesn't matter now. However, let us suppose at this point that when the price of the house was $400, the owner was a commercial enterprise whose aim was to sell property and effectively managed to do so for $1,000. Shouldn't the $600 be considered legitimate profit? Of course, it should; in fact, it is profit.
10. This is what we call fictitious profit.

However, there is an objection to this logic that needs to be overcome.[14] This objection is about something indisputable: when any merchandise is sold for a higher price than its real value, what happens is simply a transfer of value from the buyer to the seller. Thus, the profit obtained by the seller in such a commercial operation is equal to the loss of the buyer, so that the total wealth is not affected. In this case, a pure transfer of value is observed.

This is quite true, at least in relation to a commodity that is consumed immediately or soon after being bought, and thus 'destroyed'. If one buys a commodity for a price greater than its real value, one may keep thinking that no loss in purchase will take place as long as one doesn't consume the commodity and the price doesn't change. But this is pure illusion. By consuming the commodity, one has consumed its use value and enjoyed something whose value, as represented by its social wealth, is actually smaller than imagined.

However, something different happens when a commodity is not for consuming, but for adding to one's possessions or estate, and when it comes to real assets or even financial ones. These types of assets are part of one's possessions (patrimony) and if their speculative valuation is taking place while one owns them, one will feel richer than before and may count them as profit. If one of these assets is sold for an overvalued price, then the profit will effectively be money. The buyer of this asset will consider himself/herself the owner of the same amount of wealth he/she had before the purchase happened, provided no price reduction has taken place; his/her wealth would've only changed in form. It is true that from a global perspective, if the price of the asset reduces, what once appeared as profit would disappear as a result of a prejudice towards the

14 We thank Claus Germer for having presented this objection in our discussions.

owner at the time. This means that fictitious profit exists as long as there is speculative valorization of any asset, and it disappears when eventually speculative valorization disappears.

What are the characteristics of fictitious profit? There is one basic characteristic: from the point of view of an individual and isolated act, this profit is as real or true as any other. And this remains very clear if we keep in mind that one may obviously buy anything with the amount of money corresponding to this profit. The point of view of the market, which allows one to observe just an isolated individual or an isolated mercantile act, is fundamental to understanding this aspect: under such circumstances, this fictitious profit is real and does not differ from any other type of profit.

Now let us abandon our positivist limitations and make an effort to think dialectically. Let us stop thinking of the individual and isolated act, which will allow us to see just a little bit more than mere appearance, and let us analyse the phenomenon from a different perspective. Taking into account the society as a whole, is this profit real? Does it have substance derived from productive labour action? Is it a result of surplus value produced by wage labour (or an excess in value produced by non-salary workers) that makes it real? The answer is no. This profit is pure smoke. The way it appears overnight, like magic, it can disappear in the same way due to the speculative fluctuations of the value of assets.

Hilferding, while analysing speculative profit, highlighted that buying and selling titles is a phenomenon that doesn't present any influence in the production or achievement of the total amount of capital's profits:

> Speculative profit or loss, therefore, arises only from the differences in the valuation of assets. It is neither actual earnings nor shares in surplus value, but emerges from the capitalization of the appropriated surplus value differential that comes out of a company and corresponds to its shareholders ... It is pure differential profit. While the capitalist class appropriates a part of the work of the proletariat, without any compensation, thereby obtaining profit, speculators earn only from each other. The loss of one is the profit of the other. '*Les affaires, c'est l'argent des autres*'. (Hilferding, 1985: 139)

De facto, Hilferding's analysis on 'differential profit' highlights the speculative movement of the prices of assets and their independence with relation to the production of surplus value. In this sense, he approaches what we call fictitious profit here. But, there is at least one important difference: according to him, the differential profit of one implies the speculative loss of the other because it results from the transactions that amount to a sum equal to zero. For us, on the contrary, this is not necessarily true. The profit obtained by a speculative rise in the price of assets, as long as the assets exist, is profit that doesn't result in loss for anyone. Besides, the perceived interest on public debt received by capital – if the operation is not financed by primary surpluses but by growing public debts – constitutes profit for the owners of this capital without constituting a loss for anyone else, in spite of the fact that this profit doesn't come from the exploitation of wage labour. It is true that in certain speculative movements, for example, in the case of the stock market, some 'players' win and others lose. Those that buy during the low and sell during the high obviously win. But that is quite another subject, which deals with the issue of the distribution of the existing fictitious wealth among the speculators (fictitious capital).[15]

At this point, our analysis should focus on the point of view of the society taken as a whole, that is, the economy in its entirety: from this point of view, the speculative rise of the stock market causes an increment in the amount of type 2 fictitious capital and, with it, in the emergence of fictitious profit.[16] A crash of the stock market will cause a reduction in the amount of fictitious capital. And this means that the emergence of a loss that may simply represent a destruction of the previous fictitious profit, which is pure smoke.

When fictitious profit is 'produced' by speculation, it increases the volume of fictitious capital existing in the economy as a whole. When the market goes down, fictitious capital is destroyed and it appears as if real wealth is destroyed – which is, in fact, the case, but exclusively from the point of view of the individual and isolated act.[17]

We should remember – as may be deduced from chapters 21 and 22 of *Capital*, Volume I (Marx, 1887) – that the point of view of the individual and isolated act corresponds to the appearance, whereas the viewpoint of reproduction and entirety refers to the essence. Besides, it is important to reaffirm that appearance is one of the two dimensions of reality: it is not false – the observer is not fooled by appearances – and it is as real as the essence.

---

15 Although he is not referring to Hilferding's interpretation, Harribey (2005) seems to suggest a position partly similar to ours when he states: 'If there weren't markets through which real products, financial bonds or derivative products were changed, there would immediately be a winner and a loser. With these markets, all financiers can reasonably expect to be winners taking into account the frequent change in the holders of titles. In such markets, all operators promise to pay later and every time that they sell their bonds, they don't do so for money, but rather reposition them in any other virtual application.'

16 Who appropriates this fictitious capital, or a big part of it, is another problem. Obviously the big speculators are usually the winners.

17 It is necessary to highlight that the market conditions that lead to the destruction of fictitious capital also determine the destruction of real capital.

Let us go back to our overvalued real estate. With the fictitious profit from the sale, one can actually buy anything. Let us suppose that one buys luxury goods or makes an investment in fixed capital. In which case, wasn't the acquired product produced as economic surplus? Aren't these acquired goods part of the material surplus produced in society? Or, in other words, aren't these types of goods (luxurious and investment ones) not a component of the surplus produced under the form of surplus value? Isn't it about real wealth, from all points of view? It is actually, more than that, about real and material at the same time. If this is so, does this so-called fictitious profit not correspond to a surplus value that was produced at some point? In which case, it would not be fictitious profit. Actually, it does not seem fictitious. Let us make a more objective analysis.[18]

Surplus Value, Capitalist Economic Surplus and Fictitious Profit

Let us begin by clarifying some things related to the Marxist concept of surplus value, in particular the possibilities of its destination. The latter is conditioned by the material form taken by value in excess produced in a capitalist way. Perhaps it would be better to say, instead, that the decision on the surplus value's destination, which is the right of those who receive it in the form of profit or any other form (unproductive wages, rents, interest, taxes, etc.), conditions the way in which capitalist surplus should be possessed at the end of a certain productive period. If we remember the Marxist outlines of reproduction, described by Marx in *Capital*, Volume II, we easily realize that fact: surplus value needs to present a specific material content, without which there won't be an appropriate reproduction of the economy. In a certain sense, here is what Marx says: 'In one word, surplus value is only convertible into capital solely because the surplus-product, whose value it is, already comprises the material elements of new capital' (Marx, 1968: 405).

In a nutshell, we can affirm that the total amount of surplus value corresponds to a physical and material surplus.[19] To say that this surplus should be material would be an impropriety because a part of it is certainly composed of services, which are similar to any material merchandise.

18 That is strictly a sentence used by Marx in the chapter on the merchandise in *Capital* (Volume I).

19 Obviously, the expression 'valeur actionnariale' is absolutely unacceptable from an appropriate perspective of Marx's theory of the value. It would be less problematic, except for our present analyses of fictitious profit, if it referred to an appropriation of the resulting value of work in any productive sphere. About this last aspect, for beginners, it would be convenient to read the chapter on 'rent and its sources' in *Capital*, Volume III (Marx, 1894).

Thus, surplus value, after being transformed into profit, can be converted into fixed capital through accumulation because the substantive or material surplus already contains in advance the corresponding material elements. It can be transformed into circulating/constant capital because the raw material and auxiliary goods needed were produced and are part of the material surplus. Surplus value can be converted into additional wages because the workers' goods for consumption have been produced as surplus. It can be transformed into luxury goods, materials of war, etc., because a part of the surplus that corresponds to the produced surplus value is composed by these goods, or these merchandises. If we are going to use part of the surplus value for the acquisition of properties or real estate, they will have to be produced, and thus a certain part of the produced surplus will take this form.

This means that it is not possible to make a real investment if the necessary material elements for it are not physically present in the surplus value. For example, the work in the construction of a productive enterprise is completely surplus work, that is, surplus value that is in the process of being produced, from a global point of view. Therefore, any credit (interest-bearing capital) for that investment is limited by the volume susceptible to be produced as surplus in the system. Any supplemental credit for the production and investment could provoke, among other things, inflation, reducing workers' wages and forcibly enlarging the surplus.

Furthermore, when it comes to the expansion of fictitious capital, the situation is different. This capital can further increase the limits allowed by the production of wealth and surplus, by means of fictitious profit. While interest-bearing capital is limited by the available volume of the surplus, fictitious capital doesn't have that limit.

Thus, answering the previous question, fictitious profit, which bought luxury goods or fixed capital, de facto corresponds to a surplus value produced some time in the past. And that is indisputable. However, let us see now look at the other side. Going back to the example of the purchase of real estate, let us suppose that the buyer of the aforementioned property has obtained the corresponding money from direct profits generated by industrial material production, thus from real profits (it is surplus value, pure and simple). What was the destination of his/her profit? He/she bought a speculatively overvalued property. The destination of his/her profit was partly real value ($400) and partly pure fictitious wealth, that is, fictitious capital ($600). Summing up, the real profit belonged to A and was transferred to B through the purchase; and the fictitious profit remained in the hands of A, in the form of a speculative overvaluation of a real asset, the property.

Thus, it is true that the salesperson, who was benefited by the speculative valorization of the real estate, initially appropriated a fictitious profit. When buying luxury goods or means of production, he/she transformed his/her fictitious property into real wealth. But that was possible only because the buyer did exactly the opposite. He/she partially transformed his/her surplus value in the shape of money profit into the fictitious form of the overvalued property. And then, if we make a dialectical effort once again to analyse things from the entirety point of view, our answer to the previous question is that fictitious profit doesn't have anything of surplus value or anything of mercantile value in excess.

All this leads us to conclude that, all things considered, the fictitious profit generated by speculation will simply increase the aggregate value of the fictitious wealth or fictitious capital. We could even reverse the statement and it would be absolutely correct (although perhaps comprehensible only later on): in an economy, the increase in fictitious capital from one year to the next (we refer exclusively to type 2 fictitious capital here) is exactly equal to the generated amount of fictitious profit.

Moreover, the statement that the appropriated surplus, the real profit, can be used for fictitious accumulation makes sense only from the individual point of view. As a matter of fact, if the individual B gained his/her real profit and bought fictitious capital, whether it was an overvalued real estate or a public bond, then, in fact, he/she transformed his/her real profit into fictitious profit, at least in part. But that is just the opposite of the inverse phenomenon. Somebody in the economy obtained fictitious profit and transformed it into real, material surplus of the same amount. Therefore, from a global point of view, appropriated surplus value that is profit and is not consumed increases the real capital. Appropriated fictitious profit that is not reduced by an eventual devaluation of assets increases the fictitious capital to the same amount. The total consumption of luxury goods and real accumulation can only originate as surplus value, the real fruit of the exploitation of productive labour. Type 2 fictitious capital arises as a result of the fictitious profit.

In other words, all this means is that from a global point of view, the produced surplus value can only be consumed individually ('individual consumption', according to Marx), accumulated as productive or commercial capital, destroyed or wasted. Therefore, the expression 'financial accumulation of surplus value' can only be deceitful and a statement that implies a contradiction in terms.[20]

Let us ask a parallel question. What happens with the growth in the pension fund asset of wage-earning workers? Does this have to do with

20 It is necessary to highlight, however, that if *financial accumulation* is also treated as increase in the interest-bearing capital of the economy, then the expression is correct. At the same time, with the additional volume of interest-bearing capital, which is intended to finance, for example, increased production, there occurs a material surplus in the form of means of production, produced as surplus in the form of surplus value.

the rise in fictitious capital, that is, the parasitic speculative capital? A positive answer could be provided, at least if it is in relation to the increase resulting from the applications in the funds of part of the wages of the workers who are thinking about their retirement. In fact, behind the value of these applications, there is real substance that can be considered part of the socially produced value in excess or, on the contrary, part of the labour force's value. In both cases it cannot be considered an increase in fictitious capital.

However, what happens if the destination of that increase in funds is the purchase of government titles? Isn't this an increase in fictitious capital? Of course, it is. What it is necessary to understand in this case is that the global parasitic speculative capital has not been increased, but a part of what was earlier fictitious capital, or other holders' property, can be transformed, and in fact is transformed, from fictitious capital into interest-bearing capital or directly into productive or commercial investment. Therefore, from a global point of view, fictitious capital has not increased, but the distribution between real and fictitious wealth has been affected. It has partially changed hands.

Public Debt and Derivate Markets

Of course, the new public debt bonds or instruments issued by any government and used to finance whether, for example, physical investment in transports infrastructure or any other investment, possess a real corresponding part (the investment) and are the counterpart of that real wealth. Marx considers these public bonds (as well as the shares of any company) to be fictitious capital, even when they are not speculatively overvalued. However, it is a fictitious capital that has a counterpart in the world of real wealth. Therefore, we call this capital type 1 fictitious capital.

The same happens with the increase in debt if the latter is used to finance expenses in education or health, so far as it adds value to the labour force. This increase in the circulating public instruments corresponds with a produced real wealth. It is type 1 fictitious capital.

A different case is related to the public debt bonds, when the issuing is due to an inadequacy or insufficiency of funds derived from primary surpluses, for the interest payment of the previous public debt.[21] This issuing creates fictitious profit and increases global fictitious capital.

21 In the Brazilian case, for example, the interests paid by the public sector during 2006 reached the sum of US$ 160,000 million (7.7 per cent of the GDP), while the primary surplus was US$ 90,000 million (4.3 per cent of the GDP), according to the Central Bank of Brazil. So, in a year, the Brazilian state obtained about US$ 70,000 million as fictitious profit for the renting capital. Therefore, it increased the fictitious capital that operates in the country by US$ 32,000 million.

Something that could bring about confusion regarding the fictitious origin of capital composed of public instruments is Marx's statement that the public debt is a powerful mechanism for the original accumulation.[22] This statement is made in the chapter referring to that accumulation:

> The public debt becomes one of the most powerful levers of primitive accumulation. As with the stroke of an enchanter's wand, it endows barren money with the power of breeding and thus turns it into capital, without the necessity of its exposing itself to the troubles and risks inseparable from its employment in industry or even in usury. The state creditors actually give nothing away, for the sum lent is transformed into public bonds, easily negotiable, which go on functioning in their hands just as so much hard cash would ... The Bank of England began with lending its money to the Government at 8%; at the same time it was empowered by Parliament to coin money out of the same capital, by lending it again to the public in the form of banknotes. It was allowed to use these notes for discounting bills, making advances on commodities, and for buying the precious metals. It was not long ere this credit-money, made by the bank itself, became the coin in which the Bank of England made its loans to the State, and paid, on account of the State, the interest on the public debt. It was not enough that the bank gave with one hand and took back more with the other; it remained, even whilst receiving, the eternal creditor of the nation down to the last shilling advanced ... With the national debt arose an international credit system, which often conceals one of the sources of primitive accumulation in this or that people. (Marx, 1887: 529-30)

It should, however, be noted that, according to Marx, public debt can play the role of stimulating original accumulation, taking into account that the holders of the public bonds, in addition to safely receiving interest due on the money that would otherwise be unproductive, can use them, if required, to finance the industrial capital and thus obtain additional remuneration. In addition to that, Marx observes that the public debt allowed the Bank of England, with its right of issuing credit money, to '[give] with one hand and [take] back more with the other'.

To use public instruments to finance, for example, production only means to convert fictitious capital into interest-bearing capital, as clarified earlier, from the point of view of the individual holding these public bonds. The financing of the production presupposes the existence of produced value in excess. For the holder of the instruments, this conversion means that, as a counterpart, another agent transformed his/her real capital into fictitious capital. This is the appearance-essence dialectic/individual-totality act. The fact that the fictitious capital has

22 We thank Julio Gambina for presenting this question that could apparently contradict our interpretation of fictitious capital.

such an effect over original accumulation or over regular accumulation is the result of its dialectical real-fictitious nature, which is quite difficult to understand. And so, the difficulty is doubled: real/fictitious dialectic, essence-appearance dialectic.

Leaving aside public debt, let us now observe the derivatives market. The obtained profit in this type of market, by creating an important return of the parasitic speculative capital, can lead us to consider it as fictitious. However, this is not the best way to analyse it. The profit, when it constitutes returns from a loss of a proportional amount suffered by other agents who operate in those markets, cannot be considered fictitious profit, nor even profit. It is, truly, a pure transfer of value. Furthermore, perhaps most of the time, the loss is of small investors (true speculators, although some or most times, not capitalists in the strict sense of the word). Thus, this profit contributes to the increase in the speculative great capital's profitability. Therefore, like fictitious profit, it should be considered a counteractive factor in the tendency of the capital's profit rate, or at least of the great capital's profit rate, to fall. Savings of wage-earners, middle class or not, and of small entrepreneurs, used as speculative investment in derivative markets or in secondary markets for bonds or shares, can increase, by transfer, the profit of the parasitic speculative capital, without in fact being fictitious profit.

Something More about Fictitious Capital

So, in summary, we can say that fictitious profit is created annually by the increase in public debt used to finance unproductive expenses and interest payments, plus the speculative valuation (value in excess or valorization) of assets, whether it is real (real estate) or fiduciary (private bonds of different types, even shares). This profit corresponds exactly to the amount of increase in type 2 fictitious capital.[23]

There is an argument that we consider definitive to accept the category of fictitious profit and to show that it fits in with the logic of Marx's analysis on fictitious capital. It could be presented as follows: if not for the existence of fictitious profit, how is it possible for new fictitious capital to occur? How is the high increase in fictitious capital's global value possible, at least for type 2? Obviously, surplus value, or surplus value produced while being accumulated, expands the value of industrial capital and never that of the fictitious one. Thus, the only possible answer is that the increase in type 2 fictitious capital can only have fictitious

[23] This capital can grow further, but not very significantly, with the decision of the state to grant public concession to individuals on the right to operate, for example, radio frequencies.

profit as its origin. Fictitious capital is sometimes considered a simple accumulation of rights to appropriate future surplus value.[24] We hope that one understands that such a vision is false. Fictitious capital is much more than that. It is, in the present, as real as any other capital, from the point of view of the individual and isolated act. Besides, it demands or requires present and future remuneration, and, sometimes, it has in its nature an even bigger voracity than other forms of capital, at least in the short term. To consider it a form of capital that is preserved as a usufruct of future surplus value brings with it the risk of expressing a limited perspective based on the Keynesian vision, which is unable to realize the dialectics that determine and explain it.

The rise of fictitious profit and fictitious capital is, undoubtedly, essential to understand why the speculative stage of capitalism has survived until the present, in spite of having emerged two decades ago. However, this survival would not have been possible if, at the same time, an enormous rise in the exploitation of wage-earning workers had not taken place in the core and peripheral countries, in addition to a rise in the exploitation of non-salaried workers, especially in the poorest regions of the world.[25]

Capitalist logic would be completely absurd if it were simply sustained, for so long, by the simple rise in fictitious profit. Although the latter has been created in a particular and powerful mechanism to counteract the tendency of the profit rate to fall, it cannot be considered to be sustaining capitalism. The aforementioned rise in exploitation had the increase in relative surplus value as its origin (thanks to the technological development of the period), in absolute surplus value (extension and intensification of the working day), in super-exploitation (reduction of direct and indirect real wages) as well as in the increase in the misery of non-wage-earning workers.[26]

---

24 It seems to be also Katz's vision when he states: 'the financial transactions … represent expectations of the future exploitation of the labour force' (Katz, 2002: 4). This also seems to be Bonnet's position: 'In this sense the financing of the capital is at the same time a forward flight of capital in crisis – a betting on the future exploitation of work – and an answer of capital to its crisis – a disciplined offensive to prepare conditions for a possible future exploitation' (Bonnet, 2006). We agree this is capital's response to the crises and an offensive against work, but we do not agree that it is a bet on future exploitation. Capital is voracious and, today, it demands remuneration.

25 That is what Foster highlights about the increase in workers' exploitation in the USA: 'real wages for the majority of them are contained; unemployment and underemployment increase; the job creation is fragile; the government social services for the population (including education) are in regression; and the taxes paid by workers increase' (Foster, 2006).

26 We agree with Katz (2002) and Perelman (1990) in the sense that the recent financing has contributed to recomposing the general profit rate: 'The Marxist interpretation allows an understanding of how the recent financial transformations have contributed

There are two important things to point out. First, the continuity of the current stage of speculative capitalism will only be possible with the additional rise in labour exploitation worldwide and with the intensification of value transfers from the periphery to the core countries.[27] Furthermore, the eventual overcoming of that speculative stage to a new stage, in which the domination of the parasitic speculative capital could be destroyed, or at least significantly reduced, would only be possible through a process that would provoke future substantial increase in labour exploitation, although it has already reached very high levels.

What is the theoretical basis for the previous conclusion? Why do other heterodox theories, very critical of speculative capital, present other conclusions, accepting the possibility that the current capitalist stage will evolve into a new virtuous era, similar to the golden years of capital, with the prevalence of productive capital and the possibility, at least in some countries, of renewal of concessions to its workers?

The Two Critical Visions of the Capitalist Future

Our conception that the future of society, as long as it survives as capitalist, implies a rise in workers' exploitation and the absolute increase in the misery of huge sections of the population, comes directly from the Marxist theory of value, correctly interpreted. According to this theory, capitalist wealth and, in particular, capitalist profit originates and continues to originate (inevitably), in the current stage, from human labour. Technological development has an important role, but as a mechanism of transfer of surplus value (by means of extra profits and monopoly rents) and not as a producer of surplus value (except through the mechanism of relative surplus value, which has been counteracted, regarding the profit rate, because of the increase in the capital's organic composition).

Thus, the law of the tendency of the general profit rate to fall is a necessary consequence of that theory.[28] The critiques of the law, expressed on

to recovering the profit rate in the crisis process and reorganization of capital during the last decades' (Katz, 2002: 14). However, we believe this occurs not only because of the increase in exploitation, but also because of fictitious profit.

27 We agree with Katz (2002) in this respect, but perhaps his thesis about future capitalism is not as conclusive as ours and allows thinking about overcoming the current stage without major traumas, albeit with higher levels of workers' exploitation.

28 The relation among the theory of the value, the law of the tendency of the profit rate to fall and fictitious capital is fundamental in the interpretation of the financial capital crises, creating by themselves Marxist categories that perfectly explain the character of these crises. In this sense, in our opinion, Chesnais presents an analysis without a true understanding of the Marxist theory of value, when stating:

> One can also say that the theory of the financial crisis outlined by Marx – a crisis where the destruction of the value (fictitious) of bonds and a brutal credit crunch

diverse occasions and in various ways, are nothing more than 'authoritarian' and based on strange assumptions about Marx's theory itself. For this reason and taking into account that they cannot be empirically proven, makes them absolutely irrelevant.[29]

According to this perspective, fictitious profit rises as another countering factor of this tendency. Curiously, it is something that doesn't have its origin in surplus value and doesn't come from exploitation. Thus, capital approached its ideal: to win and increase without being obliged to sully its hands by exploitation. But at what cost? What would the consequence be?

In exact contrast to this, the heterodox concepts have a different vision of the source of wealth and surplus. First, they refer to Ricardo's perspective with a Sraffa slant.[30] It trivially considers wealth as a heterogeneous group of goods and surplus as a result of the technology used (the technological matrix of the technical coefficients, according to Sraffa). Alternatively, and what is worse, they only have an intuitive vision of the nature of capitalist wealth, thus of surplus, denying any relevance to the theory of value. In the latter case, they are pleased with an even more naïve vision, lacking the capacity to understand the scope of their conception.

For all these concepts and for the authors who are located in the Marxist camp but in the tributaries of the limits of Ricardo's vision, surplus value and profit rate can increase perfectly, without any problem, as a result of technological development. Therefore, there are no major problems. Capitalism can overcome the current phase and to do this, it is enough to impose limits on financial capital, through economic and political mechanisms.[31] Such concepts accept the existence of financial capital's control in current capitalism, but they believe in a possible return

---

> combine with the effect of banking difficulties and the tangle of debts and credits – is not natural to Marxian or Marxist analysis. It foretells the crisis theory of the best Keynesian theorists in the field, particularly Hyman Minsky. (Chesnais, 2006: 89)

If the author really intended to assert that the Marxist perspective is hardly able to outline a theory of crises and that this outline is only a foretelling of the Keynesian theory of crises (which is even worse), it would mean that dialectics is not able to explain them and that the scientific categories of value-work and fictitious capital are simple predictions (or perhaps subsidies, if that is possible) of the 'best' Keynesian analysis. If this is true, we believe Chesnais does not make an appropriate analysis of the Marxist theory of value.

29 See Coletti (1978: 58-91). Coletti wrote significant texts on this when he considered himself a Marxist.

30 See Sraffa (1966).

31 We consider that the concept of financial capital, disseminated mainly in Hilferding's (1985) and Lenin's (1954) works, is not enough to understand either the movement of fictitious capital or of parasitic speculative capital. This idea is also discussed in the works by Carcanholo and Nakatani (2001) as well as in the interesting article by Alves Pinto (1997).

to productive capitalism and even being able to make concessions to workers.[32]

If, in addition, according to the experts of these concepts, the conflict of financial capital versus productive capital can be realized by a different set of hands, provoking completely different factions within the bourgeoisie, things will be even easier: it will be enough to have the 'productive and progressive' bourgeois faction promoted to a dominant sector. Thus, it will become necessary to be its ally, or even better, its political subordinate.[33]

They live in a world of dreams: with the utopia of a humane capitalism. They are happy with their concepts and dreams. Sraffa's perspective, the most naïve economic vision, is the economic basis (since a long time) for the most trivial reformism. Unfortunately, for them, although they don't understand it, the magnitude of Marx's theory of value demonstrates this perspective as completely illusory. If it weren't so tragic, it would be a serious comedy.

Such concepts have an additional difficulty. They don't know very well how to treat financial capital. Actually, they don't even understand the concept of capital properly, and that seems absurd. In the best cases, they treat capital according to Sraffa's theory as a heterogeneous group of means of production and without any resulting social dimension. The counterpart to this is to understand work, not as a central concept in the theory (and not taking into account ridiculous post-modern reasons), but as a simple factor for granting inputs consumed by workers, who in terms of production, are no different from an animal or a combustion engine. If capital is a heterogeneous group of goods, what does financial capital mean, for these concepts? What is the nature of financial capital? What is its relation to productive capital and interest-bearing capital? The truth is that the life of these reformists, at least from a theoretical point of view, is not very easy!

32 For example, Duménil and Lévy (2003), although they admit that the current contradictions of capitalism can be solved by a great crisis, also believe in the possibility of a gradual extinction of the hegemony of what they call 'finance' and a return to a capitalism with certain concessions to workers, that is, a more humane capitalism, if that actually existed at some point in the past. See also Carcanholo (2004).

33 We totally agree with Bonnet in this respect: 'In our countries, these types of interpretations that mechanically set the financial and productive spheres in opposition lead us to unsustainable diagnoses and, therefore, to recycling nationalist-populist programmes focused on the protection of presumed autochthonous capitals, which are authentically productive vis-à-vis financial and transnational capital' (Bonnet, 2006). And also: 'In many analyses, the competing financial and productive capitals are associated, in a fractionalized vision, with some factions of the bourgeoisie with opposing interests and policies (see, for example, Beinstein 1999)' (Bonnet, 2002).

Perhaps, the best way to understand financial capital according to these concepts is to treat it as capital on hold, like a granting of a credit with the expectation of appropriation of a real surplus in the future. The great difficulty they face, besides the absence of an appropriate theory of wealth and value, is their incapacity to understand the dialectical method. Maybe they are delighted with Böhm-Bawerk's statements that dialectics isn't but a rhetoric resource, although that author works within a different perspective.[34]

The absence of a dialectical vision doesn't allow them to see that 'financial capital', or fictitious capital, is simultaneously both imaginary and real. The fact that this is a reality baffles them when dealing with the phenomenon. The metaphysical and positivist logic is unable to understand the fictitious-real dialectic. If it is fictitious, it can be easily overcome, and for that, an appropriate policy is enough. What happens if it is real?

References

Alves Pinto, Nelson Prado. 1997. 'O capitalismo financiero', *Revista Crítica Marxista*, 1(5): 9-26.

Beinstein, J. 1999. *La larga crisis de la economía global*. Buenos Aires: Corregidor.

Böhm-Bawerk, Eugen von. 1974. 'La conclusión del sistema de Marx', in Rudolf Hilferding *et al.* (eds.), *Economía Burguesa y Economía Socialista. Cuadernos de Pasado y Presente* No. 49. Buenos Aires.

Bonnet, Alberto R. 2002. 'El fetichismo del capital-dinero. Un comentario sobre el debate Chesnais-Husson', *Revista da Sociedade de Economia Política*, p. 10.

——— 'Leyendo la "globalización" políticamente', http://www.herramienta.com.ar/varios/8/8-8.html, 1 August 2006.

Carcanholo, R.A. 2004. 'Resenha do livro Uma nova fase do capitalismo? François Chesnais, Gérard Duménil, Dominique Lévy e Immanuel Wallerstein', *Revista Crítica Marxista*, 19: 146-51.

Carcanholo, R.A. and P. Nakatani. 1999. 'O Capital Especulativo parasitário', *Revista Ensaios*, 20(1): 284-304.

———. 2001. 'Capital especulativo parasitario versus capital financiero', *Revista Problemas del Desarrollo*, 32(124): 9-31. (Earlier version in: J. Arriola and D. Guerrero (eds.), *La Nueva Economía Política de la Globalización*. Bilbao: Servicio Editorial Universidad del País Vasco, 2000, pp. 151-170).

Carcanholo, R.A. and M. de Souza Sabadini. 2010. 'Interprétation théorique de la crise capitaliste actuelle', *La Pensée*, (364): 7-22.

[34] See Böhm-Bawerk (1974).

Chesnais, François. 2006. 'La prééminence de la finance au sein du "capital en général", le capital fictif et le mouvement contemporain de mondialisation du capital' *La Finance Capitaliste. Actuel Marx – Séminaire d'Études Marxistes.* Paris: Presses Universitaires de France, pp. 65-130.

Coletti, Lucio. 1978. 'El Marxismo y el "Derrumbe" del Capitalismo. México, D.F.: Siglo XXI.

Corazza, Gentil. 1999. 'Notas teóricas sobre as relações real-monetário em Marx', *II Jornada de Economia Política, SEP.*

Duménil, Gerard and Dominique Lévy. 2003. 'Superação da crise, ameaças de crises e novo capitalismo', in François Chesnais *et al.* (eds.), *Uma Nova Fase do Capitalismo?* São Paulo: Xamã.

Foster, John Bellamy. 2006. 'Monopoly-Finance Capital', *Monthly Review*, 58(7).

Harvey, David. 1982. *The Limits to Capital.* England: Basil Blackwell.

———. 1996. *Condição Pós-Moderna: Uma pesquisa sobre as origens da mudança cultural.* 6a edição. São Paulo: Edições Loyola.

Harribey, Jean-Marie. 2005. 'Il n'y a pas de génération spontanée du capital', *Cahier Marxistes*, (231).

Hilferding, Rudolf. 1985. *O Capital Financiero.* São Paulo: Nova Cultural.

Katz, Claudio. 2002. 'Enigmas contemporáneos de las finanzas y la moneda', www.socialismo-or-barbarie.org/teoria_de_la_revolucion/040606enigmas contemporaneos.htm.

Lénine, Vladimir I. 1954. 'L'impérialisme, stade suprême du capitalisme', in *Œuvres choisies*, tome I, deuxième partie. Moscou: Éditions en Langues étrangères, pp. 433-572.

Marx, K. 1863. 'Theories of Surplus Value', Volume IV of *Capital.* Progress Publishers. http://www.marxists.org/archive/marx/works/1863/theories-surplus-value/.

———. 1887. 'A Critique of Political Economy', Volume I of *Capital.* Progress Publishers. http://www.marxists.org/archive/marx/works/download/pdf/Capital-Volume-I.pdf.

———. 1894. 'The Process of Capitalist Production as a Whole', Volume III of *Capital.* New York: International Publishers. http://www.marxists.org/archive/marx/works/download/Marx_Capital_Vol_3.pdf.

———. 1968. *El Capital. Crítica de la Economía Política*, Libro I. México, D.F.: FCE.

Paula, João Antonio de, Cerqueira, Hugo Eduardo A. da G. and Albuquerque, Eduardo da M. 2001. 'Finance and Industrial Evolution: Introductory Notes on a Key Relationship for the Capitalist Accumulation', *Revista Econômica*, 3(1): 5-53. http://www.uff.br/cpgeconomia/v3n1/2-eduardo-hugo-jantonionota18.pdf.

Perelman, Michael. 1990. 'The Phenomenology of Constant Capital and Fictitious Capital', *Review of Radical Political Economics*, 22: 66-91.

Sraffa, Piero. 1966. *Producción de Mercancías por Medio de Mercancías*. Barcelona: Oikos-Tau.

Trindade, José Raimundo Barreto. 2006. 'Dívida Pública e teoria do crédito em Marx'. Tese (Doutorado em Desenvolvimento Econômico), Universidade Federal do Paraná (UFPR), Paraná.

CHAPTER 6

The Great Depression of the 21st Century and Fictitious Wealth

On the Theoretical Categories of Fictitious Capital and Fictitious Profit

Reinaldo A. CARCANHOLO

Federal University of Espírito Santo (UFES), Brazil

Introduction

Corporate capital believed it had found an economically different way to produce wealth, a way that no longer required the use of nature and productive work. And this is how we got where we are. The truth is that since the 1980s, capital and its ideologists, amongst them some economists, began to believe they had found a magic formula to ensure that economic wealth was being generated without the use of human labour. Some even thought that the workforce would no longer be necessary for capital to produce economic surplus and ensure its necessary profitability. Labour had thus lost centrality. Technology, information and control over knowledge were raised to the rank of magical entities that were capable of anything and became objects of worship. Capital didn't need to get its hands dirty with production in order to be realized as a being capable of generating profit by itself, that too very high profit. Nature also became secondary. And this belief is now a fact. Financial capital was somehow able to accomplish this feat. From the late 1970s onwards, it not only dominated the capitalist scenario, but its capacity of *appropriation* of profit also surpassed that of productive investments.

Capital dedicated itself frenetically to speculation and there it found the remedy for the low profitability it had faced during the 1970s. Thus, speculation was not a detour from the system, one of its shortcomings, but an attempted solution, a medicine for capitalism's structural disease, that is, the tendency of the rate of profit to fall. The magic worked for a while and corporate capital was able to achieve a real and significant recovery of its profitability rate; the empirical data available are clear on this. But, after all, this is how we got where we are. The depression experienced at the beginning of this century and the subsequent economic and financial crises the world bears today are the price that was paid for this period of speculative orgy. This price is, and will continue to be, very high, even though it is paid mainly by those who do not benefit from it at all.

What we are currently witnessing in the capitalist world is much more than a simple succession of financial or credit crises. We are living in what some call the Great Depression of the 21st Century. It is not merely a cyclical crisis, from which the system can recover and get back to normal functioning after some time. Nor is it a result of a period of deregulation of speculative capital, in which some of the world's powerful governments behaved recklessly. We are dealing with something much more important. We are currently witnessing the beginning of the collapse of a particular stage of capitalism. The financial crisis that began in the United States with the sub-prime mortgages in 2007, which spread throughout the financial system as well as the real economy sector, in addition to the crisis that the European world is experiencing in the second decade of this century, constitute the beginning of this process.

To classify the current crisis as that of overproduction or over-accumulation is to basically say nothing. If this is effectively what is happening, then what is causing this phenomenon? What reasons were or are there for it to have happened? We consider the idea of underconsumption, while extremely appealing, to be nothing more than the result of mere theoretical naiveness, which is alien to Marx's dialectical theory of value.

Marxist Interpretation and the Theory of Value

We intend to analyse the current reality of the capitalist economy rigorously from a Marxist perspective and specifically based on Marx's theory of value. What does it mean to approach reality from such a perspective and theory?

First, it means distancing ourselves from those interpretations that identify a supposed 'system deficiency' as a cause of the financial crises, a deficiency that sometimes allows the excessive greed of capital to run free, thus compromising the regular behaviour of the market. Along with this deficiency, according to such theories, there would also be the permissive policy of governments that do not regulate enough the movements and logic of this speculative and rentier capital. Thus, to have a Marxist perspective is to refuse the state voluntarism characteristic of all sorts of Keynesian views.

Keynesian interpretation has a weakness that is characteristic of neoliberalism, but in the reverse direction. While the latter shows blind faith in the market, as if it were capable of anything, Keynesianism, at the other extreme, puts its entire religious conviction on the capability of the almighty state. Marx's perspective, on the contrary, argues not only that there are internal contradictions inherent in capitalist society, but also that these contradictions worsen with time, that society's antagonism inevitably becomes increasingly severe. Thus, even though state intervention – understood as a contradictory body that is still able to represent the global interests of capital – may be able to temporarily mitigate the intensity and consequences of the crisis for capital, especially in the critical moments, it is not powerful enough to prevent this process by which antagonism grows between these contradictions inherent in the system.

To understand the current depression and the subsequent crises from a truly Marxist perspective implies identifying the contradictions existing in the present stage of capitalism and distinguishing especially the main contradiction that explains the development of this stage. In order to do this, there is no choice but to use the dialectical theory of value, understood not as a simple theory of prices (which is an elementary mistake), but as a theory of capitalist wealth and, in a broader sense, as a scientific theory that explains the functioning of this society. It also requires, and this is fundamental, an adequate understanding of the dialectics within the concepts of fictitious capital and fictitious profit, which are nothing more than necessary derivations of the theory of value.

A central issue for understanding capitalism in general, from the point of view of this theory, is the contradiction *production* x *appropriation* of wealth. Not only where the relationship between capital and labour is concerned, but also with regard to the redistribution of excess value (of which surplus value is a part) amongst non-workers and also the various factions or autonomous forms of capital. This is precisely what allows us to characterize the current stage of capitalism as speculative and parasitic, dominated by the insufficient capacity of productive capital to generate the necessary real economic surplus and deliver the payments to the so-called financial capital and capital as a whole. And this has consequences for the relationship not only amongst capitalists, but also between capital and labour.

Therefore, it seems to us crucial to understand in some depth the nature of economic wealth in capitalist society, the determinations of its production and appropriation, and the nature of capital and fictitious profit, a category that allows us to understand the dialectics of what is euphemistically called financial capital.

What Is the Nature of Capitalist Wealth?

There is no doubt that the economic wealth of any society, in any historical epoch, consists of material goods, which have a twofold origin: nature and human labour, the latter understood as the conscious human activity that transforms nature, adapting it to the needs of each individual and society as a whole. Available wealth consists of that which is accumulated in the form of buildings and facilities, machinery and equipment, vehicles, tools, stored raw materials and auxiliary materials, consumer durables, food and a wide variety of other consumer goods produced previously.[1] All these goods are economic wealth, whether for consumption or for producing new goods.

It is necessary to also consider the social productive flow, those goods that are produced and regularly consumed or stored. We cannot forget services, that is, goods that are consumed as they are produced, like transportation, education, health services and many more. These constitute the real wealth produced, even though they do not represent wealth in the nature of the physical or material, if one can use such an expression.

The aforementioned is more or less obvious and David Ricardo's explanation for the nature of wealth, for example, was limited to it. On the other hand, Adam Smith's genius allowed him to observe, in a time prior to Ricardo, that in a market society, and particularly a capitalist society, wealth is also of another kind. For Smith (2005), economic wealth is a social relationship of power and domination over alienated labour and human beings. Let us say it again: 'wealth *also* presents itself as a social relationship.' Also?

For Smith, market wealth is of two kinds: Accumulated useful goods and social relations. How is it possible that Smithian thought, limited to not knowing the dialectical perspective, admits the existence of this double determination: Materiality, on the one hand, and social relations, on the other? He finds a way by stating that market wealth is not twofold, that is, it is not both things at once. It's one or the other, depending on the intention of the owner. No dialectic thought there, but nevertheless capable of grasping profound dimensions of reality, albeit with limitations.

These conclusions of Adam Smith found fertile ground in Marx. In Marx's dialectical perspective, capitalist wealth is at once both the 'material' and social dimensions. At the same time! For Karl Marx, market wealth, and particularly capitalist wealth, is the contradictory unity of these two dimensions, these two poles: material content and social form, 'materiality' and the social relationship of domination over human beings. Unity of what he calls use-value and value.[2] These two dimensions or

1 In this society, a significant form of wealth that is not always remembered consists of a skilled workforce.

2 Many people might interpret the expression 'material content' to be a reference to materiality, a physical/material dimension of wealth, which does not include services.

poles are intimately related to each other, but not in a static or definite manner. Insofar as market society progresses or develops, the social dimension of wealth acquires increasingly greater importance, imposing itself over use-value. If, in the earlier stages of this society, the logic for the producer was much more tied to the 'materiality' of the product (remember, for example, the case of craftsmen corporations in the Middle Ages), as market relations developed and as market society progressed, the social dimension of wealth became gradually more important. The producer was increasingly subordinated to the logic of money and value, and not to the materiality of the product. From a certain historic moment onwards, this materiality was only relevant to the producer as long as it meant more money.

While producing a particular commodity, the producers are not thinking of the satisfaction that it can provide to those who consume it, they just think of the money that might be made from the sale. Or better still, they only think of satisfaction to the extent that it increases the amount of money or profit they might get from it. And it is with money that they find the way to exert power over someone else's work, over other human beings. They just think about their personal interests. Adam Smith already said this when referring to the interest of the baker, the butcher, etc.

> It is not from the benevolence of the butcher, the brewer, or the baker that we expect our dinner, but from their regard to their own interest. We address ourselves, not to their humanity but to their self-love, and never talk to them of our own necessities but of their advantages. (Smith, 2005: 19)

In a market society, wealth is increasingly more about social relations and less about 'materiality'; in capitalism, the former eventually dominates the latter. There is, indeed, a genuine process of dematerialization of wealth that begins with the emergence of market relations and develops frenetically in capitalism.[3] It is for this reason that the magnitude or

---

This would be a big mistake. By material content Marx understands the determination that capitalist wealth shares with wealth in any form of society. And to prevent any further confusion on this issue by comparing capitalist wealth with the more primitive form of wealth of previous societies, let us think of wealth in a post-capitalist, socialist society, in which services will be significant. This mistake made by many leads to the misinterpretation of important parts of Marx's work, including, or especially, the *Grundrisse*. The basic characteristic that differentiates commodity services from any other type of commodity is the fact that it needs to be consumed at the very moment it is being produced. Obviously, this consumption can be individual or productive. As we know, value is, in fact, a social market relationship expressed as social ownership of the commodity. Therefore, it would be a serious mistake to confuse value and exchange value or to use a certain amount of money as an example of value.

3 We reiterate that we are not referring specifically to the physical/material determination, but to the so-called 'material content' that involves services as well.

size of capitalist wealth, this substantial wealth that is increasingly dematerialized, must be measured by its social form and value. The magnitude of value, determined by the amount of abstract labour, becomes the measure of the size of this wealth, which is essentially domination over someone else's work. In fact, the materiality of capitalist wealth, or rather its real substance, is configured by the amount of socially necessary labour for the reproduction of this 'materiality', that is, the amount of abstract labour. Outside of that substance, there is no real capitalist wealth.

The process of dematerialization is easier to observe in the money form of capital rather than in commodities. Money in capitalism becomes increasingly dematerialized: From gold and silver to paper money, cash credit, credit cards and virtual money. This process can also be seen with capital. If earlier, the image of capital in our minds was of a factory or a big store, today, we increasingly think of 'financial' capital. The latter has no materiality, cannot be seen or touched. Where is it? Is it in the bank? It just cannot be found.

Even with this process of dematerialization, wealth in its social dimension always has a material content behind it as the substance of use-value. Always? In fact, advanced capitalist society has the curious ability to produce fictitious wealth. What is fictitious wealth?

Fictitious Wealth

In capitalism, the different economic agents (households, individuals, businesses of all types and also the state) have estates that can be measured in value and are expressed in the market in certain monetary terms. Someone's estate, or estate wealth, is made up of real assets (buildings, cars and so on) and titles (stocks, bonds, etc.) as well as money, whether in paper form (securities), coins, or as bank deposits. Furthermore, these agents are also entitled to annual returns measured in value, expressed in terms of money.

In an advanced capitalist society, the total sum of all agents' estates in the entire economy, i.e., the total social estate wealth is usually higher than the total value of the inventory of the existing, real capitalist wealth. This is precisely what preliminarily indicates this notion of nominal or fictitious wealth (fictitious capitalist wealth) and will allow us to further understand the concept of fictitious capital.

So, one thing is a society's estate wealth, another is its real wealth. And there is indeed a certain disconnect between the magnitudes of these two. The first, estate wealth, is like a cloud that floats above real wealth and is only partially a reflection of the latter. Its other part, nominal wealth, lacks substance and has no correspondence with materiality.

Is it possible at this point to give an idea of the reasons for this disconnect?

At the moment, we'll mention just one out of the many different reasons for this disconnect. This is a phenomenon that occurs circumstantially due to the speculative increase in housing prices. This is perhaps the simplest example for understanding the gap between the two forms of wealth.

Speculative and more or less sustained appraisal of a particular apartment, for example, allows the owner to see oneself and be seen in the market as richer than before. The owner's estate increases to the exact amount of the speculative appraisal and this increase will be maintained as far as speculation keeps the price of the property high. Note that if the owner sells that property and the market price remains unchanged, the buyer, the other part of the business operation, will not have transferred value to the seller, since the buyer's estate will continue exactly the same as before the purchase: earlier as cash, and now as property appreciated by speculation.

This additional wealth, which is a result of speculation and is now part of the estate that got its property value increased speculatively, is what we call *fictitious wealth*.[4] It is part of the total estate wealth, but not of the real, material wealth. Actually, we should call it fictitious/real wealth, since it is wealth that, even though it lacks a real counterpart when observed from the standpoint of the entire economy, is recognized in the market every day as real wealth, just as any other type of wealth. At this level of individual actions in the market, wealth is undifferentiated; the only thing that matters is its magnitude expressed in terms of money.

Note that this wealth is recognized by the market, but has neither nature nor labour as its origin. It has value, but is not a product of human labour. How is this possible? Is it a violation of the Marxist theory of value? Not really. It is actually perfectly understandable based on this theory. Despite the fictitious/real dialectics, as fictitious wealth is *simultaneously* both, for the sake of simplicity, we'll just refer to it as fictitious wealth.

Undoubtedly, and on the other hand, a part of the agent's estate wealth is straightaway real wealth and cannot be considered fictitious. It is like property owned by a private individual. If the speculative appraisal is

4 There is an objection to the fact that such appraisal creates fictitious wealth. It comes from the right idea that if an asset is sold for a price higher than its value, that value gets transferred, as opposed to creating fictitious wealth. We have had the opportunity to show elsewhere (cf. Carcanholo and Sabadini, 2009: 41-65) that this objection has no basis, since overvalued bonds or real estate are maintained within the buyer's own estate, while speculation keeps its price high. In the case of consumer goods, for example, once these goods are used or consumed, they are no longer part of the buyer's estate and the idea of value transfer is indeed applicable.

ignored, the owner's estate corresponds directly to real wealth. As we have seen, only the estate's additional value corresponding to speculative appraisal is actually fictitious wealth.

We insist that what has been described here is only one of the ways in which fictitious wealth exists in capitalist society. Another way is constituted by the money in the hands of people and of private companies, in addition to bank deposits, minus all debt.[5] We will discuss other ways later.

Just as in the case of an individual agent (person), a company's estate – consisting of the actual value, in labour, of the commodities in its property (materials, equipment, facilities, etc.) – is straightaway real wealth. The speculative appraisal of these assets is fictitious wealth and, in this case, constitutes *fictitious capital* because it is a value that exists within the appraisal process inside the circulation that defines the existence of capital.

Here, we are faced with one of the origins of fictitious capital; but it is only one of them and, in fact, not the main one. Thus, let us take a look, for the first time, at the existence of this extremely abstract concept: *fictitious capital.*

Illusory and Fictitious Capital[6]

The credit system that exists in any capitalist society has the curious ability to produce another form of fictitious wealth, that of fictitious capital. Let's see how that happens.

The starting point for understanding this issue is to grasp that when the existence of credit and the payment of interests is widespread in society (which occurs in any space where capitalism is already in a relatively advanced stage), they produce an illusion for the economic agents: the belief that there is capital behind any regular income earned by someone.

When there is the widespread practice of charging interests, the idea is that if any amount of money generates (or at least can generate as interest) for the beholder more money, that amount of money appears as *interest-bearing capital.* Any regular income is seen as coming from interest-bearing capital and appears to the eyes of the market as interest

---

5 Wealth appears as if it existed twice: On the one hand, as circulating money, and on the other hand, as commodities that can be bought with it.

6 Our research on fictitious capital extended itself with time. For many years, we have been thinking about this concept that Marx so rarely discussed in *Capital*. In a few aspects (not many), our current conclusions differ from those found in previous works. Nonetheless, reading such previous works must not be dismissed, since they offer dimensions and aspects on the subject of fictitious capital that are not discussed here or are discussed here in less depth.

from actual, existing capital. When it is the result of non-capital, the company produces the illusion of the existence of capital, which is *illusory capital*.

Marx refers to this matter in *Capital*:

> The form of interest-bearing capital is responsible for the fact that every definite and regular money revenue appears as interest on some capital, whether it arises from some capital or not ... This, however, is and remains a purely illusory conception, except in the case where the source ... is directly transferable or assumes a form in which it becomes transferable. (Marx, 1863-83a: para. 7)

And, in specific reference to public debt:

> But in all these cases, the capital, as whose offshoot (interest) state payments are considered, is illusory, fictitious capital. Not only that the amount loaned to the state no longer exists, but it was never intended that it be expended as capital ... Nevertheless, this fictitious capital has its own laws of motion, as we shall presently see. (*Ibid.*: para. 8)

Public concessions to private individuals, when free, constitute a mechanism of illusory capital production. In Brazil, public concessions over the right to use radio and television frequencies, given for free as a way to reward political support, are or were (it appears that the conditions of these concessions have undergone some changes) typical of this mechanism. Another example in Brazil, which seems to no longer operate this way, was public concessions over the right to manage a registry of deeds and documents, a lifelong concession that passed down from father to son, as long as the latter graduated in law. These concessions had or still have the ability to raise capital as if by magic: illusory capital.

This type of capital, although it is more or less extensively present in a capitalist economy, but in insignificant amounts, has no greater importance to the logic of society, except when it becomes what is called fictitious capital. And for this conversion to happen, it is simply necessary that regular income, the source of the illusion, be represented by a title (a document that makes it believable), which in turn can be traded in the market, that is, it should be possible to sell the title to a third party. It is necessary for the regular income to become a negotiable instrument. This simple fact, which is not so simple, produces a significant transformation, and this fictitious capital (another form in which fictitious/real wealth exists) gains importance in capitalist society.

In the case of Brazil, radio and television concessions, as long as they can be traded in the market, are one of the forms in which fictitious capital exists. Another results from the speculative appraisal of assets, as mentioned earlier. Marx explains the conversion from illusory to fictitious capital in the aforementioned quote that we repeat here: 'This [idea of being capital], however, is and remains a purely illusory conception, except in the case where the source … is directly transferable or assumes a form in which it becomes transferable' (Marx, 1863-83a: para. 7).

Thus, the illusion disappears and a new economic concept, a new form of capital appears. Does this mean that it is real capital? It is not illusory capital, but actually it is and it is not real. How do we understand this? Is it just wordplay? As a matter of fact, it's not. To clarify the issue, we must understand the dialectics involved in this concept.

A title that grants someone the right of appropriation of a regular income, a security that can be sold to third parties, *seems* to its owner to be true capital, to be real capital. And indeed, it is. It is accepted as real in the market, in everyday business transactions. It is market wealth, fictitious wealth as well as fictitious/real wealth. There is no real substance behind it, no wealth that is previously produced; there is no value and no material surplus produced earlier to which it corresponds. Thus, from a global standpoint, not from the perspective of economic agents that operate in everyday life, it corresponds to fictitious wealth. It appears as an extension to an agent's estate, but it does not constitute real wealth for the economy as a whole. Thus, in short, fictitious capital is real from the perspective of everyday commercial activities and from the standpoint of individual and isolated actions. However, it is fictitious from the point of view of the economy in its totality. It is, and yet it is not fictional; it is, and yet it is not real. This is its dialectics.[7]

There is, however, an additional aspect to be highlighted from the totality perspective. It is true that we are considering capital to be fictitious because it doesn't correspond to the real wealth produced. However, it exists because it is able to appropriate the market surplus or surplus value. Thus, from this angle, we can say that it is real. Any real capital, in its existence, has previously produced real and material substance and has the right of appropriation of the surplus value that will be produced. Fictitious capital has no real substance, but it has that right of appropriation. Thus, in short, even from the totality perspective, it is at the same time fictitious and real. It is real because it truly has one of the determinations of real capital.

It is worth remembering at this moment that the perspective of individual and isolated actions corresponds with the appearance of reality, and the totality and reproduction perspective is the only one that allows us to understand the essence of reality. It is also important to remember

7 The ridiculous idea of 'human capital' has its origin in this illusory process, except that in this case, it represents a mystification. See more details in this text's appendix.

that appearance is not the result of an observational mistake, as is often considered, but is one of the two true dimensions of what is real.

The real existence of fictitious capital and, therefore, the fact that it is not the result of a mere illusion is demonstrated when we realize that its movement and effect on the economy truly interfere with the process of appraisal, accumulation and reproduction of capital in general, as well as in the way the economy works and in its logic. In short, fictitious capital has no corresponding substance and does not contribute to the production of surplus value. But it requires compensation, that is, it is entitled to participate in the surplus value produced.

Forms of Existence of Fictitious Capital

Fictitious capital is precisely that part of an estate or estate wealth that is not directly made up of real goods and behaves like capital, that is, it has appraisal as its objective, whether as a result of speculation or merely as rentier capital earned exclusively through interests. It has various forms, besides those already mentioned till now.[8]

One of the most important forms in which fictitious capital can be found is stock shares. In this case, however, one could argue that behind their value, or at least part of their value, is the real estate of the company to which they correspond and to which shareholders are entitled as partial owners.[9] Adding the value of a particular company's shares can yield a value greater, equal or even less than the value of its real estate. In this last case, one of the basic characteristics that determine the existence of fictitious capital, as we understand it till now, would not be present: the absence of material wealth that corresponds to it from the totality perspective.

However, there is no doubt that Marx believes that shares really are fictitious capital, and his argument is very clear when he states: 'But this capital does not exist twice, once as the capital-value of titles of ownership (stocks) on the one hand and on the other hand as the actual capital invested, or to be invested, in those enterprises' (Marx, 1863-83a: para. 11). Also: 'But these titles likewise become paper duplicates of the real capital…' (Marx, 1863-83b: para. 5)

---

8 The ones already mentioned are: (*i*) the part of the value of realty or fiduciary goods derived from speculation; (*ii*) the capitalization of regular earnings when the right to them is ensured by securities that can be traded; (*iii*) cash and bank deposits of the public and banks minus their debts.

9 Here the term 'real estate' is not to be confused with the commonly understood concept of 'realty' or 'real property', defined as property consisting of lands and of all appurtenances to lands, like houses, buildings, offices, farms, etc. Here, as explained earlier in the text, it is a reference to that part of an agent's estate that corresponds to real, material wealth, as opposed to fictitious, or nominal wealth. [Translator's note]

In fact, if, for the sake of simplicity, we assume that the total value of a company's shares matches the true value of its real estate, the wealth in the market appears to be doubled.[10] An evidence of this is that both the shareholder and the company may use up its entire estate as collateral for any bank loans. If the total value of the company's shares exceeds the effective value of its estate, we would in fact be faced with two different types of fictitious capital. Each part of that value – the one that corresponds to the real estate and the additional one – is a different kind of fictitious capital. The part of the stock value that is equivalent to the value of the real, material estate constitutes fictitious capital because it apparently doubles the economic wealth of society. The other part is fictitious capital because it has nothing of real, material wealth.

This difference is highly significant and important. Hence, we will make a clear distinction, calling the first part 'type 1 fictitious capital' and the other part 'type 2 fictitious capital'. While type 1 has material wealth behind it and, in fact, contributes to the production of surplus value (at least in the case of a productive enterprise), type 2 has nothing material behind it and does not contribute to production in any way, especially the production of economic surplus. The various forms of fictitious capital fall into one of these two types. In many cases, a particular form may be a combination of both these types.

Money

In fact, as mentioned earlier, even the amount of money available in the hands of businesses and consumers is fictitious wealth or type 1 fictitious capital (if it works as capital). This occurs when the monetary system is based exclusively on currency and credit system. The holder of that money has it as part of the holder's estate or is liable to pay it to someone who earlier had it as interest-bearing capital. This value is nominal wealth. Another completely different thing is that material wealth is made up of those goods that will be purchased with that amount of money. Thus, wealth appears as if it existed twice: As a right of the lender (or simply as the owner's estate) and as commodities to be sold. After the commodities are sold, they still appear as doubled wealth: first, as material wealth in the hands of the person who bought the commodities (in case it was directly and initially the owner of the money) and, second, as money in the hands of the person who sold the commodities. All this means that the purchase-sale transaction does not create additional nominal wealth by seemingly doubling existing wealth. It means that the sum of money in the hands of its owner is indeed pre-existing nominal wealth and, in this case, type 1 fictitious capital.

10 It can appear tripled, quadrupled, etc.

So, all money in circulation and all money considered part of someone's estate – like the money deposited in banks, for example – is fictitious capital, if it is meant for appraisal, that is, if its goal is to make more money. Thus – and this is important – money-capital, the functional form of industrial capital available to businesses, is in fact fictitious capital.

> With the development of interest-bearing capital and the credit system, all capital seems to double, and sometimes triple, itself by the various modes in which the same capital, or perhaps even the same claim on a debt, appears in different forms in different hands. The greater portion of this 'money-capital' is purely fictitious. (Marx, 1863-83a: para. 22)

It is possible that the amount of money available – either circulating money/currency, or credit money deposited in banks – is in excess of the amount of money necessary for global circulation, and this occurs frequently. In this case, the difference constitutes type 2 fictitious capital (or, at least, fictitious wealth). In fact, this type of capital always appears to be in excess of real, existing material wealth.

The Case of Debentures and the Increase in Public Debt

Since we have earlier addressed the issue of companies' stock shares, we must now take a look at the issue of debentures, that is, bonds issued by a particular company and sold in the market. It is a way to obtain resources through credit, a method for a company to finance itself. People who buy debentures are attracted to them due to the interest they bear. These people are, hence, owners of interest-bearing capital. So, when a company issues debentures, is it actually creating fictitious capital?

Credit operations between private individuals, including the issuing of debentures, do not determine the creation of new fictitious capital, even though those debentures themselves represent fictitious capital. Even though it is true that the holders of debentures, or lenders, present the corresponding values as part of their wealth, the debenture issuing company, or the debtor, consider these values as debt.[11] In this case, the private wealth, that is, the global estate of the private economic agents, is not doubled as a result of a credit operation.

Let's take a closer look. Before the purchase of debentures, agent A had fictitious capital in the form of money (at a value of, say, 1); company C produces wealth in the form of means of production (value of 1) that, eventually, will be sold to company B. The corresponding value of all three agents' assets together is equal to 2.

11 With the purchase of debentures, the estate is not altered: the share that is used in the transaction was earlier in the form of money and is later in the form of credit securities (titles).

After the purchase of debentures, what is each agent's situation? A now owns fictitious capital in the form of titles issued by company B; B owns the means of production purchased from C, but owes the same amount to A; C now owns money at a value of 1, which was initially in the hands of A, was passed on to B who, finally, gave it to C. Total value of all three agents' assets after these transactions is equal to 2. There was no increase in the assets of this small group of private agents.

Let's compare this with the sale of company shares by B. A already owned fictitious capital in the form of money and, after buying the shares (value = 1), A now maintains the same value in the form of shares; company B bought the means of production and does not owe anything, since the shares sold are part of its capital; C now owns money corresponding to a value of 1 as fictitious capital. The assets of all three agents before the money transactions were equal to 2; after the transaction, it is equal to 3. Fictitious capital was created.

Therefore, simple credit transactions between private individuals do not create new fictitious capital. However, it is necessary to clarify something that is significant and that was already suggested: A certain amount of interest-bearing capital does indeed constitute fictitious capital, but its movement itself does not create additional fictitious capital. One thing is to be fictitious capital, while the other is to create new fictitious capital.

When banks create additional credit, which is a common practice amongst them, they do create additional fictitious capital, and here there should be no doubt. If they effectively finance production, they create type 1 fictitious capital, and the same happens when they discount a trade bill. When they finance speculation, they create type 2 fictitious capital.

On the other hand, let's consider the state when it issues or increases public debt. This issuance creates fictitious capital. The increase of public debt can be due to new titles, in this case bonds, issued by the state to private individuals. When aimed at financing regular expenditures, interest payments, military and similar expenditures, this increase creates type 2 fictitious capital.[12] This is one of its most relevant forms and has the most significant consequences in current capitalism. Thus, the increase of public debt increases the total volume of fictitious capital that exists in the economy.

Let us consider this calmly. If the increase of public debt had as its goal some state investment (new roads, public buildings, whatever their

[12] 'These promissory notes [public debt, RC], which are issued for the originally loaned capital long since spent … serve for their owners as capital to the extent that they are saleable commodities and may, therefore, be reconverted into [material, RC] capital' (Marx, 1863-83b: para. 4).

destiny might be – administration, health, education, safety, etc.), type 1 fictitious capital increases. This could be easily understood if we think that the state could pay the construction companies or the producers of such products directly with these new bonds (titles). Wealth appears twice: First, in the hands of the state, and second, in the hands of private individuals. If the payment to construction companies or producers is made in cash, and if this money is obtained by the sale of bonds to a third party, nothing changes.

The other part of the increase in public debt, the part that corresponds to regular expenditures or that is not meant to finance any type of real, material wealth, determines the creation of type 2 fictitious capital. For example, the state incurs expenses in purchasing consumer goods, and the regular use of these commodities eventually leads to their destruction, but the bonds that allowed the state to buy such goods are still in the hands of private individuals. These bonds make up that individual's estate, but will no longer have a material counterpart after those commodities are consumed.

The case where pre-existing public debt interests are paid is even easier to understand. Many times these interests are paid exclusively with the country's government primary balance, that is, with public revenue savings set aside to pay public debt. To pay the other part of the debt, the state issues and sells new bonds to the public, thus increasing public debt. In this case, the increase in public debt implies the creation of type 2 fictitious capital.

Another way to create type 2 fictitious debt is through military expenditure. When expenses are financed by tax funds, they constitute a reduction in the surplus value available for distribution amongst the various factions of capital and other sectors that benefit from it. When they are financed by increasing public debt, they create type 2 fictitious capital.[13] This form of fictitious capital is extremely relevant today, especially for the most powerful countries like the United States and the UK.

Let's summarize the different types of fictitious capital and the different forms in which they exist. The first form we mentioned is illusory capital, when capital exists as titles (bonds or negotiable instruments, in general) that can be sold to third parties. This form is the least important. We then referred to the speculative appraisal of assets and stock shares. We demonstrated that circulating means and the money part of agents' estates (when used as capital), including money-capital, constitute fictitious capital as well. Debentures are fictitious capital, even

[13] When the increase in public debt is meant to finance military investment, like the construction of a military base, then type 1 fictitious capital is created.

though their issuance doesn't create additional fictitious capital. Finally, we discussed public debt (and how its increase is an important way to create new fictitious capital). On the other hand, transactions that do create additional fictitious capital in society, which we mentioned earlier, are: (*i*) issuing of titles based on illusory capital, (*ii*) speculative appraisal of assets, (*iii*) increase in public debt, and (*iv*) issuing of additional money for circulation.

Each one of these forms must be considered either type 1 or type 2 fictitious capital, depending on the circumstances. The crux of the matter is that we understand that type 1 has a material counterpart, even though it seemingly doubles wealth. Whereas, type 2 fictitious capital has no real counterpart and contributes nothing to wealth production or trade, even though it is entitled to participate in its appropriation.

Moreover, it is important to emphasize the fact that nominal wealth or fictitious capital is considered real wealth in the daily activities of the market. There isn't the slightest possibility that it would not be recognized as such, as that would signify disrespecting property rights. This right should never be ignored or destroyed, except when there is a crisis or, more simply, in speculative asset deflation.

The Conversion from Fictitious to Material Capital and Vice Versa

Fictitious capital, in the hands of a private individual agent, whether it is type 1 or 2, can be converted into material capital:

> These promissory notes [in reference to public debt], which are issued for the originally loaned capital long since spent, these paper duplicates of consumed capital, serve for their owners as capital to the extent that they are saleable commodities and may, therefore, be reconverted into [material] capital.[14] (Marx, 1863-83b: para. 4)

At any point in time, the holder of a title that represents fictitious capital of any type will find in the market the possibility to convert his fictitious capital into material, real capital. It can be converted, for example, into a farm, factory, supermarket or building. To be fictitious capital is to be recognized as wealth by the market, just like any other type of property. Fictitious capital is not fictitious in the market's operations; on a day-to-day basis, it is real.

Does this mean that, from the perspective of totality, all fictitious capital can be converted into material capital? The answer is obviously

[14] Comments in brackets were added by the author to contextualize and facilitate comprehension of the citation.

no. The conversion exercised by an agent at any point in time in a specific direction has its corresponding conversion in the opposite direction by the other agent. The total amount of fictitious capital is not decreased by these conditions. We can analogize this with a hot potato game. In the end, someone is always caught with the hot potato in their hands. The potato can always be passed on to another player, but it is always in somebody's hands. At the end of the game, whoever has the potato in their hands loses. In capitalism it is the same way. In a moment of crisis, who is left with the hot potato? Usually, it is the small investor, the beneficiary of a retirement fund, etc. If that potato ends up in the hands of a powerful, big bank, the state tries to rescue it: because it is 'too big to fail'.

Obviously, if all holders of fictitious capital try to convert it into real assets, all at the same time, there won't be enough material wealth available to do so.

But, is the reverse conversion possible? That is, is it possible to transform real and material capital into fictitious capital? The answer is yes. This is exactly what happens with, for example, all military expenditure that is financed by the increase in public debt, that is, when military bonds are issued. Here, the labour utilised in military production is productive labour, and the real wealth produced becomes fictitious wealth. It's the same with past labour that is incorporated into military production.

Fictitious Profit

Let's go back to our initial rationale when we revealed that capitalism produces fictitious wealth. That is, back to the idea of fictitious appraisal of realty or fiduciary goods. We already saw that this fictitious wealth, when operating as capital (be it interest-bearing or speculative), must be considered fictitious capital.

Let's consider that a company's estate underwent appraisal due to speculative reasons, regardless of whether the increase in value was of its real estate or its titles. This appraisal will appear as an increase in profit at the end of the year. The result of this speculative appraisal will be added to the operational profit in order to calculate total profit.

Let's take a look at this profit. Does it have surplus value as its base? Is it the result of the exploitation of productive workers from some realm of economic activity? The answer is no. That is why it must be considered fictitious profit.

It is fictitious because it is not a result of surplus value or any other kind of market surplus and, therefore, has no counterpart in the material wealth that has been produced. Nonetheless, from the perspective of the daily activities of the market, from an isolated and individual perspective and just from its appearance, it is as real as any other type of revenue; it translates into a certain amount of money that has been accounted for. It can be seamlessly converted into any type of material wealth, be it realty, consumer goods or any other types of goods. However, it has no material counterpart from the totality perspective. If we look at the economy as a whole, we will see that total profit, including fictitious, is greater than the amount of surplus produced.[15]

The dialectics of fictitious profit is the same as that of fictitious capital: it is real from the perspective of individual and isolated acts, and fictitious from the totality perspective. This way, it is real and fictitious at the same time.

It is not easy to accept this concept.[16] First, because it doesn't appear in Marx's works. And second, for a more concrete reason: it is no easy task for those who are convinced of the depth and reality of Marx's theory of value to accept that there is profit that is not a result of exploitation. Nonetheless, it is necessary to remember the effort Marx put into the third volume of *Capital* in order to show the process that mystified the origin of surplus value, or better yet, of capital's profit. This process is very deep: a merely superficial analysis of the capitalist system, of its appearance, demonstrates that profit is not a product of the exploitation of labour.

It is necessary to, once again, emphasize that this conclusion is not simply the observer's or the analyst's mistake. It is a conclusion derived directly from reality and expresses what is real. The problem is that it expresses reality exclusively in a single dimension, that of its appearance. It is a conclusion derived from a one-dimensional view of reality. It is not wrong in itself; the error resides in its limiting itself to uni-dimensionality. The conclusion lacks the perspective of another dimension, that of its essence.

The market's perspective, which allows us to observe only an isolated private individual or an isolated market action, is fundamental.

---

15 Understood at the level of abstraction found in the first chapter of Marx's *Capital*, Volume III.

16 'Demonstrating the existence of fictitious profits is not an easy task, or rather, in a sense it is not possible. First, to understand its existence presupposes, in our opinion, besides the already mentioned dialectical perspective of things, a proper interpretation of Marx's theory of value, something uncommon. Secondly, to think of an empirical demonstration of its existence is something completely outside of scientific logic; it is meaningless within the dialectical perspective. Perhaps it is possible to describe it and suggest ways in which it exists, and at the same time, clarify its theoretical dimension and its relation to the other categories from the Theory of Value' (Carcanholo and Sabadini, 2009: 47-48).

We cannot deny that, from the daily perspective of the market, or the isolated and individual perspective, the profit gained by a specific entrepreneur is due to his/her competitiveness and sagacity. But this doesn't belie the fact that the total amount of economic profit available to be distributed amongst beneficiaries is, in fact, a result of the exploitation of productive labour. When we studied the transformation of values into production prices, we saw how wide the distance or the contradiction between essence and appearance (value and price) really is. In this case, the appearance is the result of a process of value transfer and, therefore, of surplus value distribution amongst capital's divisions and the companies or agents within these divisions. Marx's analysis demonstrates this with a lot of depth. It is even possible to show why the total amount of surplus value is different from the total amount of profit, as long as the latter is measured as the price of production.

Fictitious profit is an additional step in the process of mystifying the origin of capitalist profit. It is not the result of fictitious wealth transference, but of the creation of fictitious wealth. From the totality perspective, it is a mere smoke curtain. It is explained by capital's ability to produce nominal or fictitious wealth, an ability that was explained earlier in the chapter.

The existence of fictitious profit does not deny the determinations of Marx's dialectic theory of value. It just shows that appearance, one of reality's poles, has the ability to hide the essence of the system with surprising intensity. It is essential to point out here that this intense detachment between essence and appearance of the capitalist economic surplus is not free of implications on reality. If it wasn't for that, the use of dialectics could seem, not without reason, as a mere act of rhetoric, or as a deceiving instrument to explain the unexplainable. Dialectics is nothing like that.

Fictitious profit, especially when it is very high (characteristic of the current stage of capitalism), has serious implications and important consequences on the way the system works. This detachment between appearance and essence is what induces the growing antagonism between production and appropriation of economic surplus – antagonism that could become (and in the current stage of capitalism, in fact, becomes) the dominating contradiction of the system. That fictitious profit emerges in a given year temporarily resolves the mentioned contradiction, but the contradiction worsens with the increase in volume of the surplus-thirsty fictitious capital, that doesn't contribute at all to the production of this surplus.

Let's pay close attention to one important fact: Fictitious profit instantly becomes, considering the totality of the economy, new fictitious capital. It is true that someone who obtains a certain amount of fictitious profit can convert it into real wealth, but the corresponding fictitious wealth is transferred to somebody else.

The aforementioned dominance of the contradiction between surplus, or surplus value production, and appropriation explains the present speculative phase of the system, a phase in which we live, which is going through a structural crisis.

To accept the existence and relevance that the concept of fictitious profit has, it is necessary to abandon the mechanistic interpretation of the theory of value, which views the concept of value as always having a material dimension. Value is actually a social relation that is expressed as property over the product of labour that progressively dematerializes, as we already know. The dialectical perspective of the theory of value allows us to understand that profit is a product of exploitation, but capitalism is able to produce the fiction (that is real in appearance) that profit is detached from labour. But the price for this fiction must be paid in reality.

The concept of fictitious profit was also used by François Chesnais (2006) in an article published in the *Herramienta* magazine, but the author did not accept the role we assign it of a counter-tendency to the fall in the rate of profit, a process that started at the end of the 1960s.

Another important author also envisions this concept and calls it 'differential profit'.

> Profits or losses from speculation arise, therefore, only from the difference between the corresponding appraisal of interest-bearing titles. They are neither profits, nor do they participate in the surplus value, but arise solely from fluctuations in the appraisal of the part of the company's surplus value, to which stockholders are entitled; fluctuations that, as we shall see, need not to arise from the variations in profits that are indeed realized. They are purely differential profits. While the capitalist class as such appropriates a part of the proletariat's work, with no compensation, speculators make money of each other. Someone's loss is someone else's profit. *Les affaires, c'est l'argent des autres.* (Hilferding, 1985: 139)

What Hilferding doesn't realize is that fictitious profit of a certain agent does not necessarily mean someone else's loss. While speculation is in place and titles are overvalued, for example, all consider themselves rich and, in the market, they indeed are. Nobody loses; some may not profit if they sell the titles before prices rise or if they do not purchase them. Losses will only occur during crises, when the titles depreciate. At that moment, the ones who generally lose are the least powerful and the worst informed. But that is a whole different story.

Something similar can be said about housing appraisal; it does not represent losses, per se, for anyone. The case where fictitious profit is created by raising public debt is slightly different. At no point in time will there be a loss for the private agents, except in a case where the state redeems the title with tax money, with the government budget primary balance, which almost never happens. In this case, the weight falls upon those that either pay their taxes or don't benefit from that source, that is, wage labourers.

Finally, it is important to highlight that in a particular economy, the overall increase in type 2 fictitious capital is largely explained by fictitious profit. Few are the mechanisms that create new type 2 fictitious capital that do not involve the creation of fictitious profit.

Appendix

Notes on the Ridiculous Idea of Human Capital

As we mentioned before, the idea of human capital comes from the same illusion created by interest-bearing capital that gives birth to illusory capital. But in this case it is a mystification produced and maintained by neoliberal thinking, pure and simple.

In an excellent article by Alain Bihr (2007), the author identifies the origin of the idea: 'We owe the concept of human capital to the American economist Theodor W. Schultz, who invented it in the 1950s. It was popularized by his colleague and compatriot Gary Becker.' The author goes on to explain when it was publicized:

> Confined for a long time to a small circle of neoclassical economists, the notion of 'human capital' spread during the 1980s to become one of the favourite concepts of 'human resources' theorists and employment agencies. It holds a privileged place in the vocabulary of politicians... (Bihr, 2007: para. 1)

The website http://pt.goldenmap.com/Capital_humano, in its Portuguese version that we freely translate here, is more explicit about the topic and also maintains a critical attitude towards the idea:

> The concept of human capital was originated during the decade of 1950, in the studies of Theodore W. Schultz (1902-1998), who shared the 1979 Nobel Prize of Economics with Sir Arthur Lewis. The concept was developed and popularized by Gary Becker and recovered in the 1980s by multilateral entities more directly related to neoliberal thinking, in the area of education, in the context of productive restructuring. It derives from the concepts of fixed capital (machinery) and variable capital (salaries). 'Human capital' (capital incorporated into human beings, especially in the form of health and education) would be an explanatory component that is fundamental to the uneven development among countries.

And there is also a reference to Marx's *Capital* (1863-78) that is worth replicating here:

> Apologetic economists...say: [The worker's] labour-power, then, represents his capital in commodity-form, which yields him a continuous revenue. Labour-power is indeed [the worker's] property (ever self-renewing, reproductive), not his capital. It is the only commodity which he can and must sell continually in order to live, and which acts as capital (variable) only in the hands of the buyer, the capitalist. The fact that a man is continually compelled to sell his labour-power, i.e., himself, to another man proves, according to those economists, that he is a capitalist, because he constantly has commodities (himself) for sale. In that sense a slave is also a capitalist, although he is sold by another once and for all as a commodity; for it is in the nature of this commodity, a labouring slave, that its buyer does not only make it work anew every day, but also provides it with the means of subsistence that enable it to work ever anew. (Marx, 1863-78: Sec. X. Capital and Revenue...: para. 13)

Very suggestive: Even slaves owed or owe human capital!

A better citation is found in the third volume of *Capital*, where the relationship between this ridiculous idea of human capital and the illusion caused by interest-bearing capital is clear, an illusion that is the origin of illusory capital. Beyond that, Marx finds the origin of the idea (although not of the 'human capital' expression) to be from as early as the 17th century!

> Wages are conceived here as interest, and therefore labour-power as the capital yielding this interest...The insanity of the capitalist mode of conception reaches its climax here, for instead of explaining the expansion of capital on the basis of the exploitation of labour-power, the matter is reversed and the productivity of labour power is explained by attributing this mystical quality of interest-bearing capital to labour-power itself. In the second half of the 17th century, this used to be a favourite conception (for example, of Petty), but it is used even nowadays in all seriousness by some vulgar economists and more particularly some German statisticians. Unfortunately two disagreeably frustrating facts mar this thoughtless conception. In the first place, the labourer must work in order to obtain this interest. In the second place, he cannot transform the capital-value of his labour-power into cash by transferring it. (Marx, 1863-83a: para. 9)

Marx would be even more surprised if he had the opportunity to know that a certain gentleman would reinvent the idea in the 20th century, an idea that existed since the 17th century! And that is still repeated by mediocre economists and by non-economists too. It has now gained the status of a concept or category: Human capital! It appears on the arsenal of all those people who want to impress with their vocabulary and an untouchable seriousness those listeners that they consider more ignorant. Maybe that is why this certain gentleman was awarded the Nobel Prize.

References

Bihr, Alain. 2007. 'A fraude do conceito de "Capital Humano"', *Le Monde Diplomatique Brasil*, 5 December, http://www.diplomatique.org.br/artigo.php?id=74 (Accessed on 16 February 2013).

Chesnais, François. 2006. 'La prééminence de la finance au sein du "capital en général", le capital fictif et le mouvement contemporain de mondialisation du capital', *La Finance Capitaliste. Actuel Marx – Séminaire d'Études Marxistes*. Paris: Presses Universitaires de France, pp. 65-130.

Hilferding, Rudolf. 1985. *O Capital Financiero*. São Paulo: Nova Cultural.

Marx, Karl. 1863-78. 'Chapter 20: Simple Reproduction, Part 2', in *Capital, Volume II*, Marxist Internet Archive, http://www.marxists.org/archive/marx/works/1885-c2/ch20_02.htm#10 (Accessed on 16 February 2013).

———. 1863-83a. 'Chapter 29: Component Parts of Bank Capital', in *Capital, Volume III*, Marxist Internet Archive, http://www.marxists.org/archive/marx/works/1894-c3/ch29.htm (Accessed on 16 February 2013).

———. 1863-83b. 'Chapter 30: Money-Capital and Real Capital. I', in *Capital, Volume III*, Marxist Internet Archive. http://www.marxists.org/archive/marx/works/1894-c3/ch30.htm (Accessed on 16 February 2013).

Smith, Adam. 2005. An Inquiry into the Nature and Causes of the Wealth of Nations. http://www2.hn.psu.edu/faculty/jmanis/adam-smith/wealth-nations.pdf (Accessed on 16 February 2013).

Part IV

Analytical Approaches to Rebellions and Struggles

CHAPTER 7

The Dialectical Unity of Capital and Non-Capital

The Role of Overpopulation in Popular Rebellion Today

Wim DIERCKXSENS & Andrés PIQUERAS

International Observatory of the Crisis (IOC),
The Netherlands and Costa Rica

and

University of Castellón Jaume I, Spain

Throughout its history, capital has established a decisive form of discrimination that has effectively strengthened its power against labour: discrimination between an *endogenous labour force* (integrated, with certain guarantees and rights in the capitalist nexus) and an *exogenous labour force* (yet to be incorporated or incorporated as 'heterochthonous', without such guarantees and rights). We refer to the historical incorporation of the exogenous population from the non-capitalist to the capitalist nexus (with the consequent replacement capacity of the endogenous labour force) as *absolute mobility.*

The more possibilities capital has of accessing a population in the non-capitalist nexus and of being able to incorporate it through absolute mobility into the capitalist nexus, the greater its unilateralism or class domination. In contrast, when these possibilities run dry, capital is more inclined towards reformism or negotiation. However, this absolute mobility has historically been combined with *relative mobility* of the labour force, which includes various processes, of which labour force migration is a fundamental component. This chapter holds that both types of mobility are at the core of class struggles.

Theoretical Framework

While the process of widespread, incessant reproduction of capital is what gives meaning to the capitalist mode of production, this dynamic entails other coincidental processes, all of which have a common starting point in the monopolization of the means of production or means of subsistence. These are:

- Turning the maximum possible period of time in each day of collective labour into surplus work time converted into accumulated surplus value.

Which leads to:

- Exploitative control over the maximum possible proportion of living labour (namely, people).

Which, in turn, results in:

- Maximum possible appropriation of and control over their time.
- Maximum possible control over their mobility.

A constant, relentless battle between labour and capital has been fought over these processes throughout history. In this chapter, however, we will focus exclusively on the last of these in an attempt to contribute to Marxist research in this field.

Since the very beginnings of merchant capital, two concerns have been constant. The first has been about how to obtain a labour force at minimum cost for main production activities.

With European colonial expansion across the rest of the globe, and the shaping of the international pan-European system (Arrighi, 1999) that would become a global system in the 20th century, a market – first international and then global – of raw materials and use values, generally turned into merchandise, gradually spread and became consolidated; capital resources and assets would later be added. From the outset, these were accompanied by the development of an international – and later world – labour force market.

The role of intra- and inter-continental acquisition of living labour, initially to guarantee the original or primitive accumulation of capital and colonial production (slavery and other kinds of forced labour in local populations, mobility of enslaved Africans, mobility of coolie serfdom in the Asian population), and then to ensure specific capitalist exploitation (proletarian wage-dependent automobility), first gained importance in the colonies and then in the system's peripheries. Only with the industrial revolution the metropoles, or core centres of the system, became directly involved in this international labour force market, with the emigration of millions of peasants and proletarians to the peripheries. A century later, in the middle of the 20th century, these metropoles began to import labour on a mass scale from the peripheries.[1]

1 The movement of living labour to strategic economic sectors (mining of precious minerals, cotton plantations for the textile industry and food production for European

Historically, the cheapest way of introducing living labour into the capitalist mode of production was to have access to and continuously incorporate into capitalist production a labour force from outside itself; in other words, a labour force neither produced nor reproduced under capitalist conditions.[2] The implications of this process were: (*i*) the destruction of pre-capitalist economies, with the consequent 'liberation' of huge numbers of people predisposed to 'mobilization'; and (*ii*) the artificial reserve of non-capitalist forms of production at the peripheries (used for many years as huge 'Bantustans') as places for the production and reproduction of the labour force under non-capitalist conditions, and as a disposal to reabsorb this labour force when it was no longer needed for capitalist exploitation (and which also generated constant focuses of frequently endemic, popular ethnic resistance).

The channelling of labour force mobility and the way it is incorporated are, therefore, equally, if not more important than the production and creation of surplus value in the dynamics of unequal capitalist accumulation and development, since they are an essential condition for these processes to occur.

In this accumulation process, the incorporation of labour directly through its geographical or sectorial mobility is just as decisive as its occupational integration in the social and international division of labour, often used as 'raw material' in situ, to later be exploited or imported as 'objectified labour'.

The second concern has been about how to retain or 'anchor' a labour force that had gradually been freed from the bonds of vassalage, slavery or serfdom.

The retention or anchoring of living labour is a less visible, or perhaps less perceived, process, whereas, paradoxically, one of the distinguishing features of capitalism is said to be the *mobility of the labour force*. Indeed, the proclaimed basic condition of the labour force in the capitalist mode of production is that it must be mobile, in other words, capable of occupying jobs and settling where capital requires it to do so. The logic of this condition,

---

salaried workers; railway and transport infrastructure, mining and industrial production in the metropoles, etc.) was essential to the development of the system's central formations, which controlled these dynamics and the mobility and use of living labour in the aforementioned ways that, far from occurring linearly, overlapped in time and were used in combination at the system's discretion.

2 For this reason, control of women's reproductive capacity has always been so important (loss of men through forced or 'free' migration also led to a significant increase in their productive role). Control of reproduction has historically been the subject of women's struggles, through 'womb strikes' to avoid giving birth to children in conditions of slavery, servitude or, in general, overexploitation. These issues are thoroughly covered in Potts' (1990) excellent work.

needless to say, lies in two circumstances that differentiate capitalism from any earlier mode of production: (*i*) the process of dispossession of people's means of production, which leaves them disposed ('free') to be mobile; and (*ii*) the fact that the worker *owns* his or her labour force (i.e., he or she, as the *owner*, has the inalienable right to sell it). These circumstances constitute the necessary conditions for labour force to be a *commodity* (a factor alien to individuals and the basis of their alienation). In turn, the *mobility* of this commodity is claimed to be one of the basic requirements for the origins of capitalism associated with its very raison d'être: that of producing producers separated from their means of production, without structural or economic connections to either the production processes or specific places of production. Their transformation into proletarians marked the origins of capitalist mobility (from owners of the means of production to individuals dispossessed of this control and, therefore, available for wage labour or, in general, dependent labour). This is what we call *absolute mobility* (De Gaudemar, 1979).

However, from the outset, this renascent mobility had to be either curtailed to varying degrees or channelled and, in all events, controlled, to prevent people from 'leaving' their condition of commodity-labour force; in other words, to guarantee and perpetuate their dependence. When this was not possible through waged work (inevitably with insufficient wages), two forms of subjection were historically used:

1. Absolute subjection (slavery or other forms of forced labour).
2. Relative or bridled subjection, most commonly in the form of indenture or engagement, servitude, peonage, apprenticeships and migrations under contract or relegation to the employer.[3]

These impediments to mobility were imposed wherever the social relations of capitalist production did not mature sufficiently to develop the *social* field, with all the recognitions, public interventions and rights that ensure that dependent waged labour becomes an efficient way of retaining the labour force on its own.

With the development and maturity of such social relations of production, these impediments gradually ceded importance to dependent waged labour (although they did not disappear altogether and were

3 Wage insufficiency was accompanied by increased property prices and taxes in order to prevent workers from becoming independent or self-employed. Bridled: refers to the de jure and/or de facto obstructions to workers' mobility, whether geographical, sectorial, professional, social or political. The economist Moulier-Boutang (2006) implacably and comprehensively explains the process by which this labour force is *bridled*, i.e., how the formally 'free' work of the capitalist era (and extolled as such by liberal thinking) has actually been permanently subject to constrictions, in such a way that their 'freedom' is more the exception than the rule.

brought in to complement dependent waged labour whenever and wherever necessary). Meanwhile, the so-called primitive forms of mobility outside the reproduction of capital (that of people incorporated into the capital value process through their proletarianization; see De Gaudemar, 1981) would give way to other increasingly significant forms of mobility within the capitalist accumulation process. Although, generally speaking, labour force mobility tends to refer only to migratory geographical mobility, capital actually uses this mobility in at least four different ways:

1. As an adaptation to the organization's labour process requirements (different work shifts, job swaps, or the increasing social and technical division of labour in general in order to increase productivity or surplus value). In other words, to pursue technological-organizational shift of capital.
2. As a way of matching the labour force to the demands of various spheres or branches of activity, depending on expectations of the capital's profitability.
3. As a form of displacement in and out of waged labour (employment-unemployment; regulated-unregulated employment, etc.).[4]
4. As a means of subordinating the labour force to the spatial movement of capital and, within that, to its dynamics of concentration and centralization.

As a whole, therefore, labour force mobility has tended to be channelled and subjected in order to ensure that its malleability, flexibility or subordination adapts to the demands of capital accumulation. We understand this condition as *relative mobility* (De Gaudemar, 1979), a condition that was gradually combined with absolute mobility as capitalism developed and labour was truly subsumed under capital in consequence.[5] For this reason, the study of labour force mobility cannot be separated from the analysis of how ways of working were implemented and the changes in the organizational processes they involved, keeping in mind that spatial and functional mobility intersect and are permanently linked in the capitalist mode of production. The precise study of how capital is valued and the resulting forms of labour mobility at each moment in

4 The first two types of mobility have frequently involved dismissals, shift rotation, forced changes in job posts or activity and, in general, numerous hardships deriving from the real subsumption of labour to capital. The third type of mobility, needless to say, inflicts untold misery on these workers.

5 The terms labour and capital, in their capitalized forms, are understood as Marx's 'collective labour' and 'collective capitalist' and are, therefore, also opposing historical subjects.

history are also, therefore, essential to any thorough understanding of migration analysis.

In addition, not only the movement of labour force or the different procedures by which it is procured (waged labour being only one way, historically combined with forced or semi-forced labour) but also specific incorporation of the labour force in the processes of capitalist accumulation are vitally important.

The ‘free’ international migration of proletarianized labour, as part of these migratory movements, is linked to all the aspects listed above and has the following effects:

1. Reduction in capital turnover time (due to shorter production time caused by increased intensity).
2. Continuation of sectors with a low organic capital structure due to the intensive exploitation of labour.

Both these processes counterbalance the tendency of the rate of profit to fall.

In response to the tendency of profit to fall, capital introduced several mechanisms, including the rule of tendency to labour mobility perfection (De Gaudemar, 1979: 236). For this reason, it is so important to take into account migration flows as elements of the production of the labour force commodity arising over time in different social formations, and not only as the essential components in the circulation of this commodity. The more efficient and cheaper means of transport become, the greater the benefit to capitalist development through access to an increasing labour force in ever more distant markets. This is especially true if the costs of travelling and transport are borne by this peculiar commodity, the only commodity that can move by itself and finance its own mobility.

It is in this fourth way, however – capital mobility, which requires us to consider the global capitalist market – that international migrations of proletarianized labour (waged labour) become particularly relevant and visible.

Throughout the course of capitalism, dialectical materialism has understood international migration primarily as a global mechanism to supply the labour force and to provide the elements (ethnic, family, community, neighbourhood, etc.) to support its reproduction. From this perspective, therefore, migrations cannot be separated from the socio-anthropological analysis of each social formation and its cultural-identity markers; neither can we ignore the special significance of gender in the migration process, and of community ties (ethnic, national, local, etc.), which frequently become stronger.

The geographical mobility of the labour force has been exploited in many different ways, depending on the position of social formations in the international division of labour. Some of the most important historical manifestations are:

1. The expansion of capital into new geographical areas transformed local subsistence producers into waged workers. This was often accompanied by forced movements of populations between peripheral formations, and importing the labour force from areas with previous capitalist development (the latter as migration processes from the centres to the peripheries of the world system).
2. The intense accumulation of capital in the central societies generated reverse processes of global migration, from the peripheries to the centres of the system.[6]

   It has been noted that when a labour force migrates from places with more developed forces of production and, therefore, more developed labour organization and consciousness, to areas where these aspects are less developed, historically class consciousness and organization at the destination tend to be fostered. When the labour force migrates in the opposite direction, the tendency is to weaken the labour force's social negotiating power as well as its political agency.
3. Further levels of capitalist accumulation in the peripheries led to inter-periphery migration and migration of a certain type of labour force (particularly highly skilled labour) from central societies to the peripheries.
4. Finally, importing labour force has historically been linked to the strengthened or reproduced capital domination over labour in some of the system's social formations, with particular significance in central formations, through increased labour replaceability.

If the development of capitalism is associated with the arrival of a growing waged labour population, there is another subsequent condition, namely, the need to constantly replenish the reserve of labour disposed to becoming waged, given that the relative power of capital over labour

[6] The first two of these dynamics were present in the controversial debate between Luxemburg and Bauer over which of the two was integral to the imperialism of the central societies. But labour power migrations from the colonies or peripheries to the metropole (feeding the process of relative overpopulation), and the reverse flow (in pursuit of external capital investment) are not simply phenomena that coincide with the spread of capitalism and its hegemonic link with other modes of production. One or the other of these complementary phenomena has greater impact at different times, depending on the prevailing dynamics of capital and specialization in the capitalist world economy.

is moderated by the replacement rate of the commodity of the labour force that capital is capable of maintaining. Indeed, some authors, such as Marglin, have argued that

> the differential between the average rate of growth of capital, *g*, and the average grade rate of growth of the labour force, *n*, determines whether or not the capitalist economy tends continuously to extend its boundaries. If (g-n) is greater than zero [...], the relative power of workers inside the previous boundaries of the capitalist economy is likely to increase; this pressure forces capitalists to expand beyond those boundaries.[7]

However, a fifth point, frequently ignored in systemic analyses, must be added:

5. There is an element of autonomy in almost all migrations. Migration may also be regarded as a break with or escape from relations of labour, dependency or subordination, or, in general, as a 'way out' of social relations that are in principal less desirable than those hoped for through migration. This implies that migration also involves an element of sabotage of the capital-labour relations constructed at the point of departure. Migration may also inject 'turbulence' into labour relations at the point of arrival, and even into the flows linking the two points. This condition may also be expressed in the idea that there is always an uncontrollable part to the migration phenomenon that does not respond to more or less systemic interests (although this does not imply that it cannot be explained in systemic terms).

The weakening of labour's social negotiating power that tends to occur in the second point initially may, therefore, be countered by the new migrants' contrasting experience of past autonomy, both in their demands and organization. Their disruptive potential is linked to the fact that they are not integrated and are kept on the edges of political and social loyalty mechanisms (social security, citizenship, rights, regulated employment relations, etc.) in the destination country, as we shall see later. But it is here that their greatest structural weakness lies (Piqueras, 2007).

Research dealing with this fifth point draws a conclusion that is frequently absent from other analyses: migrations, on their own, do not constitute a 'reserve army' if the additional condition of bridling is absent (Moulier-Boutang, 2006), which is designed to weaken the migrant labour force's capacity to respond.

In order to understand this better, we must consider this labour force as a case of exogenous labour.

---

7 Marglin cited in Gordon, Edwards and Reich (1994: 27).

Throughout all histories of capitalist entities, we must consider the interrelationship between an endogenous labour force, with regular and stable exchange of labour, relative freedom of movement and linked to social integration mechanisms parallel to citizenship building, and an exogenous labour force, incorporated 'from outside' and forced to remain beyond the boundaries of citizenship and regulated labour conditions. This exogenous labour force has been incessantly subject to political restriction of movement or direct bridling in the absence of other mechanisms of 'subjection', including different forms of unwaged labour, demographic reserves awaiting incorporation into unwaged labour through previous proletarianization or dispossession, or internal and inter-state migrations. Their presence has been vital in allowing these different types of regulation to appear.[8]

The state itself became the guarantor and regulator of the labour force supply, and the reproducer of the dependent and exogenous nature of a varying part of this labour force. Herein lies the raison d'être of migration policies.

In effect, because the international division of capitalist labour has historically been linked to the formation and consolidation of state frontiers, states have played a determining role in the differential accumulation of capital on a global scale.

One of the elements necessary to achieve this objective is the ingrained inequality of the labour force. To this end, states will ensure that the labour force is maintained and reproduces according to its origins through institutional differentiation, thus generating a subtype of labour force that is particularly vulnerable or deprived of social negotiating power because of its assigned foreigner status.[9]

In addition, one of the notable features of the capitalist world market is that total commodity mobility does not actually occur within it (and neither is capital distributed 'freely' in all parts of the world regardless of which state its owners are from), which means that what is truly determinant in this peculiar market is the absence of any 'free' mobility of the labour force. The implication is that whereas in a state economy

8 Therefore, as this line of analysis upholds, slavery and the numerous forms of bridled dependent labour have been permanent structural companions of capitalist accumulation, not only pertaining to primitive accumulation. Robin Cohen (1999) provides a good explanation of some of these forms and also offers a detailed case analysis.

9 In its most extreme manifestation, in the words of Sassen, 'border enforcement is a mechanism facilitating the extraction of cheap labor by assigning criminal status to a segment of the working class – illegal immigrants' (Sassen, 1990: 36-37). One of the implications of this is that the national/foreign condition becomes a class position that entails more or fewer life opportunities within labour and, consequently, is a key factor in labour's internal differentiation.

all producers buy their supplies, including labour, at the same price, this does not happen in the world market because there is no free movement of labour, which, together with other reasons and consequences, allows neither rates of surplus value nor rates of profit to be uniformly distributed worldwide, but rather fragmented by states.[10]

The absence of free circulation of the labour force is essential to maintaining differentiated prices for labour and, therefore, enabling gains to be made from the real relations of exchange between the social formations and business entities that dominate the international division of labour. This factor also explains the historical interest of capital in controlling – at its own convenience – the import and export of this special 'commodity' in different local or regional labour markets.

The capitalist law of value would bring about uniform commodity prices – including labour prices – across the world if there were a world levelling of the rate of profit, which would only be viable in a homogenized capitalist world economy, with only one capitalist state. The reality, however, is that there are different markets, assembled into what we have seen fit to attribute the tendential characteristics of a 'system', and that spawns coordinated capitalist, semi-capitalist and pre-capitalist relations of production linked to each other through capitalist relations of exchange and dominated by a capitalist world market.

In summary, the increasing restrictions on mobility are a substantial part of the limitation or curtailing of individual autonomy. The extent of these restrictions is largely conditioned by the capital-labour relation, manifest in the various forms of bridling and the renewed labour force substitution capacity by means of the geographical mobility of capital and the incorporation of vast swathes of reserve populations, which intensify and extend the possibilities of importing and exporting labour.

This reached its climax with the second universalization of the capitalist system into a single world system, following the reintegration of the Second World (or 'Socialist World') and the incorporation of the entire world population into the capitalist market, as a single world labour force. This process also involved the incorporation of periphery zones that had only been partially incorporated before, with the consequent absorption, for the first time, of the world's female and peasant labour force.

---

10 In effect, if producers in one country are less efficient (with lower productivity), their prices will not be competitive and they will quickly be sanctioned by the market. In contrast, in the world market these producers may have even higher average profit rates, since they can take advantage of lower labour costs because there is no global price for labour power, among other factors. (For an in-depth economic explanation of this process and its consequences for inequality and exploitation between countries, see Valle [2000]).

The declining influence of all these populations on the labour markets leads to the loss of social negotiating power of the rest of the world's labour force, and by extension, the strengthening of capital's capacity to dominate it. These circumstances decisively contributed to a general increase in surplus value through the rise in all types of exploitation and overexploitation.

But ultimately, as we have seen, although relative mobility (specifically migration) has gradually gained importance, the labour force substitution process is inherent to the very transformation of the capitalist mode of production and has historically been expressed through a fundamental nexus: that which determines the step between the capitalist and the non-capitalist link of the economy, namely, absolute mobility.

Also today, the possibilities and limitations of absolute mobility have marked and conditioned the capital-labour relation, with all the implications it has for the social structure and the order of domination. In the following sections, we will explore these issues and also analyse the current capital-labour relation in terms of relative mobility.

Labour Force Reproduction in a Predominantly Non-Capitalist Environment

Historically, capitalist production originated and developed itself in a non-capitalist environment to the detriment of that environment. As a result, unwaged relations (indigenous communities, small farmers, artisans, retail traders) initially predominated over waged work in the active population. Today, there are few countries where the wage relation is still incipient (below 20 per cent), although it is important to note that these are also the countries with the poorest statistical records. Countries with less than 20 per cent waged labour of their economically active population (EAP) are found mainly, though not exclusively, in sub-Saharan Africa. In Latin America and the Caribbean, the only case is Haiti, and in Asia we observe this in countries like Afghanistan, Bangladesh, Cambodia and Laos.

The markets in these economies are not developed. In a non-monetized, basically communitarian economy, unwaged labour is not distinguished from waged labour. Both men and women primarily carry out unpaid work. Domestic labour is considered as another form of unwaged labour and is not yet differentiated from waged labour. The category of domestic labour actually is a recent development brought in with the monetization of social relations. The proportion of waged labour in Burkina Faso, Malawi, Rwanda and Cambodia is below 12 per cent and as such it concerns economies without the presence of a real market (ILO, 2010). It is interesting to note that there is very little difference between male and female activity rates in these countries. In fact, rates are around 90 per cent for both women and men between the ages of 15 and 60. Child labour in these countries, although very common, is more an issue of training and socialization into the local economy. Essentially these are communitarian economies where wage relations have not really penetrated and monetized relations are barely present in these incipient market economies.

In countries where wage relations are at their lowest level, as is particularly the case in sub-Saharan Africa, neocolonialism is currently an issue under debate. It concerns fragile nations, which are a relatively easy prey for neocolonial endeavours, as may be seen in the recent occupation of Haiti, the efforts to split Sudan into two parts or the invasion of Mali. The current struggles in these countries, therefore, tend to occur once again within the framework of decolonization. Subsidies for the production of staple grains in core countries lead to overproduction, which are exported to the periphery, albeit within the framework of cooperation. As long as these countries depend on these imports, any price increase in staple grains at an international level – due to speculation or the growing demand for biofuels – causes famine. Staple grain prices increased again from the second half of 2010. New famines were expected in 2012, accompanied by popular revolts in sub-Saharan countries. This may happen in the aforementioned Asian countries, Haiti and some Central American countries as well.

The Orgiastic Phase of Capital: High Labour Force Replacement Capacity

The case is different in periphery countries, whose economies are more deeply affected by market penetration and capital penetration. In this case, the dismantling of the non-capitalist nexus has advanced, with the consequent freeing up of the labour force to be incorporated into the capitalist nexus. In countries with a percentage of the EAP in waged labour between 20 per cent and 50 per cent, capital operations and domination are highly visible and exchange relations are substantially monetized. In these countries, therefore, capital has penetrated and dominates, even though wage relations are still secondary. Countries with a percentage of the EAP in waged labour between 20 per cent and 39 per cent, with available statistical information are: Cape Verde, Equatorial Guinea, Lesotho and Zimbabwe in Africa; and Bhutan, Malaysia, Indonesia, Mongolia, Nepal, Pakistan and Vietnam in Asia. In countries with a percentage of the EAP in waged labour between 40 per cent and 50 per cent, capital is somewhat more developed. In Africa, these countries are Ethiopia, Gabon and Morocco; in Asia, they are Syria,

Yemen and Thailand; and in Latin America, they are Bolivia, Paraguay and Honduras (ILO, 2010).

In those countries where the non-capitalist nexus still predominates, capitalists are able to replace or substitute a worn-out labour force with another recruited in the gradually dissolving non-capitalist nexus. The objective conditions in this case are such that capitalists are able to pay wages that are below subsistence levels even for one individual worker, let alone a family. This condemns workers to live in subhuman conditions, with no job stability or economic or social security. Consequently, the average useful lifespan of this labour force is reduced. To obtain a new job after the age of 35 years becomes very hard because of the loss of productivity due to, among other causes, unhealthy working conditions, malnutrition and appalling housing conditions, as revealed in a previous study (Dierckxsens, 1981).

When social relations are monetized, domestic work is increasingly regarded as unwaged work, as distinct from other remunerated activities. This leads to the social perception that home-based unwaged work is no longer seen as work; as this perception grows, women's participation in economic activity declines. Thus, in Pakistan, where 37 per cent of the EAP is in waged labour, the economic activity of women between the ages of 20 and 60 is a mere 15 per cent to 20 per cent. In Paraguay, where 48 per cent of the EAP is active as waged labour, women account for between 20 per cent and 30 per cent; and in Honduras, where 50 per cent of the active population is active in waged labour, female employment rates vary between 30 per cent and 45 per cent (ILO, 2010).

The destruction of the non-capitalist nexus does not advance at the same rate in all countries. In Bolivia, where barely 33 per cent of the EAP is active as waged labour, the employment rate of women during their most productive years fluctuates between 45 per cent and 55 per cent; in Indonesia, where 34 per cent of the EAP is active as waged labour, participation rates of the women oscillate between 50 per cent and 60 per cent. Zambia's EAP consists 30 per cent of waged labour and women's participation rates during their most productive years are between 50 per cent and 75 per cent. Although we cannot explore the details of each case, we may state that the strong communitarian economies in Zambia and Bolivia present more obstacles to capital expansion than the economies in Pakistan and Paraguay, which have a more advanced dissolution of non-capitalist relations. Non-capitalist ties in Zambia and Bolivia are more resistant to the penetration of capital due to the still active communitarian economy, and the distinction between waged and unwaged labour at home is, therefore, less marked. That is why female participation in the EAP remains high. Women are relatively well integrated in communal relations.

When a minority of the EAP is in waged labour, the labour force replacement capacity is very high, and especially when relations in the non-capitalist nexus are disintegrating fast. This high replacement capacity translates into the overexploitation of the labour force, manifested in long, exhausting working days, together with pitiful wages that force workers to live in insalubrious housing, or accept unstable work that prevents them from establishing sustainable family relationships, etc. Households frequently break up as a result of domestic and international migration in search of work. These households also tend to be made up of extended family, with distant family members and/or other strangers. Struggle for survival is the order of the day, and child labour is a frequent form of exploitation by the system.

When labour force replacement capacity is very high, workers are often dismissed at a relatively young age; therefore, their useful life expectancy for capital is relatively short. In the midst of this economic and social insecurity, the working class reproduces as a class, even though workers are unable to reproduce themselves with the minimum living conditions (Dierckxsens, 1982, chapter V). The constant destruction of the non-capitalist nexus also prevents them from achieving these conditions. Workers, living in extremely precarious circumstances and conscious of their perennial economic and social instability, perceive that they are not paid for their work, nor even for their labour force, and tend to rebel. However, their demands fall on deaf ears, which belong to the bourgeois class. The fact that the rebellious labour force can be substituted, with or without repression, acts to break up strike action and is an obstacle to effective organization. These countries are controlled by dictators, but the longer the objective situation of the labour force goes on, the more explosive it becomes.

The Stagnation of High Replacement Capacity: The Road to Revolution

The transition from a situation of high replacement capacity to one of low replacement capacity (where 70 per cent or more of the active population is waged) can be slow or become stagnated. The slower and more stagnated this transition occurs, the more favourable it will be for the conditions for protest to ripen and potentially turn into a revolutionary force. This is certainly the case in those countries where the market economy and capital have penetrated substantially, but not enough for the wage relation to be generalized. Specifically, these are societies with a bit more advanced wage relation (more than 40 per cent, but less than 66 per cent of the EAP) that, however, at the same time, has remained stagnant for decades, as seen in many periphery countries of Africa, Asia and particularly Latin America since the second half of the 20th century.

Today, the political situation in countries with an EAP in which the wage relation is between 50 per cent and 66 per cent will, in our view, demand great attention in the short term. We cannot give a complete picture of the situation in all these countries since statistics are not available for all of them. Figures for waged labour in some African countries are as follows: Algeria, 60 per cent; Egypt, 62 per cent; Namibia, 62 per cent; and Tunisia, 66 per cent. Available statistics for Asian countries include Fiji, 59 per cent; Iran, 51 per cent; Philippines, 51 per cent; Sri Lanka, 59 per cent; and Turkey, 59 per cent. Figures for Latin America and the Caribbean are: Brazil, 64 per cent; Colombia, 54 per cent; Dominican Republic, 54 per cent; Ecuador, 60 per cent; Guatemala, 50 per cent; Guyana, 52 per cent; Jamaica 61 per cent; Mexico, 66 per cent; Nicaragua, 51 per cent; Peru, 54 per cent; and Venezuela, 59 per cent (ILO, 2010). In other words, most of this continent can be considered as a time bomb.

In a country with a relatively large population (like China and India), greater investment is needed to achieve generalized wage relations than in smaller countries (like South Korea and Singapore). This does not mean that the demographic factor will determine stagnation of the wage relation, but the role of a country's demographic size should not be underestimated. A rapid transition process is not to be expected in China or India, with populations of over a thousand million, even when economic growth is high and sustained. India's, and especially China's, declining economic growth rates suggest that they can expect greater political instability, particularly if the world recession deepens.

Of the African and other Asian cases, rapid transition is reflected in the data for two countries (Algeria and Turkey), whereas four countries show clear stagnation (Tunisia, Egypt, Iran and Sri Lanka). In 1964, 37 per cent of Algeria's EAP was active as waged labour; in 1977, this figure had risen to 47 per cent and in 2004, almost 60 per cent. This is a rapid, but still incomplete, transition. EAP figures for Turkey in 1965 showed 22 per cent of waged labour; in 1975, 31 per cent, in 1988, 40 per cent and in 2008, almost 60 per cent. The objective scenario in both these countries is that new work opportunities are appearing, although replacement capacity and the consequent economic and social instability remain high. Without an objective economic base for reformism, political stability in these countries is not that bad but will remain fragile, particularly in times of recession. The cases of Egypt and Tunisia were without opportunities and completely stagnant. The rebellion in Tunisia and Egypt in January 2011 lit the fuse in the whole region and beyond. The Great Depression of the 21st Century augurs a situation of prolonged and deepening stagnation. From 2012-2013 on we expect to see the beginning of a period of radicalization of the popular revolts in these countries, with a clearer political profile and corresponding organization.

The Economic Base of Bourgeois Reformism and the Limits of Replacement Capacity

The more deeply capital penetrates the sectors and regions of a country, the greater the erosion of non-capitalist forms of production. The consequence of this process is the gradual transformation of the working class into an army of a waged labour force. The tendency for non-waged relations to disappear reduces the possibilities of substituting or replacing the worn-out labour force in the capitalist nexus with an ever-smaller possibility to recruit new labour force from elsewhere. In order to reproduce their labour force, a growing proportion of workers depend exclusively on the sale of the only commodity they possess, their labour.

In many countries today, more than two-thirds of the EAP is waged. All the European countries – including Russia and the eastern European countries – head this list, followed by the USA, Canada, Australia, New Zealand and Japan, where 80 per cent of the EAP is active as waged labour; and in some cases, the figure rises to over 90 per cent. A considerable number of periphery countries also fall into this range. In Latin America, these include Surinam (80 per cent), Argentina (75 per cent), Costa Rica (73 per cent), Chile (72 per cent), Uruguay (70 per cent) and Panama (69 per cent). In many Caribbean islands with small populations, over 66 per cent of the EAP is active as waged labour. These include Antigua, Aruba, Bahamas, Barbados, Cuba, Cayman Islands, Saint Kitts, Saint Vincent, and Trinidad and Tobago, all of which are over 80 per cent. Asian countries include Qatar (99 per cent), United Arab Emirates (97 per cent), Brunei (95 per cent), Macau (China) (91 per cent), Hong Kong (89 per cent), Oman (88 per cent), Israel (87 per cent), Singapore (85 per cent), Taiwan (75 per cent), Malaysia (74 per cent) and South Korea (68 per cent). In Africa, these countries include South Africa (82 per cent), Seychelles (81 per cent), Mauritius (79 per cent), Swaziland (76 per cent), Botswana and Namibia (73 per cent), and São Tomé and Príncipe (71 per cent) (ILO, 2010). This data shows the general tendency in periphery countries, where wage relations spread more easily because of relatively small populations. Economic shrinkage during the present economic downturn may, however, for the same reason, lead to greater shrinkage of the labour market and consequent political instability in these countries.

The reduction of the non-capitalist nexus to below 30 per cent of the EAP limits the labour force replacement capacity. As a class, capitalists are then obliged to extend the workers' average useful life. To maintain labour productivity throughout an increasingly extended period of life, the labour force must be conserved because the very source of profit can be sustained only in this way. The first social security system was introduced in Germany in the last quarter of the 19th century, and then spread to other European countries. In Latin America, social security appeared first in Chile (1923) and soon after that, in Uruguay and Argentina (Dierckxsens, 1981: 79 and 129). Costa Rica introduced it in 1948, when more than two-thirds of the country's EAP was active as waged labour. In 1985, Latin American countries with over 70 per cent of their EAP covered by social security were Argentina, Chile, Uruguay, Costa Rica and the Caribbean islands like Trinidad and Tobago mentioned earlier. Cuba has real universal coverage.

The extension of the average useful life of waged labour pushes up their average age of 'retirement'. For example, the average age of waged labour in Costa Rica is shifting towards 45 years, compared with an average of below 30 years in Honduras. To maintain levels of productivity at older ages, labour force preservation must be improved; hence, the social security system becomes a general necessity. Now, the reduced labour force replacement capacity in the capitalist nexus increasingly demands the replacement from one generation to another. As labour force replacement capacity falls, in the growing absence of the non-capitalist nexus, intergenerational replacement capacity has to be guaranteed through labour force reproduction within the family. At that point, the preservation and reproduction of the labour force in the family context becomes a necessary condition for the reproduction of capital. Capital can only reproduce itself as capital as long as the labour force reproduces itself, in other words, the labour force guarantees its own intergenerational replacement. From this moment on, the importance of the nuclear family acquires historical dimensions. In this period, women's participation in the labour market is relatively limited. The role of the housewife becomes strong.

As we cannot explore each individual case, some examples will have to suffice. In the 1980s and 1990s, more than 60 per cent of Costa Rican households were made up of couples either on their own or with unmarried children. The most extended households (the nuclear family with a married child or single relatives) represented 20 per cent of the total, a legacy from previous times. Single-parent families in Costa Rica accounted for less than 10 per cent and single person households, barely 5 per cent; together, these two types of households represented less than 15 per cent (Reuben, 1986: 16; Kuhlmann and Soto, cited in Barquero and Trejos, 2005). Today, single-parent families and single-person households together make up 60 per cent of all households in Germany and 67 per cent in Sweden and Denmark. In these countries, as we shall see later, labour force is no longer reproduced within the family context as a requirement for capital reproduction.

As the non-capitalist nexus disappears and labour force replacement capacity diminishes, workers' capacity for protest grows stronger. With the generalization of wage relations into more sectors and large companies, workers' organizational capacity also increases. As a result, wages tend to rise and the working day tends to be reduced. For this reason, the same type of work in a country with a low replacement capacity is better paid than that in a country where replacement capacity is high. Likewise, migration flows tend to go from countries with higher replacement capacities and more labour insecurity to those with greater economic and social stability. When the objective conditions for working class struggle rises, the bourgeoisie, as a class, becomes an interested party in the reproduction and preservation of the labour force. At this point, struggles over salaries and working conditions are less likely to take place on the battlefield and are increasingly resolved at the negotiation table. Trade unions are generally legally constituted. The picture of a peaceful relationship between two antagonistic classes begins to emerge. The state, essentially a repressive power in the past, now takes the form of a democracy. This is the era of the bourgeois democracy and the beginning of the so-called welfare state.

Increased wages, restrictions on child and female labour, the need for social security and other factors together limit the source of absolute surplus value and compromise the competitive position of the bourgeoisie relative to that of other countries where the wage relation is not so widespread. To guarantee their competitive position, the bourgeoisie have no alternative but to increase labour productivity. This requires greater technological development, which in turn demands a widespread and more developed education process, producing a skilled labour force, as distinct from an unskilled labour force.

The more specialized the labour force (physicians, for example), the fewer specialized educational institutions there tend to be (reproduction). And the fewer educational institutions there are to reproduce a certain skilled labour force, the more they will be able to influence supply in the labour market (through professional associations), their replacement capacity will be lower, and therefore, their wage in the market will be higher (Dierckxsens, 2000: 52). This leads to a situation where the higher the costs of reproduction of the labour force become, the need to preserve it becomes increasingly more urgent and important.

Increased technological development raises the demand for a skilled labour force. But because families that invest more in education tend to have fewer children than those with less education, demand of highly educated labour exceeds supply. The fact is that the unskilled labour force receives a wage to reproduce itself as unskilled, regardless of the aspirations it might have for its children. Workers with a smaller than the average family, on the other hand, are able to use the resources and the energy that would otherwise be spent on bringing up more children to ensure the upward social mobility of their (fewer) children. In effect, the costs of reproducing the labour force (within the family) are lower for smaller families compared with the average bigger family, and this saving can be invested to permit upward social mobility. So long as capital expansion continues, the state has a role in building and managing state schools. In times of economic downturn, such as the present, education and health cuts are generally the order of the day and social mobility tends to be downward.

The higher the level of education in a population, the higher its EAP participation rates will be. A continuing downturn of the replacement capacity of the (male) skilled labour force means that skilled women tend to be in demand and incorporated into the labour force. For this reason, economic participation rates of skilled women soon become high and not noticeably different from male rates. This holds for all countries, both at the centre and on the periphery. As we demonstrated empirically in the study *Del neoliberalismo al poscapitalismo* (Dierckxsens, 2000), for upward social mobility to continue from one generation to another, fertility rates must decline further. The average number of children per woman thus falls until the extreme is finally reached, in which generational replacement is not guaranteed anymore, a situation faced now by all core countries and beyond.

Capitalism not only increasingly demands a skilled labour force, but this labour force must also have experience. Part of the training that the skilled labour force receives is obtained by experience, and an experienced labour force is generally less replaceable than the one with no experience and, therefore, better paid. A more rapid technological innovation, however, implies that previously acquired experience quickly becomes obsolete, which in turn means that older adults become a hindrance to increasing or even maintaining labour productivity. Older generations (even highly skilled), therefore, again become more replaceable and are regarded as an inconvenience to capital. Capitalists, as a class, feel they must replace this labour force with a younger, more up-to-date labour force. Because the non-capitalist nexus has shrunk, the labour force can no longer be driven out in that direction. This situation has created the need to retire this labour force on old-age pensions, first introduced for the more highly skilled labour force, and later, when its replacement capacity declined, gradually also extended to the less skilled. In times of recession, when the non-capitalist nexus increases once again, there is mounting pressure to dismantle the social system in general, and the pension system in particular.

Differential Replacement Capacity in Male and Female Labour Forces

In the post-war period – the Keynesian era – the core countries experienced sustained increase in capital and with it the accelerated generalization of wage relations at a national level. This widespread incorporation of the labour force initially absorbed the entire available male labour force. In 1970, over 87 per cent of the *male* EAP in Sweden, Canada and the USA was active as waged labour; in Switzerland, Germany, the Netherlands and the United Kingdom, the figure was over 85 per cent; in Australia, New Zealand, Norway, Luxembourg, Denmark and France, it reached 80 per cent or more. Countries like Spain (73 per cent), Japan (70 per cent) or Portugal (66 per cent) came a little behind (ILO, 1990).

At that point, the male labour force replacement capacity fell sharply, and consequently, wages started to rise. It comes as no surprise that in this context, the 1970s saw the promotion of massive incorporation of women into economic activity. In Sweden, for example, from 1970 to 1991, the participation of women between the ages of 30 and 60 increased by more than 75 per cent. In 1991, female participation was slightly lower (5 per cent on average) than that of men of the same age. During the same period, Spain and Portugal still had a high male labour force replacement capacity, and consequently, the participation of women between the ages of 30 and 60 was still relatively low in the 1970s (below 15 per cent). Between 1971 and 1992, however, female participation grew notably in Spain; despite that, in 1992, female participation levels in Spain were still lower than those in Sweden 20 years earlier.

The widespread incorporation of women into the labour market had the effect of reducing the replacement capacity for the whole labour force at a national scale. In 1991, more than 90 per cent of Swedish men and women between the ages of 50 and 54 worked, as did over 80 per cent of those between 55 and 59. This reflects a very limited replacement capacity for both genders, with the result that wages tended to even out. In 1974, for example, 55.5 per cent of women in the US earned less than 75 per cent of the average wage; 20 years later in 1994, this figure had fallen to 42.5 per cent. Figures for the United Kingdom reflect a 17 per cent drop from 64.3 per cent to 53.3 per cent between 1974 and 1986. Due to the incorporation of women in the labour market, the male replacement capacity rose, which in turn reduced pressure on wage increase. As a consequence, the percentage of men in the United States earning less than 75 per cent of the average wage increased from 18.4 per cent to 27.3 per cent between 1974 and 1994. In the

United Kingdom, this percentage increased from 11.2 per cent in 1974 to 22.1 per cent in 1986, a rise of 97 per cent in 12 years. Although there are still clear differences in women's and men's earnings, the trend towards equilibrium shows two patterns: men's wages continue to fall while women's wages tend to rise (ILO, 1990).

However, the spread of paid labour among women does not mean that, as a gender group, they have left behind their subordinate position in society. Women are frequently hired for jobs serving other members of society and in subordinate roles. Executive and managerial positions have an overwhelmingly male bias. Therefore, the former subordination of unpaid labour (domestic labour) to paid labour, previously functionally used to ensure a more efficient accumulation of capital, is now substituted by badly paid jobs for women and in subordinate roles to male executives and managers in society in general.

On the surface, this situation appears to be the subordination of women to men. In effect, capital exploits different human resources depending on the productivity expected from different jobs. In other words, employers expect a better performance from women in subordinate roles than from men. This situation is changing as a result of women's campaigns and struggles, but it may take generations, in the same way as the division of labour in the household economy. As this situation is reproduced over time, labour markets become relatively segregated by gender, just as racist practices influence division on racial grounds.

With this generalization of female labour in the labour market, the family unit becomes increasingly superfluous as the unit of labour force reproduction. Women no longer need to marry in order to reproduce their own labour force, since they can do so on their own. Hence, women's 'emancipation' during capitalism is, in effect, 'emancipation' of the individual. This 'emancipation' process is presented as if each individual lives and achieves for him or herself, when, essentially, s/he lives and works for capital. Having children at an early age is incompatible with a career; it is very difficult to have more children on the basis of only one salary. For this reason, Sweden, Denmark and the Netherlands have twice as many single-person households as single-parent households. Single-person and single-parent households together represent more than two-thirds of all households in Sweden and Denmark, 60 per cent in Germany and more than 50 per cent in the Netherlands and Canada. The total fertility rate for each of these countries, therefore, is well below the generational replacement capacity. In 2010, the total fertility rate for Germany was 1.42 children per woman, in Canada it was 1.58, in the Netherlands 1.66, in Sweden 1.67 and in Denmark 1.74 (Dierckxsens, 2011: Part I).

International Migration, the Last Resort for Generational Replacement

With widespread female employment and a slow down of the generational replacement rate, mass immigration to core countries once again becomes commonplace. Immigration indirectly increases the non-migrant labour force replacement capacity, at least in the short term, and diminishes the pressure of rising wages for both men and women. Migration tends to occur from peripheral to core countries. The analysis we carried out did not take into account migration between former Soviet bloc countries. The main migration corridors identified from the periphery to the centre are: Mexico-USA, 11.6 million migrants; Turkey-Germany, 2.7 million; China-USA, 1.7 million; and the Philippines-USA, 1.7 million (Dierckxsens, 2011).

The main destination countries are the USA (42.8 million migrants), Germany (10.8 million), Canada (7.2 million), the United Kingdom (7.0 million), Spain (6.9 million), France (6.7 million) and Australia (5.5 million). The main migrant departure countries are Mexico and India, with 11.9 and 11.4 million departing migrants, respectively. Although Mexico is ranked first in absolute terms, international migration in relative terms reveals a veritable exodus from some smaller periphery countries: 56.8 per cent of the population has already emigrated from Guyana, 45.4 per cent from Albania, 39 per cent from Surinam, 36.1 per cent from Jamaica, 26.7 per cent from Trinidad and Tobago, 20.8 per cent from Portugal and 20.5 per cent from El Salvador (World Bank, 2011).

The question now is: how long will international migration act as a resort to sustain labour force replacement capacity in the core countries? In the medium term, immigration does not guarantee generational replacement capacity, and the gradual ageing of the population is, therefore, inevitable. Female migrants tend to be in their reproductive ages and so contribute better to population growth as compared with the native population. Immigrant women, however, have very similar reproduction patterns to the women of the destination country. Important waves of migration, therefore, may cushion population ageing in core countries, but not stop it. The process will continue if the total fertility rate does not guarantee generational replacement. Furthermore, if immigration is slowed down, as in the downturn of the second decade of the 21st century, population ageing will become more pronounced, which is considered a real problem.

One of the ways current neoliberal policies aim to cut expenditure on older adults is by raising the age of pension entitlement. In times of high unemployment, this leads to the increased impoverishment of the aged population. At the turn of the millennium, the average age of pension entitlement in countries with more advanced ageing populations, like Japan, was 68.5 for men and 64.7 for women, and participation rates for those between the ages of 60 and 64 were 76 per cent for men and 37 per cent for women. In the USA, pensionable age was 64.6 for men and 63.4 for women, but the participation rates between the ages of 60 and 65 were 55 per cent for men and 35 per cent for women. In the United Kingdom and Canada, pensionable age was 62.5 for men and 60.5 for women. Participation rates between the ages of 60 and 65 in Canada were just 48 per cent for men and 25 per cent for women, and in the United Kingdom, 57 per cent for men and 22 per cent for women. In the Netherlands and Germany, pensionable age was 60.4 for men and 60 for women; participation rates between the ages of 60 and 64 in Germany were only 31 per cent for men and 10 per cent for women, and in the Netherlands 22 per cent for men and 8 per cent for women. This latter figure corresponds approximately to a quarter of that for Japan (ILO, 2010).

This data clearly shows that raising the retirement age means postponing the inevitable. The problem is not that we grow increasingly older, but that the population structure becomes older as young people do not have children. If this dilemma is not resolved under the present rationale, though it appears unlikely, the core countries will soon be considered unviable since they will not be left with a future population base.

The Reverse Path: Towards Greater Replacement Capacity on a Global Scale

Today, there are two ways in which a nation may enter and remain in a situation of high replacement capacity with strong social movements. A periphery country may remain in a situation in which objective conditions for reformism have never been achieved because of permanent high labour replacement rates. Or, as in the central formations, societies can follow the 'reverse path' through a backward shift in socio-economic and political stability. This occurs when in countries where reformism has already been established, a considerable and relatively long-lasting growth in the labour force replacement capacity takes place with high and sustained unemployment rates. The first of these two was examined earlier; we now turn to the second path, that is, reversing low labour replacement rates.

The world in the 21st century is different. In the 19th century and the beginning of the 20th century, only the first of these situations was possible, since reformism was just beginning to emerge. In the second half of the 20th century, there is only one specific example of a shift from reformism in retreat to pursuing socialism through elections, namely, the case of Chile with president Allende. However, 21st century capitalism is completely different. Many countries nowadays have a strong and more or less prolonged record of reformism, and unlike in the 20th century, we no longer have real existing socialism as a reference, as was still the case when Chile decided to become a socialist project. Consequently, in light of the present crisis and probable depression of capitalism, the key question is: Is it possible to shift from reformism to a radical change in economic rationale? This 'reverse path' process typically starts off from a more or less consolidated phase of reformism but is inclined to deteriorate significantly due to the prolonged downturn. We explored this issue in Dierckxsens (1981) to analyse revolutionary potential in the 1980s. In the present world recession, it is pertinent to bring the diagnosis up to date.

Since the end of the 20th century, the labour force replacement capacity has continued to grow on a permanent basis. Employment flexibility in the core countries began with a process of simultaneous outsourcing of capital and investments along with immigration policies; the latter process came to an end with the current economic depression. Until 1980, national economies were relatively autonomous and consequently the labour market operated primarily within national boundaries. Between 1980 and 2010, however, the population of the globalized world economy – in other words, the population available to the interests of big capital – more than doubled. The globalization of this world labour market was reflected in the migration flows from the periphery to the centre and in capital flows from the centre to the periphery.

Since the mid-1980s, the population of the globalized world economy has risen from 2.5 thousand million to 6 thousand million people. According to an ILO study, the working class potentially available for transnational capital exploitation doubled from an EAP of 1.46 thousand million in 1985 to almost 2.93 thousand million in the year 2000 (Goldstein, 2009). In essence, then, the globalization of the world labour market meant a greater labour force replacement capacity across the world. This led to a worldwide trend – both at the centre and the periphery – in falling wages, increased working hours and deteriorating working and socio-economic conditions.

Since 2008, signs of a new World Depression have been evident with a dramatic rise in unemployment rates and the consequent worsening of economic and social instability, particularly in the core countries. In Spain, Greece and the USA, real unemployment rates of 25 per cent are seen among the general population, rising to 50 per cent amid the younger population (between the ages of 16 and 24). In this context, it is pertinent to raise the issue of a possible popular challenge to the prevailing economic rationale in the core countries. A prolonged downturn will erode many socio-economic rights acquired in the past, the result of which will be a crisis of legitimacy of the existing social relations. This will reopen a political space in the core countries for (new) left-wing movements and parties that may question the very essence of the current economic rationale.

However, under reformism, faith in the peaceful path towards greater well-being was established and consolidated, and this faith will not be destroyed overnight. For this reason, initially the popular masses continue to firmly believe in the previous situation based on existing social relations. Defence of the former socio-economic situation at all costs and at any price, even at the cost of others, falls on fertile ground and may spawn ultraconservatism. When faced with an exclusive system, the first challenge is not to the excluding system, but to exclusion itself. The more economic and social rights gained previously, the greater the sense of a right to inclusion. By defending the inclusion of some on the basis of constructed historical rights, anyone who did not participate in their construction is condemned to exclusion.

It is this thinking that gives rise to the greater 'right' to inclusion demanded by full citizens over immigrants; by men over women; by state formations with an older, more developed citizenship (Germany) over those with a more recent, less consolidated reformism (Greece, Portugal, Spain, etc.); by one culture (Western) over all others, etc. This situation leads to an 'every man for himself' ideology, which becomes stronger the closer the 'economic ship' comes to sinking. The first-class passengers – the population of the core countries – appropriate the entitlement to be 'chosen' when the global economy ship (the Titanic?) goes down. This involves an ultra right-wing ideology inclined towards (neo-)fascism, or at any rate, authoritarian regimes.

Might the reverse path not only lead to a resurgence of neo-fascism, but also bring about a widespread challenge to the present social relations of production? Two trends can be seen with regard to the Great Depression of the 21st Century. In the Nordic countries, where reformism developed most profoundly and over the longest period, replacement capacity has been low for many years. Drastic labour flexibility policies were required to achieve international competitiveness. In other words, the socio-economic conditions of the working population had to be heavily curtailed in these countries so that capital could be competitive in labour costs. Countries such as Sweden, Denmark or the Netherlands cultivated this faith in bourgeois democracy – the peaceful, socially inclusive and tolerant society – more than anywhere else. At the beginning of the downturn, the popular masses reaffirmed their faith in the sacred existing relations of production and reminisced about times gone by. Since then, they have constantly demanded a return to the good times, no matter how or at what cost.

The uncompromising defence of the status quo at any cost, that is, at the cost of tolerance and solidarity of any kind, has led to the xenophobia and the right to save one's own skin at the expense of everyone else now being witnessed in Europe in the widespread attitude towards the Mediterranean countries. It is precisely in the coalition governments of Sweden, Denmark and the Netherlands that clear traits of neo-fascism can be seen.

Obviously, this tenacious defence, using all available means – including military – was to be expected from the country that is now conclusively losing its hegemony: the USA. As the Observatorio Internacional de la Crisis (2010) reports, the threat of a new large-scale war is not beyond the bounds of possibility. Indeed, it is a real possibility, given that the first two world wars followed global depressions, although it is also true that, historically, the break with the prevailing rationale grew more radical during the inter-war period.

We are not claiming that the neo-fascist trend is absent from southern European countries, or in the peripheries where reformism is more recent, or in those countries where democracy exists formally (Latin America) but not in substance. It is true that reformism in many countries has been neither deep-seated nor lasting, and in other cases it has only had a token presence. In Latin America, for instance, during the neoliberal era, many dictatorships were replaced by formal democracies, but these were in name only. Nonetheless, in more than one of this type of formal, content-less democracy, the electoral route has opened up scenarios of disconnection, processes that under a dictatorship might have only been achieved through revolution. The electoral route to an alternative has, therefore, gained political topicality.

In this context, it is also not surprising that social discontent arose first in the south of Europe. The downturn started to deepen 2012 onwards, and a radicalization of this indignation may become apparent in more political approaches. In central European countries, in the short term, the trend towards conservatism seems to be stronger than the emergence of a revitalized left to challenge the core of the system's rationale. However, the longer the crisis lasts and the deeper it grows, the more radical the political landscape will become.

Final Considerations

In sum, the factors outlined earlier have, for the moment, led to the proletarianization of most of the world's population. They have kept the labour force in an objective condition of widespread competition within its own ranks, due particularly to its increasing substitutability or replacement capacity offered by the vast global *reserve army* ready and waiting to enter the capitalist nexus (absolute mobility). These factors have also contributed to the constant and growing willingness to migrate, besides other forms of relative mobility. All the trends of a declining late capitalism (with the predictable death rattles of transnational capitalism) indicate that, in the absence of a rejoinder from labour as a historical subject, the difficulties people face in planning their own movements, enjoying freely assumed mobility (automobility) or even choosing immobility (De Gaudemar, 1979 and 1981) are far from diminishing; in fact, they may substantially increase. It is for precisely this reason that autonomy of movement is increasingly becoming a distinctive class factor (Bauman, 2001; Boltanski and Chiapello, 2002) in a world with increasingly restricted freedom, in which people have been universally transformed into this special commodity known as the labour force, with different prices and, therefore, available to facilitate unequal accumulation in the various social-state formations that humanity is now divided into.

All of this would be impossible without the growing proletarianization and incorporation of increasing sectors of humanity, or without the highly regulated restrictions on their free cross-border geographical mobility, or without state intervention to ensure their unequal status and socio-political condition.

Hence, for now, the unequal value of the world labour force is maintained, together with its debilitated social negotiating power and its weakened possibilities to arise as a force of opposition.

But this reconstitution of labour as a historical subject, expressed in collective autonomy, is the only one that can reverse the growing restrictions on individual autonomy. Similarly, this means that class struggles must also necessarily lock into the network of living labour exogenization mechanisms in pursuit of the permanence or elimination of the differential class position grounded in (or in the different life opportunities outside) the 'national' division (autochthonous-heterochthonous) of labour. And, why not? They could turn around the process of absolute mobility from inside to outside the capitalist nexus.

The present universalization of the capitalist market and its consequent formation of a single world labour force entail new challenges and possibilities, taking the capital-labour class relation to a global scale, opening up possibilities for the reconstitution or redefinition of labour agency also on a worldwide scale.

References

Arrighi, Giovanni. 1999. *El largo siglo XX*. Madrid: Akal.

Barquero, J. and J. Trejos. 2005. 'Household Types, Family Life Cycle and Poverty in Costa Rica' (Translation of Spanish Version). The Population of the

Central American Isthmus in 2003 Conference Papers. Los Angeles: California Center for Population Research.

Bauman, Zygmunt. 2001. *La Postmodernidad y sus descontentos*. Madrid: Akal.

Boltanski, Luc and Ève Chiapello. 2002. *El nuevo espíritu del capitalismo*. Madrid: Akal.

Cohen, Robin. 1999. *The New Helots: Migrants in the International Division of Labour*. Aldershot: Ashgate.

De Gaudemar, Jean-Paul. 1979. *Movilidad del trabajo y acumulación de capital*. Mexico City: Ediciones Era.

———. 1981. *La movilización general*. Madrid: La Piqueta.

Dierckxsens, Wim. 1981. *Política y Población*. San José: DEI.

———. 1982. *Capitalismo y Población*. Mexico City: Nuestro Tiempo.

———. 2000. *Del Neoliberalismo al poscapitalismo*. San José: DEI.

———. 2011. *Población, fuerza de trabajo y rebelión en el siglo XXI.* Bogotá: Ediciones Desde Abajo.

Goldstein, Fred. 2009. *Low Wage Capitalism*. New York: World View Forum.

Gordon, David, Richard Edwards and Michael Reich. 1994. 'Long Swings and Stages of Capitalism', in D. Kotz, T. McDonough and M. Reich (eds.), *Social Structures of Accumulation*. Cambridge: Cambridge University Press.

ILO. 2010. *Key Indicators of the Labour Market* (KILM). Sixth edition. Geneva: ILO.

———. 1990. *Anuario de Estadísticas de Trabajo 1945-1989*. Geneva: ILO.

Moulier-Boutang, Yann. 2006. *De la esclavitud al trabajo asalariado. Economía histórica del trabajo asalariado embridado*. Madrid: Akal.

Observatorio Internacional de la Crisis. 2010. *El mundo en la encrucijada de la Gran Depresión.* San José: DEI.

Piqueras, Andrés. 2007. *Capital, migraciones e identidades*. Castelló: Universitat Jaume I.

Potts, Lydia. 1990. *The World Labour Market: A History of Migration*. London and New Jersey: Zed Books.

Reuben Soto, Sergio. 1986. 'Política social y familia', Contrapunto No. 8, http://ccp.ucr.ac.cr/seminario/pdf/reuben.pdf.

Sassen, Saskia. 1990. *The Mobility of Labour and Capital: A Study in International Investment and Labour Flows*. Cambridge: Cambridge University Press.

Valle, Alejandro. 2000. 'Desarrollo desigual y competitividad', in J. Arriola and D. Guerrero (eds.), *La nueva economía política de la globalización*. Bilbao: Universidad del País Vasco.

World Bank. 2011. 'Migration and Remittances Factbook'. Accessed at: http://www.worldbank.org/prospects/migrationandremittances.

CHAPTER 8

Notes on the *Class Struggle* in Late Capitalism

Andrés PIQUERAS

University of Castellón Jaume I, Spain

On the Structural Limits of Capitalism

In the central social formations at the end of the 1960s, and particularly following the 1973 economic-oil crisis, the Keynesian growth model, linked to what was known as 'organized capitalism', began to show signs of demise, which also brought about the predominance of the reformist or 'social democratic' option in capital/labour relations.

That collapse can be explained by certain structural factors that have ultimately worsened to leave capitalism increasingly degenerated; however, these factors are not addressed in institutional explanations of the crisis.

Automation, or the general tendency of forces of production to develop, which is inherent to capitalist accumulation (and which underlies the permanent weakening of social relations and the created structures involved in this mode of production), presents various contradictory processes:

1. On the one hand, automation generally leads to a greater use of (and innovation in) capital intensive technologies, or in other words, less use of labour force per unit of invested capital, and in sum, less living labour in the direct production and restructuring of the labour force's qualifications. Implicit in this process are:
    a. The devaluation of labour, replacing workers' knowledge with machinery.[1]
    b. A structural tendency towards the elimination of jobs.[2] But at the same time, and with the significant reduction in manual

[1] Science goes beyond collective labour to establish universal labour, which accumulates infinitely across generations, forming a stock of free knowledge that increasingly intervenes in production and is privately appropriated by capital (see Martins, 2009).

[2] This results in growing demands for increased GDP to guarantee the creation of jobs (which also sustains the tendency to destroy more jobs during each capitalist recession

labour, automation redefines the social demands of labour, shifting them towards intellectual work, linking productivity to the increased value of the labour force, which then depends on the increased time spent training workers. Capital counteracts this contradiction by reducing the price of intellectual labour through importing cheaper qualified labour. It does so as well by the restructuring of education to lower the cost of providing this labour force (see the Bologna process in Europe). The widespread expansion of a specific technology takes care of the rest, by increasing the quantity of qualified labour consistent with this expansion and weakening the value of this labour force with each new advance.

c A chronic process of over-accumulation of invested capital per unit of value that it is able to generate. As the relative weight of fixed capital to variable capital increases in the organic composition of capital, the profit it is able to generate falls proportionally. In other words, as the mass of value represented by the labour force decreases, the impacts of increased productivity on the rise in the rate of surplus value become increasingly restricted, and the conversion of extraordinary surplus value into extraordinary profits, the basic aim of capitalist investment, is also limited.[3]

---

than can be regained in the subsequent recovery (Katz, 2010). In both the United Kingdom and the United States, for example, unemployment among unskilled young people is around 22 per cent. The number of people in involuntary under-employment in these two countries is currently around 14 per cent. A great deal of investment and cyclical reversal capacity is required to enable them to enter the labour market in a normalized ('competitive') way.

3 One of the main explanations of this process is as follows. As the organic and technical composition of global social capital increases, the rate of surplus value also increases (the proportion of *excess labour* to *necessary labour* is higher). However, the total mass of surplus value does not increase in the same proportion. This is because the necessary labour (that which workers are paid for to reproduce their labour power) left over for capitalization shrinks dramatically as this investment and organic composition of capital advances. In other words, 'necessary labour' decreases at the same rate as the increase in 'excess labour' (i.e., that worked by producers exclusively for the profit of those who buy their labour power). But as this necessary labour diminishes, appropriating the remaining labour becomes more costly. 'Through each advance in labour productivity, part of the remaining collective working day is reduced; this necessary labour time becomes surplus and is appropriated by capitalists in the form of surplus value for the purposes of accumulation' (GPM, 2012: 1). This leads to a fall in the general rate of average earnings, regardless of whether certain capitalists might increase their profit rate (for a more in-depth, numerical explanation of this issue, see Piqueras [2011]). This arises as a result of a growing 'over-accumulation' of capital in relation to its capacity to generate profits.

2. On the other hand, and as a result, an increasingly onerous R&D battle is unleashed, since rapid technological obsolescence does not allow invested capital to be amortized satisfactorily.

These processes underlie the *crisis of value* of capital that triggered the decline of Keynesianism and are the source of the profound or historical cause of the anguished prolongation of capitalism's current degeneration, a decline that the capitalist system has only been able to escape fleetingly or 'fictitiously', as we explain later.

On Attempts to Escape the Limits: 'The Class Struggle' from Above

In effect, since then capital as a historical subject has attempted to recover its profit rates through an interwoven array of measures that represented a new disorganization of the mode of production, which, at the same time, achieved global heights and involved a unilateral class offensive on all fronts against the population that lives by its labour.

A new model of accumulation came into being, known as the neoliberal model, some of the main foundations of which are as follows:

1. Increased exploitation of the labour force.

This occurs both extensively (length of working day, extra hours, increased number of days worked per year, raising of the retirement age, etc.) and intensively (through the technification of production processes and, in general, through the development of forces of production).

These changes met with little resistance from the population due to the high labour force replacement capacity afforded to capital by essentially three factors:

- Mass importation of labour and, in general, the creation of a global labour force with increasing migratory potential, ready to act as a universal reserve army;
- the growth of this universal reserve army when the Second World (USSR, China, etc.) entered the capitalist sphere, providing a far cheaper workforce; and
- business relocation, which entails companies emigrating to places where the labour force is cheaper, the fiscal demands less stringent and raw materials and energy resources are closer at hand.

As a result, the working population's social bargaining power plummeted everywhere, and trade union strength was seriously diminished. (The unions, moreover, had adapted their structures and strategies to agreements and institutionalized conflict).

This is clearly seen in the loss of purchasing power among the general labour force, and the redistribution of social wealth in favour of capital that has taken place during the neoliberal era.[4]

2. Exacerbated spatial displacement of capital.

'Exportation' of part of the surplus capital to the peripheries of the system, where the over-accumulation process has not yet occurred (because of the lower organic composition of capital, or the incorporation of sectors that are still not entirely organized on capitalist lines), with a view to making a profit there, and where production costs are also lower.

Such capital has been mainly exported either in the form of direct investment (with a high repatriation of profits) or as loans that guarantee future interests to be collected (such as interests on interests, etc.).[5]

3. Accumulation by dispossession or universal plundering (as in the 'primitive' accumulation of capital).
    - Privatization of social and cultural wealth accumulated over generations (among other aspects, this affects public services such as health, education, transport and communications; public infrastructure like rail networks or installations; and built heritage).

---

4 In Spain, the refined participation of salaries fell from almost 75 per cent to 61 per cent of the GDP, calculated at factor costs, between 1967 and 2007, which is consistent with the fact that the average real salary has been practically stagnant since the beginning of the 1980s. The number of hours worked has also risen: according to the figures for the years 1999 and 2002 from the CIS (Spanish National Survey of Working Conditions), 46.4 per cent of workers worked longer than the nominal working day, and a fifth of all salaried workers (22.3 per cent) were not paid for these extra hours. According to Eurostat, full-time employees work an average of 8.5 extra hours per week, of which 4.7 hours are unpaid (meaning that more than 10 per cent of the regular working day, determined through negotiated agreements, is given to the employer at no cost) (on these data, see Schweiger and Rodríguez [2007]). This does not refer to temporary work or the general precariousness of the Spanish labour market, which is one of its most significant characteristics, affecting 30 per cent of low-skilled jobs in 2009 compared to the EU average of 17 per cent; and 23 per cent of higher-skilled jobs, compared to 11 per cent in Europe. The rate of temporary work is much higher among immigrants with a job contract. Spain registered a 44 per cent rate of temporary employment among immigrants as compared to an average of 24 per cent for the Spanish-born population, which sets it apart from other countries.

5 So-called development cooperation has been the traditional tool and channel used in both processes, with striking persistence in the latter, which generates huge amounts of repayable debt from the peripheries to the centres of the system. In the mid-1990s, the peripheries were repaying around 200,000 million dollars a year solely as interest on debt (a large part of which had been caused by 'development aid'. In 2007 the total amount of debt (public and private) of all peripheral social formations amounted to 3 trillion 360,000 million dollars.

- Privatization of natural heritage. Commercialization of nature in all its forms (dramatic reduction of available resources).
- Land-grabbing. Elimination of communal or collective properties. Displacement of peasant populations (replacing peasant or family agriculture with agribusinesses; and disappearance of alternative forms of production and consumption).
- Commercialization of genetic resources.
- Intellectual property rights or patents taken out on others' resources.
- Corporatization and privatization of public institutions (such as universities and even government administrations).
- Direct military appropriation of the most sought-after resources and raw materials.

This dispossession also includes the regressive policies that concentrate wealth in the hands of the capitalist class (distribution of collective wealth to the capitalist class), which has, among others, the following pivotal points:

- Reduction in employers' social security contributions.
- Regressive tax reforms.
- Increased opportunities for surplus capital investment through mass privatizations.
- Cuts in the corporate contribution to society as a whole. Essentially, more tax exemptions for high capital rents and the rich in general, while the tax burden on the working population continues to grow.[6]

---

6 In Spain in 1995, labour was taxed at 16.4 per cent, whereas tax on capital was 7.4 per cent, less than half that amount. Thirteen years later, in 2008, the situation had hardly changed: 16.7 per cent for labour taxes and 8.6 per cent for capital taxes. This means that tax collected today from the working population is more than nine times the total amount collected from capital, without taking into account consented tax evasion, such as consented tax havens. According to GESTHA, the organization of technical staff and inspectors of the Spanish Department of Taxation (http://www.gestha.es/), tax evasion by large Spanish fortunes and corporations totalled 42,771 million euros in 2010 alone. If evasion by small- and medium-sized companies is added to this figure, according to the same source, the total rises to 59,030 million euros. When social security fraud perpetrated by the informal economy is included, the huge sum of 90,000 million euros is reached (subsequent rectifications to the data take the first of these two sums up to 70,000 million euros and the total to somewhere over 100,000 million euros). In the period 2010-2013, the PSOE (Spanish Socialist Workers' Party) government introduced social cuts of 50,000 million euros. In other words, all cuts could be avoided if the agents of capital paid their share (which is already proportionally low compared to tax paid by the rest of society). Even before the crisis at the end of the first decade of the new century, Spanish data shows that

4. Techno-organizational displacement towards what is known as 'immaterial' production, leading to a certain 'software-ization' of the economy.[7]
5. Substantial reduction of capital channelled into investment in production. Because the profitability of productive capital is increasingly less secure due to the process of over-accumulation, capital has taken flight towards loans and stock market 'gambling', that is, basically speculation, relying on the mistaken belief that money can continuously generate more money on its own, independent of production. But behind this illusion, what it actually generated was a colossal inverted pyramid of credit-debt and speculative capital in relation to real capital. In other words, a huge amount of fictitious capital was created, actually the main driver of the brief and timid neoliberal boom in profit rates, which is why we term it 'fictitious' here (and which is another mechanism for appropriating generated collective wealth without having contributed in any way to its generation).

In the *BIS Quarterly Review* of June 2011, the Bank for International Settlements reported receiving banking data till December 2010 for a total of 601 billion dollars in issued derivatives, which represents more than 10 times the global GDP. However, other sources estimate this amount of fictitious capital to be around 30 times the 'real' global wealth (see Dierckxsens, 2011b).

This has been possible because of the deregulation of the banking and financial systems, which allowed growth funded by borrowing (a process known as 'leveraging'; in this case we refer to 'fictitious growth', since leveraging was done with 'fictitious' capital). At the same time, states relinquish their sovereignty, allowing central banks their independence, and issue debt securities in the global financial markets. States are, therefore, ranked alongside all other financial entities in the 'international risk ratings' determined by private agencies and are obliged to implement orthodox monetary and fiscal policies that are subjected to the interests of international financial capital.

This package of measures as a whole has required the elimination of controls over world capital flows, which implicitly entails the

---

expenditure on social protection was reduced from 22.8 per cent to 20.8 per cent of the GDP between 1994 and 2005 (Navarro, 2009). Although much higher initially, EU expenditure on social protection also fell between 1993 and 2002 from 27.4 per cent to 26.9 per cent of the GDP (Colectivo IOE, 2008).

7 The 'computer revolution' was at the basis of what was termed the 'new economy', which would supposedly trigger a virtuous cycle of growth, but which ended at the end of the 1990s with the cataclysmic dot-com stock market crash.

transnationalization of productive, commercial, financial and speculative capital. Concern for governance or governability for capital on a global scale is determined by this transnationalization, to ensure that this set of interventions can be implemented without labour revolt.

But the combination of this latter aim with the previous ones can only be achieved at the expense of a significant reduction in the quality of democracy, even in the realm of consumption or the circulation of capital (see note 7), along with the degradation of citizenship. Indeed, the really decisive agencies increasingly fall outside any citizen election or intervention possibilities because they are supra-state entities, distanced from any election process or citizen control, whereas elected bodies are gradually losing meaningful content. This is also in line with capital's increasing renouncement of any mediation by administrators, managers or bureaucrats (increasingly termed the 'political class', however erroneously) in order to further their class domination. Instead, capital has moved towards taking direct control of managing society, opting increasingly to use the state as a class instrument and making the process increasingly visible, a strategy that, on the other hand, may undermine its legitimacy.

But at the moment perhaps, capital's greatest problem with regard to governance and management of accumulation at a global scale lies in its inability to provide a ruling-administrative body for this global dimension (as the state was for the national dimension).

On the Persistence of Limits: Degenerative Capitalism

No less of a problem in the sphere of immediate reproduction is the fact that the organic composition of capital has continued to rise despite all the efforts described earlier and the resource of extensive exploitation of both the old and the new labour forces. The increase in the ratio of machinery to labour has taken place in all sectors involved in transnational business activity. The computerization of production processes, specifically that which was initially designed to trigger a new cycle of capital accumulation, was especially responsible for this change.

This has made the link between capitalism and employment an increasingly difficult one.

By the year 2006, the 'replacement effect' – the replacement of manual work by computers or computer systems – was occurring at an annual rate of 7 per cent in the service sector, bringing an end to secure employment in the 'more advanced' capitalist countries.

This process of substituting waged labour left

> the job market [...] currently polarized: A great many of the middle-skill jobs that used to support a solid middle class lifestyle have been automated – leaving

> us with high skill/high wage jobs that require lots of education and training and lots of low skill jobs with very low wages. (Ford, 2011)[8]

All of this hinders the creation of sufficient jobs and adequate wages to maintain a robust final demand. The high possibilities for the existence of middle classes in advanced capitalist countries has declined because the conditions that created these classes no longer exist, namely, secure jobs and decent salaries.

Therein lies the great capitalist drama, since in the end it depends on who makes the final consumption, which only has a fleeting connection with the state (as an intermediary), and in the final instance largely rests with citizens themselves (without whom state consumption would also dry up). The serious systemic contradiction of capitalism (the great weakness of capital against labour) is precisely that producers and consumers are the same agents. The more the producers' purchasing and general living conditions deteriorate, the more their very bases for functioning as a system are undermined.[9]

For this reason, the attempt to solve the crisis of value by impoverishing the population and curtailing public spending has generated yet more obstacles to the creation of profits (that can only be raised through sales). This is known as the 'crisis of realization', which, despite all attempts to avoid it through credit, built-in obsolescence of products or luxury consumption, among other options, has only been aggravated by mounting social and wage cuts. As a result, the now chronic crisis of value has become even deeper, entering into an overproduction-underconsumption loop that in other moments in history was only abandoned by means of economic expansion into new territories, or war.

Far from combating this loop, the measures taken are procyclical, in other words, they perpetuate and reinforce the crisis. Hence, the growing timidity of state investment, the depletion of social services, the lowering of salaries, the increased taxes for the working population, the widespread loss of purchasing power among the population and the dramatic drop in consumption, all contribute to worsening the crisis of realization (i.e., by obstructing sales, which is how capitalist profits are made). Similar to and consistent with this process is the substantial loss of quality of

---

8 Martin Ford refers to the paper by Autor and Dorn (2011).

9 Also for this reason, the only democracy that capitalism has been able to put forward is a *schizophrenic democracy*: opening fees can be gained in the sphere of circulation or from realized surplus value, where people are susceptible to becoming *consumers-citizens*, but the system cannot offer any democracy in the sphere of production or generation of surplus value, where people are *labour force commodities*, deprived of decision and vote in the production-distribution-consumption process.

democracy in the system as a whole and an increase in repressive aspects of the system in response to the growing difficulty to integrate through consumption (this means that democratic options are also reduced in the sphere of circulation: as consumers' possible 'choices' decline, likewise the possibilities for constitution and options as citizens also decline and associated political rights are jeopardized or they deteriorate).

In summary, the class war from above, unilaterally unleashed by capital when in the central societies labour had sleepily become integrated in the capitalist consumer order (although in recent decades this was due to credit – also fictitious to a large extent), only proclaims the exhaustion of the possibilities of reformism.

We now turn to some other considerations that reinforce this limit. On the one hand, the chances of consumer capitalism based on the central society model spreading to the rest of the planet are practically nil, and are increasingly fraught in the centres of the system, given that:

a. The earth's carrying capacity is exhausted with the present global population of 7,000 million people. There is no 'natural' way of preventing this figure from rising to 10,000 million by 2050 (except through environmental or health catastrophes or war).[10]

b Many of the basic energy and material resources that sustain late capitalism have reached or are close to their peak extraction levels.

[10] I am grateful to my colleague Paulo Campanario at the Observatorio Internacional de la Crisis for pointing this out. According to a study published in 2010 by Global Footprint Network, an organization with a long history of monitoring human impact on the environment and whose scientific methodology is described on its website, the world ecological footprint was 2.7 hectares per inhabitant in 2010. In contrast, the biocapacity (the resources actually available on the planet per surface area and citizen) was calculated at 1.8 hectares per person. In other words, on average each person is consuming one hectare more than the actually available resources, which translates in an overexploitation of the planet with potentially dramatic consequences. This consumption, however, is clearly not evenly distributed; 15 per cent of the population, located mainly in the central formations, consumes 6.1 hectares per inhabitant when its biocapacity is half that amount. In contrast, the ecological footprint of the remaining 85 per cent is practically the same as its biocapacity. In other words, the vast majority of the planet's citizens live sustainably in their environment. Only 15 per cent upset the balance, which they can afford to do only by consuming the resources of others. According to Global Footprint Network, 22 August 2012 was earth overshoot day, the date when the planet entered into ecological deficit. The available resources for that year had been used up in less than 9 months. The report's warning for the immediate future is that 'even with modest UN projections for population growth, consumption and climate change, by 2030 humanity will need the capacity of two Earths to absorb carbon dioxide waste and keep up with natural resource consumption' (Global Footprint Network, 2011, emphasis original). For the central social formations to continue consuming these scarce resources, everybody else has to stop doing so. To achieve this objective and also prevent their hegemonic, economic and political-military decline, the only option left to these declining centres is war.

Other resources will reach these levels in the decades up to 2050 (Dierckxsens, 2011a).[11]

On the other hand, if the periphery economies (with scant internal demand, not easily reversed at present) linked to the two drivers of globalization, the USA and the EU, were incorporated, it does not seem likely that they would substitute the central formations in medium-term growth and global demand by continuing to follow this systemic logic.

The separation of other social formations would then follow another socio-economic logic outside the capitalist law of value (or at least limiting it considerably), which for future continuity would also require regional integrations of great scope and intensity (such as a Latin America union).

This separation could be favoured by the growing delegitimization of the capitalist mode of production and its intra- and inter-state forms of domination, similar to the substantial and generalized decline of possibilities for consumption and claiming social benefits in its centres (with degraded citizenships). These central formations will predictably also lose the capacity to attract the rest of the planet through the 'demonstration effect' of wealth and 'welfare' that the capitalist system is capable of generating and has flaunted to date.

In addition to the processes described above, the outcome is a serious deterioration of some of the connections that capitalist-Western civilization had spread across the world and that have become practically synonymous with capitalism:

- capitalism and growth
- capitalism and welfare
- capitalism and democracy

To these must also be added the increasingly widespread and profound questioning of:

- the myth of development

Taken together, they explain the now declining capacity of late capitalism to:

- employ the population that it proletarianizes[12]

---

11 Also, in general, the work of the Observatorio Internacional de la Crisis (http://www.observatoriodelacrisis.org), and work on political ecology. See also, for example, Fernández Durán (2011) on this subject.

12 Since the mid-1980s, the population of the globalized world economy has more than doubled, from 2,500 million to 6,000 million people. According to the International Labour Organization (ILO), the working class potentially available for exploitation by transnational capital doubled from an economically active population of 1,460 million in 1985 to almost 2,930 million in 2000. The ILO report of 2011 stated that on a

- transform money into capital.[13]

Equally, the idea that quality of life is enhanced by the incessant production of commodities or the infinite reproduction of the exchange value is also increasingly challenged. In contrast, in a world of finite resources (with an ever-smaller biocapacity), only the prevalence of values of use, of forms of production with a high possibility of natural replacement, can open channels of acceptable survival for all humanity.

But that would unquestionably require abandoning the present mode of production and embarking on a widespread post-capitalist transition.

The possibilities for this transition seem necessarily linked to some unavoidable key questions: what is the link between deterioration and majority rebellion? How and when might widespread disaffection occur? What possibilities will this disaffection have to put forward projects for a different mode of production?

The negative response that has been given to the first question is largely explained by the potential for restraint that global capitalism has shown to date thanks to its enormous labour replacement capacity,

---

global scale, the employment-to-population ratio, which indicates whether a country or region's capacity to generate employment is increasing or in decline, fell from 61.7 in 2007 to 61.2 in 2009, and in 2010 it was around 61.1 per cent. Of the 64 countries for which quarterly data was available up to the second quarter of 2010, twice as many had a declining employment-to-population ratio as those with a growing ratio. In 56 countries for which data was available, according to the ILO report, the labour market was 1.7 million young people short of forecasts based on long-term observed trends. This finding reflects a considerable increase in despondency among young people, who are not included in unemployment figures because they are not actively seeking work. In consequence, references are now made to a 'lost generation' in an increasing number of countries. International unemployment figures, which stood at around 210 million in 2010, are only a pale reflection of the real situation, since these do not include the huge contingents of people who make up the informal, grey, black economy, the self-employed or mere subsistence economy, nor those who remain beyond the boundaries of their own capacity to reproduce.

13 Capitalism today has no 'engine', no 'locomotive' to pull it, no 'universal' economic sector that could impact all other sectors and take it forward, as did the railways in the 19th century or the motor industry in the 20th century. The 'light' nature of the IT sector, which has expanded universally across the entire economy, seems to be a constraint to its development of this role. The aerospace industry is a possible candidate for this challenge, but it is still in its early stages and currently may be more a source of losses than profits (for further detail, see Rojo [2011]). The large-scale arms industry is clearly a resource for activating profit, as long as it is accompanied by the widespread use of arms and their continual replacement, which is also currently limited due to its destructive repercussions. For these reasons and the permanent over-accumulation generated in late capitalism, money is increasingly left out of production, as money-commodity, ready to inflate the fictitious-financial side of the capitalist economy. (World financial assets in 1982 were 13.9 billion dollars. In 2004 they amounted to almost 150 billion dollars, i.e., three times the world GDP, which stood at around 50 billion dollars).

its overwhelming success in achieving the ideological subordination of labour, and in consequence, to the serious gap between labour and its forms of organization and consciousness to keep step with such capitalist universalization.[14] It does not seem likely however, that the constant reliance on substituting one labour force for a cheaper, more docile one will be able to prevent or oppose the reaction of increasing masses of the world population faced with the dramatic deterioration of their living conditions or even possibly written off as consumers.[15]

Forced by the offensive of capital, we are in all probability entering into a new era of class confrontations with unforeseeable consequences.

References

Autor, David and David Dorn. 2011. *The Growth of Low Skill Service Jobs and the Polarization of the U.S. Labor Market*, http://econ-www.mit.edu/files/1474.

Colectivo IOE. 2008. *Barómetro social de España: Análisis del periodo 1994-2006*. Traficantes de sueños. Madrid.

Dierckxsens, Wim. 2011a. 'Población, fuerza de trabajo y rebelión en el siglo XXI. ¿De las revueltas populares de 1948 en Europa a la rebelión mundial actual?', in Andrés Piqueras and Wim Dierckxsens (eds.), *El colapso de la globalización*. Barcelona: Viejo Topo.

———. 2011b. *Cómo salvar a los pueblos y no a los banqueros*, http://www.observatoriodelacrisis.org/.

Fernández Durán, Ramón. 2011. *El Antropoceno. La expansión del capitalismo global choca con la biosfera*. Barcelona: Virus.

Ford, Martin. 2013. *Job Automation: Is a Future Unemployment Crisis Looming?* http://www.huffingtonpost.com/martin-ford/job-automation-is-a-futur_b_832146.html.

Global Footprint Network. 2011. http://www.footprintnetwork.org/en/index.php/GFN/page/2010_living_planet_report.

GPM. 2012. 'Producción y mercado, ¿qué es lo determinante?, http://www.nodo50.org/gpm/OtroSiDigo/06.htm.

Katz, Claudio. 2010. 'Las tres dimensiones de la crisis', http://lahistoriadeldia.wordpress.com/2010/05/03/claudio-katz-las-tres-dimensiones-de-la-crisis/.

14 Consciousness also appears to be outdated in some social formations, depending on the degree of capitalist decline or socio-economic deterioration they are experiencing or will experience in the immediate future.

15 Life's resistance to being denied has historically been a factor in generating agents of opposition in any socio-economic order. In capitalism, this 'agency' gave rise to historical subjects that were able to provide alternative global projections, which can be drawn on today (accumulative legacy?) in response to the new heightened antagonisms.

Martins, Carlos Eduardo. 2009. 'A teoria da conjuntura e a crise contemporânea', *Polis*, (24): 385-401.

Navarro, Vicenç. 2009. *El subdesarrollo social de España*. Madrid: Ediciones de Diario El Público.

OIT. 2011. *Tendencias mundiales del empleo*, http://www.ilo.org/global/publications/ilo-bookstore/order-online/books/WCMS_150442/lang--es/index.htm.

Piqueras, Andrés. 2011. 'De las crisis del capital al capital en crisis. Agotamiento de las posibilidades de reformismo en el capitalismo tardío', *Actuel Marx. Intervenciones*, (10), http://www.observatoriodelacrisis.org/.

Rojo, Jose Luis. 2011. *Los problemas estructurales no resueltos en la economía mundial llevan a una recaída*, http://www.socialismo-o-barbarie.org/economia/110929_a2_ problemasestructuralesnoresueltos.htm.

Schweiger, Hans and Antonio Rodríguez. 2007. 'La participación de los salarios', *Taifa, seminari d'economia critica*, (4), http://informes.seminaritaifa.org/.

Part V

China: A Case Study

CHAPTER 9

Financial System and 'Chinese-style Market Socialism'

Tony ANDREANI & Rémy HERRERA

University of Paris VIII, France

and

National Centre of Scientific Research (CNRS), France

According to the official discourse, the People's Republic of China is still at the 'primary stage' of socialism, that is, market socialism with Chinese characteristics or 'Chinese-style market socialism'. It is particularly important to examine whether the present Chinese financial system, which plays a key role in the overall economy, exhibits specific features, as elsewhere, to the point that these features fit into such a perspective and if they contribute to explain the impressive expansion of this country, especially when this 'success' is measured by the rate of growth of the gross domestic product. We discuss here very briefly some of the problems and challenges facing the Chinese financial system today.

What is the Place of Market Finance in a System that Remains Based on Credit?

Nowadays, the financing system of the Chinese economy remains largely based on banking credit – even if it tends to move away relatively rapidly. This was the case in other countries too for a long time, such as in France, until the measures of disintermediation and deregulation were taken in the 1980s – including by so-called 'socialist' governments – in order to replace partly indirect financing (via the banking credit) by direct financing (through calls to the markets of equities, bonds and derivatives). A number of Chinese economists link the introduction and the expansion of market finance to the transformation of the state-owned enterprises into joint stock companies, which then implied the creation of stock exchanges and, more generally, to the new needs of funding by these firms (particularly in the bond market or in hedge products).

Why did this 'equitization' of enterprises happen? Several major reasons are usually formulated. Though one tried to pretend, these production units could no longer be permanently financed by the state, when they came out of the administered economy and the allocation of capital and credits by the Plan. So they needed to not only be self-financing and get resources from banks, but also find and develop external investors. As they became autonomous economic entities, these enterprises had to abandon the rules, mechanisms and guidelines of the Plan in order to adopt new management criteria, a market-type clarity and, for that, model themselves on the way Western capitalist firms are managed – focused at obtaining maximum profitability and, ultimately, at ensuring shareholders' control. Furthermore, the presence of private shareholders intended to guarantee that the state could no longer constantly interfere with their management and reduce their autonomy, even for 'good reasons'.

It would only be as a second step that, from 2005 onwards mainly, the Chinese public banks were reformed to follow this model themselves. Their capital was open not only to the mass of local shareholders looking for dividends and stock market gains, but also to great banking establishments of the North – staying always in minority and controlled – in order to train the Chinese institutions in handling financial transactions (market finance) and to simultaneously impose on them the rules of 'corporate governance'. For example, prior to the introduction of the three biggest Chinese banks into the stock exchange market, there was the entrance into their capital structure of powerful strategic investors, such as Goldman Sachs (for the ICBC), UBS (for the Bank of China) and Bank of America (for the CCB), with the intention to improve both 'business culture' and 'governance' through a diversification of shareholders.

Market finance is obviously playing an increasingly determinant role in the Chinese financial system. And this is being done in two ways: at the level of financing of the enterprises, whether financial or non-financial, and at the level of the activity of banks themselves, which increasingly develop their market transactions along with their activities of deposit and credit. Many economists and, more importantly, Chinese political officials, seem to consider that this is a 'modernization' desirable and almost inevitable. According to them, the former system based on banking credit was built on various reasons, which were legal (in particular, business laws that remain incomplete and misapplied), cultural (in conjunction with the old Confucian cultural tradition mobilizing interpersonal relationships much more than commercial contracts) and social (following the argument that the Chinese would be too 'conservative' and would not dare to take risks).

Yet, it is important here not to confuse, under the pretext of necessary 'reforms', a supposed 'modernization' with the outright adoption of the capitalist way or one of its variants – even if it has Chinese colours – which would lead in fact to give up the socialist project and the social advances that it, and only it, can allow and grant.

The Chinese authorities claim that they are currently trying to strike a 'balance' between the two models – banking credit and market finance – because if the funding by the financial markets were to weaken or to present failures, banking finance would then recover all its importance. However, this raises, in our opinion, a series of problems that should be emphasized in order to avoid misunderstandings and even some disappointments. It is known that the expansion of the Chinese economy, observed for several decades now, was not achieved without recurrent economic crises, sometimes very dire, as in 1989-1991, 1997-1998 or 2008. Crises, especially those of the later years, increasingly related directly to the growing 'financiarization' of the Chinese economic model and to its tight and contradictory integration into the capitalist world system. Crises that have also and above all else forced the Chinese monetary authorities to react firmly to limit their destabilizing effects, especially at the social level, by gradually changing the institutional framework, while providing powerful tools for monitoring and pursuing the consolidation of the national development project. While numerous uncertainties continue to surround the definition of such a project, both internally (how to articulate these institutional evolutions on the planning of 'market socialism'?) and externally (what will be, for instance, the orientations of the exchange rate policy of the country?), the fact is that the People's Republic of China is today one of the (rare) economies of the South where the ruling classes implement a true 'development strategy', which is reflective, consistent, and – we hope – destined to benefit the entire population.

Are Financial Markets More Efficient in Allocating Resources than Banking Credit?

The thesis of 'the efficiency of the financial markets', which is rooted in the orthodox theoretical corpus in economics (that is, the neoclassical current) and asserted its domination from the 1970s at the beginning of the neoliberal era, argues that financial markets would play the same positive role of so-called optimal information, evaluation and allocation as the commodities markets. And this is so by following the same argument that has been driving the massive deregulation of the financing systems, which led to the form of capitalism, 'financiarized' and dominated by the huge financial oligopolies, that we know nowadays. Nevertheless, these two types of markets are very different: one involves goods (productive capital), and the other one is based on expectations or promises of gains (financial capital and fictitious capital).

In addition to being theoretically questionable, this thesis of the efficiency of the financial markets is rejected by the whole history of the recent decades, which shows that these markets are unable to provide consistent prices – and even less 'fair' prices – for financial assets of any kind, whether bonds with interest rates, stock market shares or exchange rates between currencies. We limit ourselves simply to recalling here their mistakes and failures concerning the securities and proofs of the European sovereign debts, currently estimated in a rather irrational manner (do the 'PIGS' [Portugal, Italy, Greece and Spain], as some 'experts' have so sympathetically named them, deserve the interest rates inflicted on them?), the bursting of the 'new economy' bubble in 2000 and the fluctuations of exchange rates disconnected from the objective 'fundamentals'. Another example is the sharp de-valorization of many firms in the stock markets, even though they are getting billions in profits.

We, therefore, reject the confidence often expressed by many Chinese economists in the assumed virtues of the financial markets: self-appointed subjects of history, experiencing mimetic behaviours, pouring into the self-fulfilling prophecy, ignoring even the adjustment forces that frequently operate on the commodities markets, leading to purely speculative practices by diverting the primary function of coverage or 'hedge' instruments, the financial markets generate disasters – the subprime crisis being here a paroxysmal manifestation.

According to us, there is anyway a significant advantage in banking credit: in other words, banks – when they are state-owned and doing their job well – know and follow their customers much better than the 'market analysts', who scrutinize only the financial data and can easily be 'intoxicated' by the managers and leaderships of the enterprises. Moreover, that which belongs to the 'Chinese culture', namely, the primacy of personal relationships and, thanks to it, the climate of confidence and trust that is established, seems in this case more a strength than a weakness for the Chinese financial system and, more broadly, the economy of the entire country. It is true that there are also disadvantages: connivance, sometimes corruption, and other adverse effects, such as the risk of multiplication of 'bad loans'. The sanction by the markets in the allocation of capital and bonds might seem more anonymous, thus more 'objective'.

However, the fact is that corruption is no less – to put it mildly – in the private sector. Here, the financial history in recent years has provided many illustrations of well-known scandals, which have implicated even these 'judges' of the markets that would become the rating agencies. Therefore, we believe that the valuation on the stock markets can be an indicator, at best. In our opinion, it would be more pertinent to improve the functioning of the system of banking credit, in particular through a greater intervention in banks' management of the representatives of the staff, users and customers (that is, the stakeholders), who would exercise control over their activities, thanks to a strengthening of the various criteria of credit distribution by the intervention of external specialists involved in the projects in question.

Would it be useful in this regard to introduce in the banks' capital structure some 'qualified investors', that is, other banking entities – including foreign ones – in order to optimize the investors' 'philosophy' of the capital market? If this means that the Chinese banks would have something to learn from these institutional investors, it may be true in the case of certain financial transactions, especially intermediation; but if the aim is copying the practices of Western capitalist banks, then we can fear the worse, knowing what they have done with credit distribution – we could use the recent case of Spain as an example. However, if the goal is to reproduce the activities of business banks, then the lesson is likely to lead to abuses. It is sufficient to remember how the financial oligopolies of the North have been involved in the Libor and Euribor manipulation scandals. If this is the price one will have to pay for the 'strength' and 'vitality' of capital markets, we think it is better not to pay it.

Do the Chinese State-owned Enterprises Have to Be Managed as Private Companies?

'Market socialism with Chinese characteristics' is based on maintaining a very powerful public sector, which plays a strategic role in the whole economy. All indications lead to the belief that this is clearly one of the 'secrets' of the outstanding performance registered by the Chinese economy in terms of growth, against the neoliberal arguments in favour of private property and maximizing profit. This is probably related to the size of these enterprises, which are really of gigantic proportions, such as in the sectors of energy (electricity, oil and gas), raw materials (steel and chemicals), semi-finished products, construction or even maritime transport, that is, where the economies of scale reduce costs of purchase, production and sales. And these are the companies that provide very cheap inputs to a myriad of small and medium enterprises. This allows them not only low wages (which account for only 2 to 10 per cent of the selling prices), even if they tend to grow very rapidly, but also competitive production conditions that make them so successful on the global markets. But this is not the only reason.

Another explanation is that they are clearly not managed as the Western large private companies – with shares quoted on the stock exchange – seeking, above all else, to maximize 'shareholder value' (that is, the distribution of dividends and the stock market value of shares). A return on investment of such a level (15 per cent and beyond) is only possible because they oppress chains of local and/or relocated subcontractors. If China's state-owned enterprises behaved as rapaciously, this would be to the detriment of the entire local economy, which is obviously not the case. In addition, we would be dealing with an extreme form of 'state capitalism' (this is what we hear in the North), and we do not see how and why such a system would be superior to private capitalism. Nevertheless, it clearly appears that if state-owned enterprises are (or have once again become) profitable, their only compass is not making their shareholders rich, but rather new productive investments and the good service actually rendered to their customers. So, basically, it is not so much about whether they realize more or less profits than their Western capitalist competitors, but whether those profits are finally used to stimulate the economy as a whole rather than to increase the number of billionaires.

And we can find the proof of this argument in the fact that these enterprises pay taxes, but distribute only few dividends to their main shareholder, the state (seemingly 10 per cent on average), unlike some of the Western public enterprises, for example, in France, that serve as 'cash cows' to the state when they make profits. In our view, the payment of dividends to the state, inspired from the capitalist practices of the North, is not the right formula. It would perhaps be better if the state implemented a tax on capital as a sort of rent for the provision of these goods. Those enterprises that would work well could then keep a larger part of their profits to direct them towards productive investment and research and development (R&D), knowing that the corporate tax is already a levy that is proportional to their gains.

A recent World Bank report recommends increasing these dividends and, in China, the regulatory commission of the stock exchange seems to be moving in that direction. This appears to be a bad policy because the state-owned enterprises would then be deprived of one of their major advantages, and despite being controlled by the state, they would tend, like most Western capitalist firms, to distribute more and more dividends in order to win the favour of their private shareholders. This would be true also for financial companies like banks.

Another superiority of the Chinese state-owned enterprises is, according to us, participation – albeit limited – of their staff in the management of the production units, through its representatives within the framework of the supervisory board and the workers' congress. The development of shareholder logic could only go against such participation. Furthermore, employee ownership, frequently used in the large companies of the North, is still very exceptional and does not provide any real weight to the management. It puts the workers in a permanent contradiction between their interests as wage-earners and 'shareholders'.

A third superiority of the Chinese state-owned enterprises is that they can more easily meet the objectives of planning. It would probably not mean imposing additional duties for political purposes that would throw their autonomy into doubt and affect their results. And the Plan could also direct the activity of the private enterprises through indirect means (taxation, subsidies and support of all kinds). Nevertheless, controlling the appointment and the management of the senior executives, the public authorities, the state in the broad sense, that is, central government and local governments (provinces and districts), on which a large number of China's state-owned enterprises are depending, can afford to ensure that they act appropriately. This is especially important when 'public service missions' must be achieved, but also when they are operating in purely commercial sectors, as private companies often find ways around such missions. In the capitalist economies of the North, we have a lot of examples of degradation of public services as a consequence of their (even partial) privatization and we know that private companies will do anything to distort 'competition' on the markets to their advantage (for example, by 'tax optimization' and useless or misleading advertising).

Ultimately, why have state-owned enterprises if they must be managed like private companies? We sincerely hope that the Chinese authorities will know how to resist the lure of neoliberalism in this matter. Here, the very future of the 'Chinese-style market socialism' is at stake. For, beyond some positive benefits associated with the implementation of market mechanisms, particularly in terms of faster economic growth – helping to legitimize the strategy currently adopted – we believe that the choice of the capitalist route by the Chinese government would be the surest way to guarantee the complete failure of its development strategy, and thus not prevent the aggressive rise of the US to sustain its hegemony against the South in general, and against China in particular. This is the reason we are quite sceptical about the different recommendations of 'changes' in the international monetary and financial system formulated by some 'reformists' like Joseph Stiglitz. His recommendations were made explicit in the final report of the Commission of the United Nations, which was recently chaired by this Nobel laureate in economics. This report does not call into question the fundamental principles of the currently existing financial globalization (flexible exchange rates, free trade, the dominance of the US dollar, the domination of the financial oligopolies and the diktats of the so-called 'corporate governance').

To return to the issue of the financing of enterprises, we understand that credit and cash flow may not be sufficient, but we think that the appeal to large foreign investors should be as limited as possible. Most importantly, the former should not lead to an alignment with the practice of the 'shareholder value' (calculated as what needs to exceed the risk premium demanded for financial securities). Chinese savings are certainly abundant enough to be mobilized by the intermediary of national institutional investors, to which the public authorities could eventually impose limits of profitability. This would not necessarily be the same as those required by the state operating as a shareholder.

Should the Interest Rates Be Completely Liberalized?

The advantage of administered interest rates is that one can control them. The disadvantage is that they do not allow a flexible adjustment of supply and demand for credits and bonds. Today, in China, interest rates are 'semi-administered'. Some rates have been largely liberalized (such as those of the interbank market, treasury bills and bonds issued by the financial institutions). In the case of bonds, however, the public control of supply remains strong, since the vast majority of bonds are issued by the state, the central bank and public financial intermediaries. But the other rates are not liberalized. The floor level of the interest rates of the credits is still largely controlled by the central bank, as well as the ceiling level of the interest rates on deposits.

It is only very recently that a new step was taken towards further liberalization of the interest rates: now, the Chinese banks may indeed offer their customers some higher rates on deposits, superior by 10 per cent to the central rates, and lower rates on loans, inferior by 20 per cent to the interest rates of the central bank. According to official statements, the purpose would be to create competition and attract more investors. The aim is also to remove some facilities for banks to collect and drain savings very cheaply – the remuneration of deposits being inferior to the inflation rate – so that Chinese households do not offset the devaluation.

If these reasons are quite understandable, the actual problem is complete liberalization, which seems to be the primary objective of the upcoming reform. However, we know what it led to in the North: aberrant interest rates, particularly with regard to sovereign debt securities. We wonder how China would protect itself against these 'errors' or aberrations of markets. One might assume that this task would be ensured by the Banking Regulatory Commission. This, however, is not the case in Western capitalist countries, where such commissions often limit their role to the implementation of some prudential rules and standards, such as those established by the Basel Committee, which are based primarily on the respect of a ratio of stockholders' equity, in the same logic as the shareholder value. Nevertheless, to reach this goal, it should be necessary that the Commission is truly independent of banks, instead of being in a situation of collusion, or at least of 'understanding', with their interests (and especially since their members are generally made up of former bankers). Consequently, it seems, a regime of semi-administered rates would be better, mainly if one can make it evolve.

Moreover, the Chinese monetary policy, which obviously adheres to specific requirements destined to safeguard national sovereignty as a priority, is openly and increasingly being penetrated by instruments commonly used by the capitalist central banks of the North, and it even fixes objectives very similar to those of the latter, starting with the fight against inflation. Acknowledging that inflationary pressures remain a real threat to the expansion of the fast-growing Chinese economy, we have to keep in mind that inflation itself derives from the balance of powers in society – or the class struggle, we shall say quickly, from a Marxist point of view. We, therefore, believe that it is absolutely fundamental to submit, by political will (that will take into account the needs of the people), the national monetary policy to development objectives that are geared towards the strengthening of social policies. In other words, it is extremely important to refuse the prioritization of the instruments of economic policy imposed by neoliberalism, which places as top priority the external and internal components of the monetary policy. The budgetary and fiscal policies come in only as secondary items and, at the very bottom of the list are social and infrastructural policies. In our view, the inversion of this hierarchy or pyramid of neoliberal priorities should characterize China's development strategy. This is especially desirable because Western capitalist economies are now offering the spectacle of a total failure of interest rate policies. The fact is that the ultimate determination of these rates is placed in the hands of the authorities of the financial oligopolies and no longer in those of the states. The reductions in interest rates practised since 2008 and the erupting of the systemic crisis no longer lead to the recovery of productive investment and economic growth.

Should Chinese Banks Be Universal Banks?

The recent history of – mostly public – Chinese banks shows that, since the turning point of the early 1990s, they have been increasingly venturing into market finance and other similar areas (such as insurance or real estate) – like the Western capitalist banks when the governments ended their professional specialization. At that time they were forbidden to do so between 1992 and 1995 in response to disturbances resulting from the crisis of 1989-1991, but they were again allowed to undertake certain 'mixed operations' (both by banking credit and on the financial markets). This choice would have been made 'by necessity', facing competition from the largest foreign banks, outside and inside the country, along with the licences that have been distributed to them to operate there.

However, we know that the liberalization of banking activities is one of the main causes of the systemic crisis that hit the world economy, in the interrelationship between real and financial spheres. A crisis of extreme gravity required massive and repeated interventions of capitalist states, which have left small banking establishments to fail, but are now considerably in debt to save oligopolies, which are called 'too big to fail'. The latter risked bringing down the entire financial system with them.

This led to the questioning of the model of the universal bank, of which some bankers are very proud, forgetting that the state has often had to come to their rescue. Two major reforms are underway in the North. The first is the implementation of the 'Volcker rule', which started to be applied in the United States in 2012. It consists of prohibiting banks from trading for their own account, that is, the possibility of using savers' deposits to make themselves rich with risky activities in the markets. Nevertheless, it would be necessary to know where the 'risky' operations begin and how to build a 'firewall' against them. The second provision, or 'Vickers reform', initiated in the UK and will not be applied until 2019, seems more advanced. Commercial banks (with people's deposits) would be housed in a subsidiary, subject to strict obligations, only to be guaranteed by the state. It could no longer be used to bail out those subsidiaries that would have failed in risky market transactions. The problem is that this simple legal separation between commercial banks and investment banks, tolerating all kinds of arrangements, leaves considerable discretion to investment banking. Thus, many experts believe that it would be better to return to a complete separation between commercial banking and investment banking. Such a separation would not mean that commercial banking is confined to credits; it could also supervise investments for the term deposits, but in the framework of operations that are regulated and perfectly clear to the users.

The Chinese monetary authorities seem to be moving towards another solution: 'mixed or joint operations at the group level', but 'separated in the subsidiaries'. Therefore, the group would be equipped with a holding structure, and the failure of a particular specialized subsidiary is no longer likely to drive the whole group to bankruptcy. This 'solution' would approach the Vickers reform in a more generalized way. We understand that the Chinese authorities are reluctant to cut down their large universal banks, but we are not at all convinced that such a reform would provide a 'good solution'. It would, first of all, require that the central bank and the banking commission remain free from external influences and pressures and stay extremely vigilant to ensure the rigor of this division. This is certainly easier than in the Western capitalist economies since, in China, the largest banks are public – which should prevail everywhere because the use of deposits and banking credit represents 'public good' and the banking establishments have thus a 'public service mission' to deliver.

It is, however, extremely difficult to control what a bank is doing from outside, particularly regarding conflicts of interests or moral hazard. The Western experience shows regulators constantly overwhelmed by financial engineering and unable to control the flows of funds during high frequency trading – even if they are registered somewhere. As for the consulting companies, audit and accounting firms and other rating agencies, we know how they can fail and be indulgent. We come back to the same argument: control must first be an internal one, which requires a plurality of actors (stakeholders), starting with the workers themselves. A system dominated by finance – placed above states – means not only a loss of economic control, but also a setback for democracy, politically. Going in the direction of 'financiarization' means to give up the strengthening of the people's participation in most basic decisions about their collective future. In the North, we have many examples of criticism from the ranks of banking sector workers themselves, who have been completely neglected and, over the last decades, there has been a constant degradation of the bank employee's job. He or she is not to listen to the customers anymore, but rather sell them the maximum number of contracts that they cannot make sense of.

Should the Renminbi Be Internationalized?

Finally, we offer some brief concluding remarks about an important point related to the internationalization of the renminbi, whose monetary unit is the yuan. An internationalized renminbi, especially to turn it into a reserve currency at the global level, would require the adoption of a series of very strict conditions. These include: (*i*) the opening of the capital account as well as the flexibility of the exchange rate; (*ii*) the integration of the Chinese financial markets into the capitalist world system; (*iii*) macroeconomic policy decisions designed to gain the 'confidence' of the financial markets (especially in the fight against inflation and by limiting public debt); and (*iv*) a critical size of the economy to justify this ambition of internationalization of the domestic currency. The first two requirements are sine qua non conditions; the next two are not. And, they are not and have not been systematically respected by the capitalist countries of the North with currencies used as international reserve.

The implementation of these conditions certainly brings benefits to the country concerned, as a 'seigniorage right', particularly visible in the case of the United States. However, such a decision would mean a further submission to globally dominant finance capital and, therefore, a relative loss of control of the monetary policy. How the People's Republic of China will be able to reap the benefits of an internationalized renminbi without being forced to pay a heavy price for it – namely, renounce the full exercise of its monetary sovereignty and the definition of an autonomous development strategy? Indeed, what we see is that high finance needs a strong state during the neoliberal era, but a strong state that turns completely against the interests of the people. The recent reactivation of the role of the neoliberal state with its anti-crisis policies is an illustration: its purpose is less to save the people than the financial oligopolies.

Today, in China, the pressures for liberalizing financial markets, advocated by many economists or politicians (in Shanghai as a big financial centre, in particular) can be mitigated by reassuring speeches in favour of the control of the reform process underway and on the need of 'modernization' of the financial system of the economy in order to move towards the stated goal of an internationalized renminbi. Nevertheless, such pressures are still very worrying for the future of 'market socialism with Chinese characteristics' when they correspond exactly to the recommendations formulated for China by the International Monetary Fund (IMF) or by some neoliberal leaders in the capitalist countries of the North. Such is the case with the former President of the French Republic, Nicolas Sarkozy, who, as we recall, pleaded at the G-20 Summit in Cannes in November 2011, both for the adoption of neoliberal measures in China and for the integration of the renminbi in the basket for determining Special Drawing Rights of the IMF.

References

Andreani, Tony, and Rémy Herrera. 2013a. 'Système financier et socialisme de marché "à la chinoise"', *La Pensée*, (373): 65-75.

———. 2013b. 'Un Modèle social-démocrate pour la Chine', in Patrick Theuret (ed.), *La Chine et le monde – Développement et socialisme*, 208-241, Paris: Le Temps des Cerises.

Ding, Fiyang. 2013. 'Le Système financier chinois', *La Pensée*, (373): 21-35.

Herrera, Rémy. 2014. "Quelques Aspects problématiques de l''émergence' de la Chine", *Marché & Organisations*, to be published.

———. 2013. "Neoclassical Economic Fiction and Neoliberal Political Reality", *International Critical Thought*, 3(1): 98-107.

———. 2012. "Reflections on the Current Crisis and its Effects", *Economic and Political Weekly*, XLVII(23): 62-71.

Nakatani, Paulo and Rémy Herrera. 2009. 'Critique des politiques anticrise orthodoxes', *La Pensée*, (360): 31-42.

CHAPTER 10

Some Problems (and Paradoxes) Related to the Internationalization of China's Economy

Rémy HERRERA

National Centre of Scientific Research (CNRS), France

Introduction

The apparent success of China's economy, or what is called its 'emergence', illustrated by a very fast GDP growth rate – in fact, the highest in the world on average over the last three decades – and by the leadership role it tends to occupy within the BRICS group, is often commented upon in the media as well as in the academic literature today. Yet, some kind of 'mystery' continues to surround such a major phenomenon, especially because the contents, the forms and sometimes even the reality of the debates between Chinese economists – debates which are extremely controversial and correspond to the entire political spectrum from Marxism to neoliberalism – are not adequately perceived by Western commentators.[1] The latter must indeed rely generally on statistical data or information sources that are themselves built by Western institutions, or largely reduced to external visions of China.

In addition to this, other difficulties come not only from the uncertainty concerning a number of terms (such as 'emergence') or categories (starting with 'BRICS') used about China's economy, but also from the in-determination in characterizing this country's current system itself (between 'market socialism' and 'capitalism with Chinese characteristics', among other appellations). Such indeterminacy – not to mention, confusion – is further worsened by the ideological terminologies

[1] Read Kin Lau Chi Ping and Huang (2003), and especially Wang Hui's article.

frequently used in the discourses of the official authorities, whether Chinese or Western.

In this context, a consensus seems to be established about some 'evidences' (e.g., China would have an 'imperialist' behaviour, its currency would be significantly undervalued, exports would constitute the growth engine of its economy). By questioning such a 'consensus', this chapter attempts to clarify – with caution, and without pretending to dispel the complexity of the related issues – some of the problems facing the Chinese economy since its opening up and its insertion into the global system. As a matter of fact, China's recent internationalization remains articulated on a development strategy that is quite coherent and turned inward, but which has not been implemented without difficulties; and it has produced, especially through merchandise and capital exports, contradictory effects, both in the North and in the South of the capitalist world system, as we shall see later in the chapter.

'Emergence', Growth, and Crises

One of the most widespread ideas concerning China today is that the country 'emerged' recently, or, more precisely, just after Mao Zedong's death, with Deng Xiaoping permitting the economy's openness and reorientation by following the 11th Congress of the Chinese Communist Party in 1978. In saying this, one implicitly endorses the argument that China 'emerged' principally thanks to this recent change and reorganization, that its economy stagnated during the Maoist period of socialism and that it took off almost as soon as it was oriented towards one of the variants of capitalism.

Three main facts are consequently occulted. The first one is that China actually 'emerged' as a major civilization and unified nation-state several thousand years ago (and not thirty years).[2] It represented a significant share in worldwide production and exchange in the late 18th century.[3] The second fact is that if economic growth indeed accelerated from the 1980s – to the point of having placed China, in spite of its low per capita income, well ahead of socialist countries or 'historically planned economies' during this decade – the growth rate of net material product was relatively high during the 10 years preceding the decision to open up the economy to the world system (Marer *et al.*, 1992). This growth rate (about 6.8 per cent in per annum average from 1970 to 1979, according to statistics from

2 See here, for example, Chi Tsui (1949).

3 See, among others, Immanuel Wallerstein (1980), Paul Bairoch (1999) and Lin Chun (2006).

the World Bank) was more than twice the GDP growth in the United States for the same period (3.2 per cent) (World Bank, various years).[4] The third fact to remember here is that when growth in China exceeded a 10 per cent average in the 1980s (as compared to only 3 per cent in the United States), most of the structures and institutions of socialism were still in place in the country.

The 'take-off' of the Chinese economy is often attributed to the opening up to globalization. Yet, it should be added – which is rarely the case in the literature on the subject – that it has been made possible due to the achievements of the previous period. These achievements are of the socialist revolution, which explain, to a very large extent, the special place now occupied by China within the group of the so-called emerging Southern countries. Apart from social and infrastructural progress, China's success with large-scale industrialization and, above all, the effectiveness of the response to the agrarian question have been the most fundamental developments for this country, until now. Let us note, in this regard, that China is one of the very few countries in the world to have secured, and continues to ensure, in law as well as in its application, access to land for the vast majority of the peasant masses. This is unparalleled in its Asian neighbours, except those that have seen a radical agrarian reform associated with a socialist revolution, like Vietnam. Numerous attempts to reduce access to land as well as violations of law (in particular, with cessions of public land and expropriation of families) have certainly been observed in recent years, but these cases have encountered fierce resistance from peasant masses that are often self-organized outside the Communist Party. This gives an idea of the crucial importance of the issue of land access within the internal debates of the Chinese political leadership (Wen Tiejun, 2001).

We also perceive here the inability to understand the evolution of this country without placing the peasantry – more than 700 million people presently – at the heart of the analysis. Therefore, the main constraint that weighs on China today is the duty of feeding about 22 per cent of the world's population with only 6 per cent of total arable land of the planet and a per capita cultivated land of 0.25 hectares in rural areas. Compared to this, India has almost double and the US a hundred times more (Amin 2008). One of the key explanations of the strategy that has allowed this challenge to be met is to be found in the affirmation of access to land to the Chinese peasantry, which is probably the most valuable contribution of the Maoist legacy. Although the present methods of organization, production and distribution in the Chinese agricultural sector, penetrated by market mechanisms, no longer have anything to

4 Data expressed in 1980 constant yuan.

do with the Maoist period, the fact is that today, landownership remains *collective* – frequently in degraded forms. Here is a fundamental point that distinguishes the situation – and success – of China from other 'emerging' countries with a similar continental size, such as India or Brazil, or regionally dominant countries, like South Africa, where the agrarian question is far from having found the conditions of its solution, not even partially.

The demographic weight (about 1.35 billion inhabitants in 2012 and 1.41 billion estimated population in 2050) and the geographic vastness (9.60 million km^2) force one to temper the ambitions of comparing China with the only country in the world that has similar characteristics, that is, India (1.25 billion people in 2012, 1.60 billion estimated in 2050 and 3.29 million km^2). However, seen at a glance, the base statistics for these two countries allow us to make a series of general observations. First, the birth control policy implemented in China has succeeded in preventing its population from continuing to grow at a high rate, contrary to what has happened in India, where the demographic transition doesn't seem to be fully completed. Second, the trajectories of the gross national product levels in the two economies, which were roughly equivalent at the time of their respective and almost simultaneous opening (1978 in China and 1984 in India), exhibit a significant divergence, with the benefits to China increasing. The latter's per capita gross national product surpassed that of India in as early as the beginning of the 1990s. Finally, the growth rate of the Chinese economy has always been higher than that of the Indian economy over the past three decades, with the exception of the years 1981 (very slightly) and 1989-90 (hardly more).

Among the multiple and complex explanations of such divergences, referring in particular to historical, institutional or policy factors, it is worth re-emphasizing here the importance of the differences in land tenure (private landownership in India vs public property in China) in economies that still remain – beyond their 'emergence' (or rather 're-emergence') – largely based on agrarian social structures. Indeed, in 2010, 37 per cent of the Chinese active population was rural, contributing to 10 per cent of the domestic production; while the agricultural sector still occupied nearly two-thirds of the Indian population and represented about 20 per cent of the total production. In India, the liberalization of agriculture has converted regions formerly self-sufficient for basic products such as rice into food dependent areas and exacerbated deep internal contradictions that this country will probably not be able to solve without redistribution of landownership – this is a fundamental claim of the Indian peasant society.

Figure 10.1: Growth Rate of the Gross Domestic Product in China, 1977-2011 (per cent, in real terms)

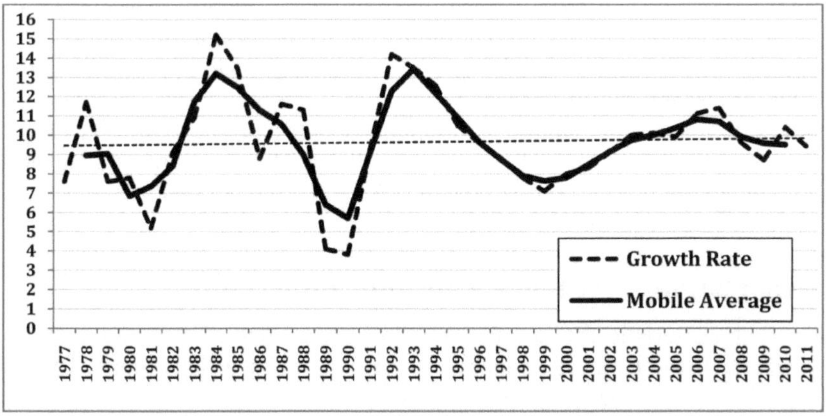

Source: Graph constructed by the author using data from the National Bureau of Statistics (various years).

By emphasizing the role of the peasantry, our approach goes against the tide of most currently available interpretations of modern China. However, it is justified by the historically huge contribution that agriculture made to the economic development of this country, taken as a whole – through the enormous surplus transfers in terms of both material and human resources destined to industrialization, but also by the central and recurrent attention that the political authorities have paid to rural areas after each slowdown of the economy (Wen Tiejun, 2001).[5] In fact, if the Chinese GDP has grown extremely fast, approaching an average of 10 per cent between 1978 and 2011 and accompanying a deepening of the industrialization process, the economy itself has gone through downward periods compared to a medium to long run trend of its GDP growth rate, especially in 1979-80, 1989-90, 1993-94, 1997-98 and 2008 (Figure 10.1). Whereas the annual growth rate remained relatively high during these periods (more than 5 per cent, except in 1990, that is, always more than the maximum reached by the United States over the same period), these divergences correspond to the regular return of crises in capital accumulation (South-South Forum, 2011). Although the volatility of the growth rate has narrowed over time, these cyclical crises have had their effects, which worsened along with the progressive 'financiarization' of the Chinese economic model. As a matter of fact, since the failure of the (soon interrupted) 'liberalization' experience in 1989-90, omnipresent state interventions (and by the party)

[5] For India, read Chandra (2009).

have constantly corrected the imbalances in the growth process, through a massive expansion of public infrastructure (including, and above all, in rural areas) and the promotion of medium-sized inland urban centres or the adoption of policies favourable to the rural population (following a strategy known as the '*San Nong*').[6] As a consequence, in response to the 2008 crisis, the net income of rural households increased, as measured in real terms and per capita, significantly faster than those in urban areas (in the rural areas, by 10.9 per cent in 2010, 11.4 per cent in 2011 and 13.0 per cent in 2012, compared to 8.0, 8.5 and 10.0 per cent, respectively, in the urban areas) (CEIC, 2012).

Exportations, Exchange Rate and 'Imperialism'

A characteristic that is often put forward to describe the internationalization of the Chinese economy is the dynamism of its exports. Export expansion since the early 1990s, and even more since the 2000s, draws an exponential curve that was interrupted only by the impact of the global crisis in 2008-2009. In this context one concludes sometimes too quickly that exports of goods and services would have become the main engine of growth in China. One forgets that the development strategy, conceived and applied with consistency and pragmatism by the Chinese leadership, is based on a 'model' that is relatively more self-reliant and consistent than any other economy of the South (and East). This 'model', which is officially called 'market socialism with Chinese characteristics', relies – and this is one of the 'secrets' of its performance in global markets, whatever the neoliberals may think – on the maintenance of a powerful state sector (including in the financial system), with a very dynamic role for the entire economy, especially for the small and medium enterprises of the local industry.

Most Chinese private entrepreneurs in manufacturing sectors seem to be primarily interested in the internal markets for their products. It is basically the expansion of domestic demand in recent years, stimulated by increasing household consumption and activated by massive capital expenditures of the state (especially in infrastructural programmes), that guides their investment plans to optimism. So, within a general scheme evolving from 'made in China' towards 'made *by* China' (Dufour, 2012), the accelerated pace of labour productivity gains (which annually averaged 5.2 per cent between 1980 and 1995, 6.7 per cent between 1995 and 2005, and 9.7 per cent between 2005 and 2010 [World Bank, various years]) allows for the extremely rapid growth in industrial wages expressed in real terms (Figure 10.2) – without significant deterioration of competitiveness due to the increase in labour costs in China relative to

6 On this point, see Wen Tiejun (2009), then Erebus Wong and Tsui Sit (2012).

other Southern competitors (such as South Korea or Mexico). Exports as well as foreign direct investments (because more than half of the exports are still due to foreign firms operating in China) play a supporting role in economic expansion. And this allows us to understand that, in 2011, their negative net contribution to the GDP growth (-5.8 per cent) broke neither the latter (which remained extremely dynamic, with a rate of almost 10 per cent) nor the increases in profit margins of local manufacturing companies (Kroeber, 2011).

Figure 10.2: Annual Growth in Real Industrial Wages in China, 1997-2010 (per cent)

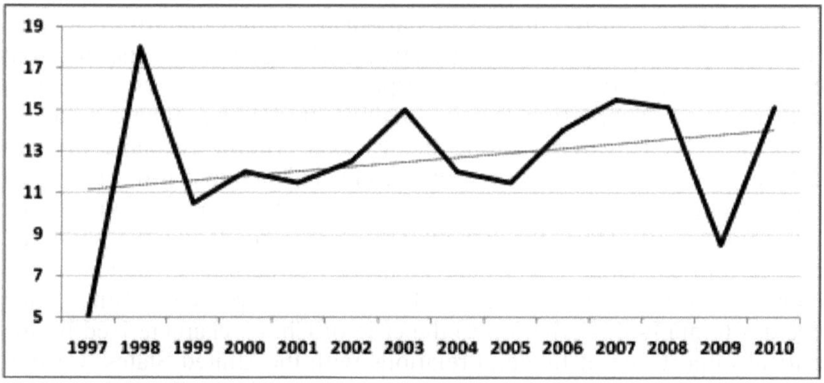

Source: Graph constructed by the author from CEIC data (various years).

Nevertheless, the upward trend of exports in the long run, which relies partly (and only partly) on the pattern of China's growth, is sufficient to crystallize an additional point of tension in international economic relations today. Indeed, one pretends that the Chinese currency, called 'renminbi' – whose monetary unit is the yuan – would be greatly undervalued, as we read in many reports disseminated by Western banks and international organizations, as well as in the dominant media. One adds that this undervaluation of the renminbi would be at the origin of persistent bilateral trade deficits of the Northern economies, and especially the United States.[7] Generally accepted estimates suggest an undervaluation by about 15 to 50 per cent.[8] Thereby, the continuous pressure exerted by Washington – helped in this task by the governments of the European Union – in the direction of an appreciation of the renminbi against the dollar meets Beijing's resistance. It has actually led

7 For example, Crédit Suisse (2012).

8 See the reports on this subject by the US Congressional Research Service.

to successive revaluations of the Chinese currency during the past decade (the last one occurred in April 2012, after that of July 2005). Between the summer of 2005 (when the monetary authorities in China decided to stop linking their currency fluctuations to the US dollar) and March 2012, the value of the renminbi has appreciated in real terms by 32 per cent as compared to the key international currency.[9] While the US Treasury recently said it recorded a weakening of the dollar against the renminbi by nearly 40 per cent since early 2005, the leitmotiv still declares that the products exported by China, already quite cheap due to relatively low labour costs, would be made more competitive in world markets by an artificially depreciated currency.

It is known that the discussions about the 'fair value' of currencies (for example, on the so-called effective exchange rates of the different currencies) are very controversial, especially when they are articulated with arguments supporting decision-making in foreign policies, including trade or debt. However, among the various criteria available in such debates, the ratio between current account balance and gross domestic product seems today to be widely used by the experts advising the US government. Thus, the benchmark chosen to define the so-called equilibrium exchange rate would be a ratio of surplus or deficit of the current account balance to the GDP +/– 3 or 4 per cent. But, if one decides to apply this criterion to the case of China, characterized by the critical importance of bilateral relations with the United States, we find that the Chinese ratio changed from 10.6 per cent in 2007 to 2.8 per cent in 2011, and to only 1.4 per cent in the first quarter of 2012. Forecasts give a ratio just over 3.5 per cent, suggesting that this test will continue to be met in the near future (Figure 10.3).[10] As a result, the 'significant undervaluation' of the Chinese currency would not be so obvious – in contrast to the deterioration of the country's terms of trade in the long run (Figure 10.4) – when we refer to one of the benchmarks most frequently used by the US administration. This did not prevent the United States, despite the external (and internal) imbalances characterizing its economy, to pursue what many observers call a 'currency war'. A 'war' that takes place through the depreciation of the dollar in foreign exchange markets, trying to impose on Beijing the terms of what looks like a 'capitulation' (Nakatani and Herrera, 2009) with immediate implications, that is, the sharp devaluation of huge amounts of China's foreign currency reserves. These reserves are still largely held in dollars (in late 2011, more than 60 per cent were in dollars compared to less than 30 per cent in euros). The question is, for how long?

---

9 This information is sourced from the Bank for International Settlements (BIS).

10 See the estimates elaborated by the World Bank (2012) and IMF (2012).

Figure 10.3: Ratio of Current Account Balance over Gross Domestic Product in China, 1997-2012 (per cent)

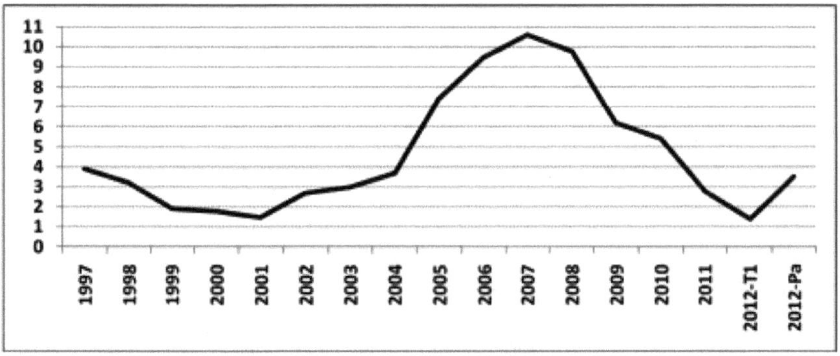

Source: Graph constructed by the author using date from the National Bureau of Statistics (various years).
Note: 2012-T1 = first quarter of 2012 (realized); 2012-Pa = annual forecast for the year 2012.

Figure 10.4: Changes in China's Terms of Trade, 1980-2010 (in index, 2000 = base 100)

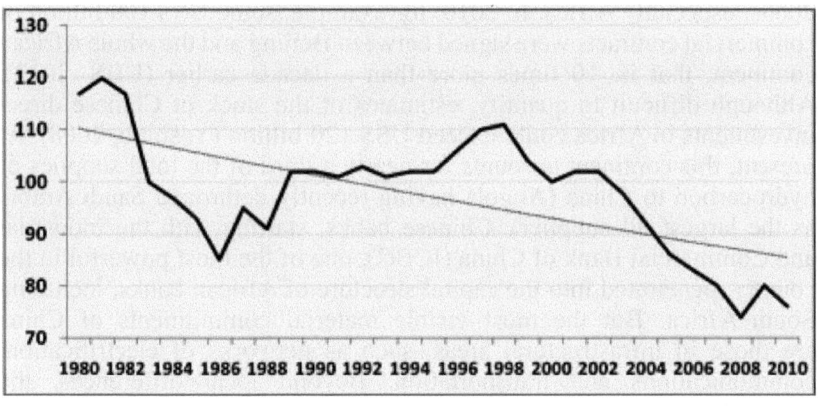

Source: Graph constructed by the author from CEIC data (various years).

Another very frequent attack against China denounces its supposedly 'imperialist behaviour.'[11] Such criticism is prompted not only by its commercial power, but also by the tremendous changes in its capital exports (Figure 10.5), making it play a major role in the refinancing plans of the US Treasury and in negotiations to restructure sovereign debts

[11] See, for example, 'The Dangers of a Rising China', *The Economist*, 4 December 2010.

Figure 10.5: Cumulated Chinese Exports of Financial Capital in the World, 2000-2010 (US dollars in billion)

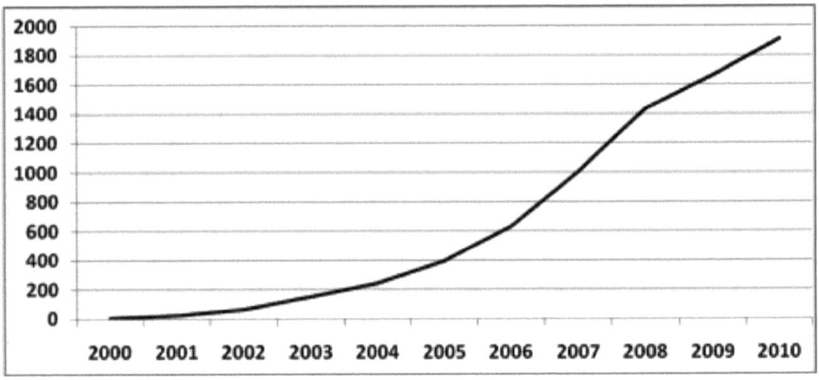

Source: Author's calculations based on IMF data (various years).

in Europe.[12] It also comes from the reactions – not always positive, nor even objective, but heavily publicized by the Western dominant media – to China's penetration into many Southern economies since the early 2000s, especially Africa. In 2010, for example, some US$ 100 billion of commercial contracts were signed between Beijing and the whole African continent, that is, 10 times more than a decade earlier (UBS, 2012). Although difficult to quantify, estimates of the stock of Chinese direct investments in Africa could exceed US$ 120 billion (Yoshino, 2008). At present, this continent accounts for nearly a third of the total supplies of hydrocarbon to China (Angola having recently dethroned Saudi Arabia as the largest oil supplier). Chinese banks, starting with the Industrial and Commercial Bank of China (ICBC), one of the most powerful in the country, penetrated into the capital structure of African banks, including South Africa. But the most visible material commitments of China are those in infrastructural areas, such as networks of electrification, communications and transportation. Beyond local differences, the outstanding fact is that China has become a major economic and political partner for Africa – as well as for the other continents of the South.

As we mentioned earlier, such a penetration has been criticized – sometimes rightly, sometimes not – in the North, but also in Africa, where influential traders or intermediaries often protested loudly against the 'yellow peril'. However, most of the political elites, as well as a large majority of the popular classes, went beyond criticism and discovered

12 Among other newspaper articles, see 'More UK equities for China?', *Financial Times*, 3 June 2011.

some benefits. Despite real and multiple problems – which could be overcome by a more controlled use of policy tools at the disposal of the states – these new relationships, albeit complex and filled with contradictions, are an opportunity for Africa. The recovery of the GDP growth rate of many African countries between 2000 and 2007 (until the outbreak of the world systemic crisis) can be partly explained by the dynamism of trade with China over the period. The positive effects of these exchanges are registered through various channels: increased trade in volume and value (the prices of exported goods have shot up due to the strong Chinese demand and competition among client countries), construction of infrastructure (a part of the contracts includes as a special component 'public works for natural resources'), and a reduced debt burden (through Chinese credits granted at very low interest rates). Furthermore, such exchanges are certainly interesting for China itself, which gets an access to strategic resources needed to support its fast growth (oil, minerals and rare metals) and finds the opportunity to hire some of its surplus labour.

Are these China-Africa exchanges fair? The substitution of 'barefoot doctors' of the Maoist revolution by (successful but also conscious of profitability) entrepreneurs at the present time has not gone without a radical change of values. However, attenuating the dependency links of the Southern countries with respect to those of the North may produce stimulating effects on them. In contrast to some arguments formulated by apologists of free trade, the functioning of the circulation sphere has demonstrated that intertwined power relationships (between countries, classes, etc.) are involved in the actually existing global system. From the Chinese point of view, which is shared by more and more numerous leaders of the South, one of the solutions to the North-South imbalances would imply promoting South-South cooperation at all levels (trade, energy, technology, etc.), and with the condition that such South-South exchanges could avoid repeating some of the defaults characterizing current North-South relationships. Would it be acceptable that a country of the South behaves towards another as a dominant power, or by putting pressure on the dispossession of natural resources and environmental destruction?

Meanwhile, China has decided to strengthen its strategic partnerships with its main neighbours, in particular within the 'Shanghai group', as well as with the other BRICS. For instance, on 29 March 2012, the Fourth Summit of the BRICS took place in New Delhi, around the theme of 'Partnership for world stability, security and prosperity'. It was attended by the then concerned heads of state or government, surrounded by large delegations: Hu Jintao, Manmohan Singh, Dimitri Medvedef, Dilma Rousseff and Jacob Zuma, together representing 45 per cent of the world's population, cumulated GDPs almost equivalent to that of the United States and two-thirds of world's economic growth. The summit ended on a strong consensus, revealing the unanimous will of these five powers to overcome some of their major points of contention and to better coordinate their positions on the international scene in order to defend a broader representation of the developing countries within the framework of the United Nations' bodies and the idea of a reform of the international order – a message that was at the heart of the discourse of the Chinese delegation.

In economic terms, the most valuable manifestation of this convergence was 'point 13' of the 'Delhi Declaration': the announcement of the setting-up of a team, under the authority of the five finance ministers, with a mission to explore the feasibility and viability conditions for a new multilateral credit institution that would be managed by the BRICS, whose creation could be announced at the next summit in 2013. This development bank, aiming at mobilizing resources for financing infrastructure and sustainable development projects in the South (but also in the East and perhaps even in the North) is part of the logics of seeking coordinated responses to the current systemic crisis and autonomous decisions of the BRICS' governments as compared to the 'solutions' proposed by international financial organizations. One of the purposes here is also to reduce the importance of the US dollar as an international currency for payment and reserve; and one of the means to achieve this goal is to promote bilateral trade denominated in local currencies and to facilitate their exchanges' connection. Clearly, the reaction of most Western commentators and 'experts' – who often simply recalled the 'high quality of services' provided by existing financial international organizations and denounced a supposed 'lack of competences' on development loans by the BRICS – was not equal to the event announcing the construction of a multi-polar world (Arrighi, 2009).

Conclusion

In this chapter, we did not want to deal with the delicate question of the nature of the Chinese political and economic system today, which would deserve a specific and thorough treatment. Due to the contradictions they carry, the traditional expressions of 'market socialism' and 'state capitalism' indeed allow the slight tightening of the range of possibilities existing between the opposite extremes of 'socialism' and 'capitalism'; but they leave uncertain the definition of this unique institutional mix, whose success tends to present it as a 'model'. What is clear, however, is that the future of the Chinese system remains largely undetermined not only because of its own dynamics, but also because the present capitalism of the financial oligopolies of the North seems to come more frontally into conflict with it, despite their close interdependence.

The relationships between the power exerted by the apparatus of a party still claiming to be 'communist' and the social block on which it is based – that is, the middle-class beneficiaries of the ongoing development, but also the private entrepreneurs – on the one hand, and the masses of workers and peasants, on the other, are unique and complex. Their evolution in the direction of a restoration of capitalism or, conversely, in that of the reactivation of a social compromise more favourable to the working classes, in conjunction with the content that will have to take the forms of democratization in this country, opens up prospects for large-scale confrontations between political forces and on quite divergent trajectories of the structures of the Chinese economy. How will the Chinese leading elites, whose legitimacy is seen greatly enhanced by economic growth and its multiple benefits, reach to find new means to confirm the country's extraordinary 'success story' without relying in one way or another on a radical change in the relationship of internal forces in favour of the working classes? That is, without redirecting the 'national project' completely to give priority to social – not to say 'socialist'– policies? In other words, would not such a choice for a 'capitalist' way assumed by these elites, which would most likely lead to the breaking of the dynamic balance characterizing the evolution of this political-economic system and to losing control of the increasing contradictions, be one of the most reliable means to ensure the failure of the previously adopted development strategy in China?

More generally, in a context where conditions seem met for one of the major consequences of the global system's systemic crisis, which is the accentuation of the North-South confrontation (Herrera, 2010), another question – or concern – arises: which attitude will the United States adopt, politically and strategically, especially from a military point of view, when faced with the rise of the 'emerging' countries, and within them, the BRICS led by China? For, as a matter of fact, Washington does know perfectly well the weaknesses of the new superpower, spreading from the 'Chinese Taipei' to Xinjiang province – in the Northwest, with its Muslim populations – through Lhasa and Xizang (Tibet).

References

Amin, Samir. 2008. *Les Luttes paysannes et ouvrières face aux défis du XXIe siècle*. Paris: Les Indes savantes.

Arrighi, Giovanni. 2009. *Adam Smith in Beijing: Lineages of the Twenty-First Century*. London: Verso.

Bairoch, Paul. 1999. *Mythes et paradoxes de l'histoire économique*. Paris: La Découverte.

CEIC. various years. *China Premium Database: Macroeconomic, Industry and Financial Time-Series Databases for Global Emerging and Developed Markets*. Beijing: CEIC Data Company.

Chandra, Nirmal Kumar. 2009. 'La Chine et l'Inde: convergence entre la croissance économique et les tensions sociales?', *Recherches internationales*, (86, April-June).

Chi Tsui. 1949. *Histoire de la Chine et de la civilisation chinoise*. Paris: Payot.

Crédit suisse. 2012. *China Market Strategy*, February.

Dessus, Sébastien and Rémy Herrera. 2000. "Public Capital and Growth: A Panel Data Assessment", *Economic Development and Cultural Change*, 48(2): 407-418.

Dufour, Jean-François. 2012. *Made by China: Les Secrets d'une conquête industrielle*. Paris: Dunod.

Foster, V., W. Butterfield, C. Chen and N. Pushak. 2009. 'Building Bridges: China's Growing Role as Infrastructure Financier for Sub-Saharan Africa', Trends and Policy Options, (5). World Bank-PPIAF, Washington, D.C.

Herrera, Rémy. 2013. "Between Crisis and Wars – Where Is the United States Heading?", *Journal of Innovation Economics and Management*, 2013(2), 151-174.

———. 2012. *Gastos públicos y crecimiento económico*, Caracas: Ediciones del Banco Central de Venezuela.

———. 2011. "A Critique of Mainstream Growth Theory: Ways out of the Neoclassical Science(-Fiction) and Towards Marxism", *Research in Political Economy*, 27(1): 3-64.

———. 2010. *Un Autre Capitalisme n'est pas possible*. Paris: Syllepse.

———. 2006. "The 'New' Development Economics: A Neoliberal *Con*?", *Monthly Review*, 58(1): 38-50.

———. 2004. "Good Governance *vs.* Good Government?", CETIM – American Association of Jurists Joint Written Statement, United Nations Commission on Human Rights, June, Geneva.

IMF. various years. *International Financial Statistics*. Washington D.C.: International Monetary Fund.

Kroeber, Arthur. 2011. 'China's Next Decade', *Dragonomics Research & Advisory*, February.

Lau, Kin Chi and Ping Huang (eds.). 2003. *China Reflected*. Hong Kong: Asian Regional Exchange for New Alternatives Press.

Lin Chun. 2006. *The Transformation of Chinese Socialism*. Durham: Duke University Press.

Marer, Paul, Janos Arvay, John O'Connor, Martin Schrenk and Daniel Swanson (eds.). 1992. *Historically Planned Economies: A Guide to the Data*. Washington D.C.: World Bank.

Nakatani, Paulo and Rémy Herrera. 2008. "Structural Change and Planning in Venezuela", *Review of Radical Political Economics*, 40(3): 292-300.

———. 2005. "De-dollarizing Cuba", *International Journal of Political Economy*, 34(4): 86-97.

———. 2004. "Dollarization in Cuba", *International Finance Review*, (5): 115-134.

National Bureau of Statistics. various years. *China Statistical Yearbooks*. Beijing.

South-South Forum. 2011. 'China's Real Experience: Course of Industrialization; Eight Crises with Subsequent Soft Landing in 60 Years'. Mimeograph. Lingnan University, Hong Kong.

UBS. 2012. *China Economics: Outlook 2011*. Hong Kong: UBS Investment Research.

Wallerstein, Immanuel. 1980. *Le système du monde du XVe siècle à nos jours: Capitalisme et économie-monde*. Paris: Flammarion.

Wen Tiejun. 2009. *The 'San Nong' Problem and Institutional Transition*. Beijing: China Economic Press.

———. 2001. 'Centenary Reflections on the "Three Dimensional Problem" of Rural China', *Inter-Asia Cultural Studies*, 2(2): 3-11.

Wong, Erebus and Tsui Sit. 2012. 'Rethinking "Rural China", Unthinking Modernization', Mimeograph. Lingnan University, Hong Kong.

World Bank. various years. *World Development Indicators*. Washington D.C.: World Bank.

Yoshino, Yutaka. 2008. 'Africa-Asia Trade and Investment: Opportunities and Challenges', Mimeograph. Washington D.C.: World Bank.

Conclusion

Wim DIERCKXSENS, Rémy HERRERA &
Paulo NAKATANI

International Observatory of the Crisis (IOC) and Ecumenical Research Centre (DEI), The Netherlands and Costa Rica

National Centre of Scientific Research (CNRS), France

and

Federal University of Espírito Santo (UFES), Brazil

In 2010 and 2011, it looked like the European Union and the Eurozone might collapse. Both of them seemed at the verge of being consumed by the tentacles of the financial octopuses of Wall Street and the City of London. At the end of 2012, the Eurozone was 'saved', in extremis and temporarily, but its destruction of social services is still in process. Then, at the beginning of 2013, we faced the threat of the United States' bankruptcy. Indeed, the growing size of the inverted pyramid of portfolio titles and fictitious capital, which is built on an ever-shrinking base of real wealth, is coming to an end. The strategy of the financial oligopolies of Wall Street in New York and the City of London, which possess this gigantic pyramid of assets, was to incorporate as many mechanisms as possible that allow them to hoard the lion's share of the productive or real wealth before (or just when) the collapse takes place.

These Anglo-American forces tried, first of all, to snatch the real assets of Europe through the business of speculating with the public debt and looking for the bankruptcy of ever-larger countries in Europe. This is a politics of subordination to the global financial networks of not only the key countries of the periphery, like Latin America in the past, but also the economic superpowers, even in Europe. The creation of a Eurozone and the European Union was a political attempt by this continent to avoid being absorbed by the Anglo-American financial octopuses. Since the eruption of the systemic crisis, the threat of bankruptcies of states exists in the very heart of the capitalist world, in the European Union and even the United States. This demonstrates that not even the metropolis can stay safe from the encroachment of the global financial network under the control of the oligopolies. These networks function like 'private states' without borders and citizens and are unaccountable to no one and nobody. According to us, this is a new form of capitalism without citizenship or democracy.

Global financial capital was able to put the European economy back on track after the experience with the Greek crisis. Through the rescue plan of the PIIGS, it was possible to transfer the risk of the peripheral countries to the central countries of the Eurozone. The Germans, Finnish, Dutch, Austrians and the French should pay tax to stabilize the peripheral countries of Europe. In actuality, it was all about rescuing German and French banks. It is in this context that a German-French project emerged with different measures to create the fiscal integration of Europe. The ultimate goal of the German-French project was to avoid falling under the aegis of Anglo-American financial capital. The real battle within the Eurozone crisis is between the big bankers at a global scale. Will the German-French alliance survive or will the Anglo-American global financial forces triumph, or will a more radical social movement emerge at a global scale against the bankers in general? Anglo-American forces meanwhile tried to snatch the real assets of Europe through the business of speculating with public debt and looking for bankruptcy of ever-larger countries. If they did not win this bet, the burden of the probable collapse of fictitious capital would fall on Wall Street and the City of London.

Entering 2013, the German-French axis continued to consolidate itself as a power bloc with a relative hard currency and a growing fiscal integration to prevent its subordination to these Anglo-American global financial forces. To preserve their domain over the real economy the German-French project confronted Anglo-American global capital with a politics of adjustment-savings-investment-production-export-surplus, at the very cost of its population principally in the Mediterranean countries. Europeans found in the BRICS (Brazil, Russia, India, China and South Africa) tactical allies for their project. The greatest fear of the Anglo-American financial forces is that the Eurozone will not only transform itself into 'Great Germany', but, worse, it may do so in alliance with China and Russia as part of the Euro-Asian Continental Bloc. The constitution of this Bloc would imply the definitive defeat of global Anglo-American capital.

The strategic objective of the Anglo-American project is not only to destabilize the euro, but even the dollar, as is becoming clear today. These global bankers want to take advantage of the panic, which implies replacing the dollar and the Federal Reserve Bank with a global monetary authority controlled by the global bankers themselves, free of any state control, even of the US government. Conservative US anti-globalist forces, especially the Tea Party, need to maintain the dollar as the leading international reserve currency, guarantee their domination through the military-industrial complex and the Pentagon, control the Middle East to tap into oil reserves and deepen their intervention in Latin America. They are losing space.

Amidst this confrontation of the forces of capital, a space has opened for more radicalized progressive forces that fight for de-globalization and a decoupling from neoliberal globalization. The Great Depression of the 21st Century has provoked a crisis of legitimation of global proportions. Western civilization itself will be put to question and so also the Eurocentric dominant worldview with its deep-seated, near religious, belief in efficiency and sophistication. This Eurocentric worldview will soon be in its last stages, as China reaches the Western level of efficiency and sophistication in science, technology and institutions. In this context, there is a threat of a 'great war', that is, a war between core countries. It will be perpetrated specially against those powers that could represent a threat to the established Western civilization, which means China and probably Russia. The Great Depression of the 21st Century will probably lead to the collapse of neoliberal globalization and will open new avenues for alternatives.

Western civilization is based on capitalist society and, therefore, on the myth of economic growth. Without growth, sustainable accumulation is impossible. Strategic natural resources are becoming scarcer and are concentrated in the South; some of the most important ones are in China. Ever scarcer natural resources will put limits on global economic growth. It means a crisis of the very Western 'civilization' itself. The Great Depression of the 21st Century is closely related to the limits of the development of fictitious capital. The era of dominant fictitious capital over substantive or real capital is coming to an end, and its collapse will be the climax of the Great Depression.

Since 2008, signs of a new World Depression have been evident, with a dramatic rise in unemployment rates in the core countries and the consequent worsening of economic and social stability, which will lead to the end of middle-class and political stability. Democratic options are becoming more and more difficult and a growing de-legitimacy of the capitalist mode of production is the consequence. The political space for left-wing parties will grow in the central countries, and these will question the very essence of the current economic rationale. In Latin America, social and economic insecurity is a very old concern, political instability has been a common issue and the current economic rationale tends to question the past. In more than one of the formal, content-less democracies, the electoral route to an alternative economic rationale has, therefore, gained political topicality.

There is a very high probability that the present crisis will become more acute as a systemic crisis of capital, since all the conditions are there for that to happen. Capitalism is in danger, including at the centre of the system. One could say that there have been many other capitalist crises and that the system has always come out of them stronger than before, more monstrous and more monstrously concentrated. Yes, it is true that there have been even pre-capitalist crises. We are not announcing the end of the world here. It is yet another fantasy – perhaps due to impatience – to believe that capitalism is going to collapse from the effects of the current crisis: the monster is going to survive and will continue to kill.

The present situation does not resemble the beginning of the end of the crisis, but the beginning of a process of a long period of collapse of the present phase of capitalism, which is oligopolistic and financialized. And this process of collapse opens up great possibilities for a transition, in which the class struggle will become tougher and more complex. This will force us to reconsider the alternatives of post-capitalist social transformation, which more and more of us, in spite of our differences, wish will be socialist in nature (if not something more).

Now, if the structural problem for the survival of capitalism is indeed that of downward pressure on the rate of profit, and if financialization is not a sustainable solution, the only thing that this system will offer, until it is on its deathbed, is the worsening exploitation of labour. Fictitious capital demands to be remunerated and it obtains this by transferring the surplus of productive capital and by putting constant pressure to increase the exploitation of the labour force. To be able to relaunch a cycle of expansion at the centre of the global system, the crisis that we are currently experiencing must destroy the absolutely gigantic amounts of fictitious capital, most of it parasitical. But the contradictions of the global system have now become so deep and so difficult to resolve that such devaluation will risk pushing it towards collapse.

The extreme seriousness of the current crisis hitting Europe, especially in the Eurozone, caused by the so-called sovereign debt crisis in Greece and Italy, among many others, begs the following question: do not the people of Europe have something to learn from the experience of some of the developing countries and the anti-crisis strategies that the latter have adopted? For, the fact is that till now, it is the North that has offered its formulas, supposedly universally valid, to the economies of the South – even if they very rarely fit them. However, times have changed.

The neoliberal solutions of widespread austerity programmes and the slashing of public services that have been offered today – or rather, have been imposed – in an attempt to save capitalism in crisis and revive growth, are absurd. These are the surest ways to aggravate this crisis and push the system even more quickly over the edge. And this is done while encouraging the rise of the extreme right everywhere – which is racist, demagogic and always in collusion with the established order.

In this context, the crisis now thundering through the Eurozone should be seen as closely linked to the very foundations of the process of European integration. Without a state, without even the existence of a politically united Europe, it was believed that a single currency could be created. The original error was right there in that Europe claimed it could weld together vastly different economies without reinforcement from political institutions at the regional level or promotion of social equalization from above. It is, therefore, logical that this 'bad Europe', which turned against the people and became anti-social and anti-democratic, is ever more openly rejected.

Yet, it would be fostering illusions to continue to believe in the possibility of a new 'Keynesian compromise'. The previous one, agreed to after World War II, was not a gift from the big capitalists, but was torn from them by popular struggles, multiple and intersecting. Today, the high finance that has reacquired power is unwilling to make any concessions. Keynesianism – that some people would certainly like to see in place – has no reality and no future. It is now the financial oligopolies that dominate and dictate their law to the states for setting interest rates, creating money or, when necessary, nationalizing.

Faced with the systemic crisis and the dangers it brings – including the extreme right wing gradually taking control of the government – the time has come for the progressive forces in Europe, as well as in the North more generally, to shift gears to the offensive by once more formulating alternative proposals for a radical and internationalist left, oriented towards the reconstruction of social programmes and solidarity in struggle with the global South. It would be a lie to say that such a break could be achieved easily. Nevertheless, it would also be a lie to say that such a path is doomed. As a matter of fact, the South dared to break the rules of the existing international monetary system without causing chaos at home. It is precisely this path of breaking away – even temporarily – from the neoliberal dogma that allowed them to empower themselves and recover.

Many of the South's recent experiences have shown that by reclaiming elements of national sovereignty (monetary, among others) and by showing political will when faced with the dictates of financial markets, these countries have created room to manoeuvre, which allowed them to get out of dramatic socio-economic situations that had been caused to a large extent by the very operation – unfair and unacceptable – of the world capitalist system. We are thinking here, for example, of the process of de-dollarization in Cuba or the distancing of Venezuela vis-à-vis the IMF or the creation of the Bank of the South (Bancosur) around the countries of the Bolivarian Alliance for the Americas (ALBA), such as Bolivia and others.

But one can also cite the case of countries with less radical governments, such as Argentina, which declared itself insolvent in late 2001 and whose economy has quickly returned to growth, without it getting isolated from world trade. Cessation of payments, currency devaluation and a debt conversion plan were the measures that saved the Argentinian economy from neoliberal disaster. We also have to think of Ecuador, where the government arranged an audit of external debt, cancelled 'odious' debts (that is, illegal and/or illegitimate), used the suspension of payments to reduce the public debt burden and free up resources for social and infrastructure programmes.

In all these experiments, the government's recovery of its decision-making policy regarding the economy allowed the country to dig its way out of the quagmire in which it was stuck, without any disaster. As was the case in Malaysia after the Asian crisis of 1998, when the government (which was not 'left' at all) put limits on the orders of the IMF and managed its anti-crisis policy as it saw fit. So, why not in the North? Is there really no alternative?

Of course, the situations differ from one continent to another, but there are alternatives in the form of post-capitalist, democratic and social transitions, in solidarity with the South. The imperative is not to develop miracle or turnkey solutions, but to reopen spaces of debate on the left. It is high time one finally spoke, without taboos or complexes, of anti-crisis solutions to serve the European people: a revival of progressive regionalization in the North open to the South; currency devaluation and possible new common currencies; recovering control of the financial flows and resource allocations; redefining the political role of central banks; nationalization of the banking system and of certain strategic sectors of the economy; arranged cancellation of public debts; a deep redistribution of wealth; reconstruction of public services; development of popular participation and real democracy at all levels, including inside the enterprises and in all the processes of decision concerning people's collective future; but also and above all, the rebuilding of a strong and internationalist solidarity between the workers of the North and the peoples of the South. For us, therefore, it is time to reconstruct alternatives and radical proposals – on the left. Because, actually, it is right to talk about the sovereign people and not about sovereign debt.

Editors and Contributors

Editors

Rémy Herrera

Rémy Herrera is Researcher at the French National Centre of Scientific Research (CNRS), teaches the Masters course and supervises PhD theses at the University of Paris 1 Panthéon-Sorbonne. He has also been a consultant at the OECD and the World Bank. He is currently Executive Secretary of the World Forum of Alternatives.

Wim Dierckxsens

Wim Dierckxsens is Coordinator of the International Observatory of Crisis. He is also a senior researcher at the Departamento de Investigación Oeucumenico, Costa Rica; former administrator for the United Nations; and professor at the National University of Honduras and the National University of Costa Rica.

Paulo Nakatani

Paulo Nakatani is Professor at the Department of Economics, Federal University of Espírito Santo (UFES), in Vitoria, Brazil. He has been President of the Brazilian Society of Political Economy (SEP, Sociedade Brasileira de Economia Politica) and Director of the academic review of the SEP.

Contributors

Paulo Campanario

Paulo Campanario has been a professor in demography in various universities in Honduras, Nicaragua, Mexico, Costa Rica and Brazil. He received his PhD from the University of Montreal, Canada. He is also Consultant in Population and Development and Researcher at the Centro Latinoamericano de Demografía CEPAL-UN.

Antonio Jarquín

Antonio Jarquín is a physician who received his diplomas from the universities of London and Vienna. He is Vice-President of the International Physicians for the Prevention of Nuclear War (the federation received the Nobel Prize in 1985). He has also been Ambassador of Nicaragua in the United Nations. He is a member of the Transcendt Association.

Reinaldo A. Carcanholo

Reinaldo Carcanholo was Professor at the Department of Economics, Federal University of Espírito Santo (UFES), Vitoria, Brazil, and part of the post-doctorate programme in social policies. He has been a professor in economics in Honduras, Nicaragua, Costa Rica and Chile. He was also Collaborator of the MST in Brazil.

Mauricio de Souza Sabadini

Mauricio de Souza Sabadini is Professor at the Department of Economics, Federal University of Espírito Santo (UFES), Vitoria, Brazil. He did his PhD in economics from Panthéon-Sorbonne University, Paris. He is also Tutor of the Programme SESU PET-UFES.

Andrés Piqueras

Andrés Piqueras did his PhD in sociology and social anthropology. Currently, he is Professor in economics at the University of Castellón Jaume I, Spain. Founder of the Permanent Observatory of Immigration, he is also coordinator of the research branch on globalization, new identities and collective subjects.

Tony Andreani

Tony Andreani is Emeritus professor in political sciences and sociology at the University of Paris VIII. He is Co-Director of *International Critical Thought*, a journal of the Chinese Academy of Social Sciences, edited by Routledge. He is also a member of the scientific committee of *La Pensée*.

Business & Innovation

The creation of new activities, of news production and consumption modes, of new goods and services, of new markets and new jobs (etc.) depends as much on the heroic action of entrepreneurs as on the strategies of big corporations which develop their activities at a global scale. Innovation and business are interlinked. The main themes of the books published in this series are: Entrepreneurship, enterprise and innovation; Innovation strategies in a global context; Innovation policies and business climate; Innovation, business dynamics and socio-economic change. The synergies between innovative entrepreneurship, firms' strategies and innovation policies is of major importance in the explanation of technological paradigms change and of the transformations in economic and social structures of wealthy and less wealthy countries. In this series are published books in English or in French specialized in economics, management and sociology of innovation and also dealing with change and entrepreneurship in a local, national or international perspective.

This series is supported by the Research Network on Innovation.